SPIRITPOWER

BOOKS BY VERNON COLEMAN

The Medicine Men (1975)
Paper Doctors (1976)
Everything You Want To Know About Ageing (1976)
Stress Control (1978)
The Home Pharmacy (1980)
Aspirin or Ambulance (1980)
Face Values (1981) Guilt (1982)
The Good Medicine Guide (1982)
Stress And Your Stomach (1983)
Bodypower (1983)
An A to Z Of Women's Problems (1984)
Bodysense (1984)
Taking Care Of Your Skin (1984)
Life Without Tranquillisers (1985)
High Blood Pressure (1985)
Diabetes (1985)
Arthritis (1985)
Eczema and Dermatitis (1985)
The Story Of Medicine (1985)
Natural Pain Control (1986)
Mindpower (1986)
Addicts and Addictions (1986)
Dr Vernon Coleman's Guide To Alternative Medicine (1988)
Stress Management Techniques (1988)
Overcoming Stress (1988)
Know Yourself (1988)
The Health Scandal (1988)
The 20 Minute Health Check (1989)
Sex For Everyone (1989)
Mind Over Body (1989)
Eat Green Lose Weight (1990)
Toxic Stress (1991)
Why Animal Experiments Must Stop (1991)
The Drugs Myth (1992)
Why Doctors Do More Harm Than Good (1993)
Stress and Relaxation (1993)
Complete Guide to Sex (1993)
How to Conquer Backache (1993)
How to Conquer Arthritis (1993)

Betrayal of Trust (1994)
Know Your Drugs (1994)
Food for Thought (1994)
The Traditional Home Doctor (1994)
I Hope Your Penis Shrivels Up (1994)
People Watching (1995)
Relief from IBS (1995)
The Parent's Handbook (1995)
Oral Sex: Bad Taste And Hard To Swallow (1995)
Why Is Pubic Hair Curly? (1995)
Men in Dresses (1996)
Power over Cancer (1996)
Crossdressing (1996)
How To Get The Best Out Of Prescription Drugs (1996)
How To Get The Best Out Of Alternative Medicine (1996)
How to Stop Your Doctor Killing You (1996)
How to Overcome Toxic Stress (1996)
Fighting For Animals (1996)
Alice and Other Friends (1996)
Dr Vernon Coleman's Fast Action Health Secrets (1997)

novels
The Village Cricket Tour (1990)
The Bilbury Chronicles (1992)
Bilbury Grange (1993)
Mrs Caldicot's Cabbage War (1993)
The Man Who Inherited a Golf Course (1993)
Bilbury Revels (1994)
Deadline (1994)
Bilbury Country (1996)

short stories
Bilbury Pie (1995)

on cricket
Thomas Winsden's Cricketing Almanack (1983)
Diary Of A Cricket Lover (1984)

as Edward Vernon
Practice Makes Perfect (1977)
Practise What You Preach (1978)
Getting Into Practice (1979)
Aphrodisiacs - An Owners Manual (1983)
Aphrodisiacs - An Owners Manual (Turbo Edition) (1984)
The Complete Guide To Life (1984)

as Marc Charbonnier
Tunnel (novel 1980)

with Dr Alan C Turin
No More Headaches (1981)

with Alice
Alice's Diary (1989)
Alice's Adventures (1992)

SPIRITPOWER

How To Find Freedom And Give Meaning
To Your Life

Vernon Coleman

European Medical Journal

First published in the United Kingdom by the European Medical Journal, Publishing House, Trinity Place, Barnstaple, Devon EX32 9HJ

ISBN 1 898947 49 X

A catalogue record for this book is available from the British Library.

Printed by J W Arrowsmith, Bristol

To Vicky

CONTENTS

PART THREE
How to Get What You Want Out of Life

Preface
What Do You Want Out Of Life?
(You Can Have It If You Really Want It)

'Believe nothing, no matter where you read it, or who said it! No matter if I have said it. Unless it agrees with your own reason and with your own common sense.'

- Buddha

We are all composed of three parts: body, mind and spirit. In my book *Bodypower* I described your body's astonishing self healing powers – and explained how you can take advantage of those powers to stay healthy and to defeat nine out of ten physical illnesses. In the sequel, *Mindpower*, I explored the powers of the mind, described how you can harness positive emotions and conquer and control weaknesses and destructive emotions and explained how you can use your mind to heal your body and teach yourself mental self defence. This book, *Spiritpower*, deals, as the title makes it clear, with the third and most abstract of the 'body, mind, spirit' trilogy. I have deliberately taken a practical and pragmatic attitude to this topic for I believe that the freedom of the spirit is constrained by very real, practical barriers. I believe that individual liberty and intellectual freedom are essential foundations for a healthy spirit, and that self awareness, self sufficiency and personal privacy are vital ingredients in the development of a healthy spirit. In the first part of this book I explore and explain the history and background to our current rather stagnant spiritual environment. In the second part of the book I go into the specific reasons for our loss of freedom and personal dignity. And in the third, and most important, part of the book I describe precisely how you can regain your physical, mental and spiritual freedom.

Vernon Coleman 1997

FOREWORD
Today's Handbook For Tomorrow's Revolutionaries

'When a wise scholar hears the Tao
He practises it diligently.
When a mediocre scholar hears the Tao
He wavers between belief and disbelief.
When a worthless scholar hears the Tao
He laughs boisterously (and foolishly) at its wisdom.'
- Tao Te Jing by Lao Tsu

'To constitute the millionth part of a legislature, by voting for one or two men
once in three or five years, however conscientiously this duty may be performed,
can exercise but little active influence upon any man's life and character.'
- Samuel Smiles

We live in a demanding, harsh, high pressure world where today's valued qualities are very different to those of a generation or two ago; where no one has any time; where loyalty, friendship and compassion are archaic qualities, emotional history rather than practical values.

Today, everything moves at a faster pace than ever before. Expectations are higher and more materialistic; success is judged not by personal achievement but in crude material terms.

In today's world you are more likely to win society's respect not because of your capacity for goodness or kindness or for your capacity for friendship; not through your sensitivity or through wisdom or love, but through the size and age of your motor car, the size of your home, the number of fashion items in your wardrobe and the source of your most recent top up suntan.

These are cold, rough standards by which to measure yourself – and in our competitive society your accomplishments and achievements will never be enough. There will always be someone who is richer, or who has better hair or a more perfect body.

The most potent source of pain, distress and dissatisfaction in our modern world is toxic stress – the sort of stress over which we have no personal control (and which I described in some detail in my book *How To Overcome Toxic Stress*). Toxic stress creates guilts and enormous feelings of failure. It is often toxic stress which turns ordinary men and women into workaholics, overachievers, depressives and inadequates. It is toxic stress which is largely responsible for the epidemic of mental disease in our society and the unending variety of stress related physical disorders – asthma, high blood pressure, heart disease, peptic ulceration, irritable bowel syndrome and so on. It is toxic stress which creates the anger, violence and mindless, self destructive rage which are such a part of our society.

In *How To Overcome Toxic Stress* I explained how we have created a world in which society is more important than the individual, and I described the simple ways in which toxic stress can be overcome. But even when toxic stress is overcome most of us are still slaves of, and tied into, the depersonalizing system which measures personal success only in material terms and puts the abnormal needs and expectations of the state above all else.

***

There are, it cannot be denied, more things to worry about today than there have ever been before. When our descendants look back on this period in human history there will be little for them to be proud of.

Superficially, the last few years have been a period of growth for a civilised, developed society. Millions of people own their own microwave ovens, video recorders and television sets. But the second half of the twentieth century will be remembered with shame and embarrassment. Our time in history will be remembered as the decade when people stopped caring, stopped trusting one another and started thinking only of themselves. The second half of the twentieth century will be remembered for poverty and extravagance; for hatred and jealousy.

The incidence of violence in our society is increasing faster than at any previous time. The incidence of child abuse is on the increase. Every winter thousands of old people die because they cannot afford to feed themselves or keep themselves warm. The number of people committing suicide is rising faster than ever. The number of people who have no jobs, and no hope of employment, has never been higher. The incidence of baby battering is on the increase. The number of sexual crimes rises constantly.

A baby born today is, when grown to adulthood, more likely to be admitted to a mental hospital than win a place at university. Thousands of people are homeless and have no hope of finding homes. There are now more alcoholics around than ever before – and the incidence is increasing every year.

We have polluted our environment, fouled our seas and filled our world with indestructible rubbish. We have more laws than ever before, and civil liberty is now merely a phrase from the past, but crime rises constantly. The greatest threat to personal liberty now comes not from crooks or bandits but from the courts and the police. Although we now have more social workers than ever before in our history, social problems are endemic. We spend more on healthcare than ever before but people are sicker than ever, and thousands die because they cannot get the treatment they need.

Most citizens have forgotten how to care and have become zombies; more concerned about their chances of winning the lottery than their responsibilities for the world.

Big companies that sell food, lend money or manufacture goods care nothing about their customers. They sell them food that will kill them. They lend them money they can't afford to pay back. And they sell them goods that are shoddy and poorly made. They lie and they cheat to maintain their profits.

The second half of the twentieth century will be best remembered for a meanness of spirit, a lack of generosity and an absence of honesty. But most of all our time will be remembered as the years when hardly anyone really cared.

We have lost our way. The maps have been altered. And the rules have been changed.

**

For years I made the mistake of assuming that most people were sensitive, compassionate and understanding. This was a grave error and one which has caused me much heartache. I care and you care, but most people do not. Most people are stupid, selfish and insensitive.

You do not have to go far to find the evidence to substantiate this assertion.

A recent survey showed that 88% of the population believe that schools should teach children to obey authority. The same survey showed that 65% of the population support the censorship of films and magazines and exactly the same percentage approve of capital punishment. Most people approve of giving more powers to the police – even when those powers bite deeply into their own rights to freedom and privacy. The people who 'think' this way also support and approve of a generally insensitive attitude towards poverty, suffering and sickness. In the new, late twentieth century canon these are signs, not of misfortune, but of weakness. The modern solution is more jackboot than kindness, more gas chamber than caring.

We may live in rich, allegedly developed countries but our governments treat the ill, the poor and the unfortunate with derision and contempt.

The medical profession, parts of which used to treat the Hippocratic Oath seriously, has sold out and become a marketing arm of the pharmaceutical industry. Doctors, nurses and other health care professionals have become a part of the selfish, uncaring society. Social workers are a sick joke; so obsessed with incest, daily meetings and their own sense of importance that they have completely lost touch with the real world and forgotten what compassion means. Lawyers, school teachers and others who might have been expected to fight for freedom are now interested only in preserving their own professional status. Religious leaders now abstain from moral authority – they have presumably been told that morality is no longer a marketable commodity.

Revolutionaries who dreamt of freedom, peace and compassion when they were twenty dream today of new triple-tufted carpets, double glazing and ABS brakes. (Today's twenty-year-olds have missed out the dreams of freedom, peace and compassion and gone straight to the dreams of triple-tufted carpets, double glazing and ABS brakes.)

Nero was accused of fiddling while Rome burned. At least he did something creative. Today's free citizen spends several hours a day watching television and no longer believes that he can make a difference.

Over my shoulder I see the forces of darkness arraigned in suits of every shade of grey. And yet while these evil forces crowd daily closer, the over-promoted talents of the television age dedicate their lives to endorsing violence and sucking people dry for cheap programming. The magic box is dominated by self important, intellectually deprived presenters with expensive haircuts and cheap brains. Salacious and hypocritical but rarely courageous or original, they have turned a potentially powerful medium into a tool of the state. The government is safe as long as the voters are more concerned with soapland than with reality. The electors sit slumped in front of their nightly five hours of watered down, two dimensional entertainment because they are too frightened to speak up; they are convinced that they cannot make a difference. They may occasionally still feel anger, frustration, alienation and bewilderment. But they dare not speak out for they fear for their own safety. They know that unemployment – and worse – beckons for those who stand up and speak.

**

It is a mistake to assume that most people are automatically and inherently good. They aren't. The world is inherently evil. Power and money corrupt and we live in a corrupt world.

The trouble is that most 'bad' people do not regard themselves as 'bad'. Indeed, they often think that they are doing a worthwhile job. People who work for arms companies or tobacco companies don't think of themselves as 'evil' even though what their company is doing may be evil. They find all sorts of excuses for what they do and they slowly lose sight of truth and decency. The most evil people in our society don't think they are evil. They think they are just doing their jobs. They think that someone else is doing all the evil things which are ruining the world. They do not realise that the evil emanates from them all along.

The fact is that evil is not just about being evil; it is also about allowing other people to behave in an evil fashion. Evil is not caring and not saying anything. For so many people in our society 'just doing my job' means cheating the poor and making life difficult for other people.

Lawyers who represent dishonest corporations are evil. Civil servants who abuse and do not serve the people who pay their salaries are evil rather than civil.

Apathy and silence are just as much a sin as torture and murder. Standing by silently is a sin.

* * *

I received a letter the other day from a reader who wanted to know why I am so outspoken.

'I agree with much of what you say,' he wrote. 'But you would make far fewer enemies if you were more tactful. You make people feel uncomfortable.'

I am sure that reader is right.

I've been a newspaper and magazine columnist for thirty years and in that time I've been fired well over forty times. (I've also resigned quite a few times too). One editor once told me that he was getting rid of my column because I made people think.

I am old enough to know that I have two main problems.

The first is that I am honest. I say what I believe. And I don't care whether it is politically incorrect or culturally insensitive.

And my second big problem is that I care passionately.

Neither of these are, I realise, fashionable virtues.

Indeed, I am sure that some people would regard honesty and passion as vices.

We live in strange and rather awful times.

Most people don't seems to give a stuff about anything any more.

The world is full of people who don't care, won't take responsibility and are frightened to say what they think.

Unlike their predecessors modern politicians no longer resign.

And they get away with it because not enough people care.

Our streets are full of people who are homeless and impoverished.

No one gives a damn.

Our hospitals are decaying. Patients are treated without compassion or respect.

The educational system is a sick joke. Illiteracy is commonplace. Huge swathes of our population are unemployable because they can neither write a letter nor add up a column of figures.

Go into a shop to buy something and the chances are that you will be served by a surly, ignorant assistant who doesn't care a jot whether you buy something or not. If you do buy and the product goes wrong they won't care about that either.

We live in a world controlled by bureaucrats and faceless morons who neither think nor care about what they do. Have you tried telephoning a government organisation or a large company to complain recently? It's like talking to cotton wool.

Bored complacency is endemic.

A friend of mine has just received a cheque from his insurance company. The accident which resulted in this modest payment occurred years ago. Over the months he has spoken and written to an endless series of grey faced bureaucrats. None of them seemed to care a jot about the delay.

Another friend is waiting to go into hospital for an operation on her hip. She has been on the waiting list for over a year. No one gives a damn. When she rings up to try and find out what is going on the hospital staff are rude and offhand. They clearly regard all patients as a bloody nuisance.

We live in a world which is run by the incompetent and the uncaring, the unthinking and the unfeeling. No one seems to care any more.

Well I refuse to apologise for the fact that I care. And you should not apologise for the fact that you care either.

I have nothing but contempt for people who sit on the fence and won't say what they think.

***

As I write fur is back in fashion. Affluent women everywhere are pulling their fur coats from the back of their wardrobes and swaggering along the streets wearing the skins of thirty or forty dead animals with pride.

A few years ago the dirty looks, the catcalls and the occasional can of red paint forced fur owning women to put their dead animal skins back into the closet.

Not any more.

The rich bitches are getting away with it because fur is now yesterday's cause; yesterday's shame and horror. The wholesale slaughtering of living, breathing, sentient creatures so that rich bitches can swagger around looking like rich bitches is no longer a big story. It is dead news.

And nobody cares. A recent survey showed that nearly half the population admit that they would not be prepared to take any sort of action – even for a cause they believe in.

But, that isn't too surprising. No one seems to really care about anything very much any more.

There is much tut tutting in the smart suburbs when news comes in of another atrocity in Africa. 'Golly,' they murmur, as they tuck into the highly processed but tasty chemical, faeces and cardboard pie they think of as food. 'Isn't that terrible.'

And then the atrocity in Africa merges into last week's atrocity in Asia and the previous week's atrocity in South America. There is much frowning and shaking of heads when the evening television news is full of reports of ethnic cleansing in distant parts of Europe, the names of which only newsreaders can pronounce.

'Well, I never,' they mutter, as they down another can of beer and wonder whether they've won the lottery this week.

And there is much disgust and disapproval when another senseless piece of violence is reported: when another mad gunman mows down a dozen or two innocent victims or when a passer by is knifed to death for daring to whistle a happy tune.

'Terrible, isn't it,' they say to one another, quickly blaming the government, the church or the killer's relatives or neighbours, and then forgetting about the horror when their favourite TV theme tune starts.

When it really comes down to it no one really gives a damn. No one cares enough to do anything.

And as each new horror story gets publicity so the old horrors are forgotten. Yesterday's carnage, cruelty and destruction becomes simply yesterday's news.

To some extent all this is understandable. Because every day brings new examples of wickedness we can no longer cope. There is just too much horror and awfulness to bear.

Today my mail brought me a photograph of a bear in Turkey who has had its legs broken so that it can be forced to walk about on crutches to entertain the tourists. I received a photograph of a tiger in China tied up in a cage prior to being beaten to death so that shopkeepers can turn its bones and organs into highly priced quack remedies.

And no one cares.

No one allows these horrors to affect them too deeply. They quickly forget and push aside these terrors.

But the wars, the localised, personalised violence and the sheer cruelty are just a part of it.

The entire insane world is corrupt. Politicians around the world are found guilty of taking bribes. The food industry now sells garbage which causes cancer, heart disease and other deadly diseases – and kills more people than Hitler ever did. Why are so many people silent? Children are getting leukaemia and other cancers which could have been prevented. Most cases of cancer are avoidable. Doctors now do more harm than good.

People hear the messages and read the words but they don't do anything – partly because they can't cope with all the information, partly because the truth is inconvenient (if you believe that cancer is caused by specific foods then you will have to make big changes to your life) and partly because they don't think that what they hear is really going to affect them.

Cigarettes are still sold freely in corner shops, supermarkets and pubs even though they kill millions. Drunk driving continues unabated – despite the slaughter on the roads.

And people ignore it all. After all, what can they do?

They blame the politicians. They blame industry. They blame fate. But people never want to take any of the blame themselves. They have handed over responsibility, washed their hands of the world, and let the politicians take charge.

If *they* don't make the world a better place then it is *their* fault.

But nothing does gets done of course because the politicians don't care. Modern politicians are, almost by definition, ruthless, dispassionate and uncaring people. The only word they really understand is 'compromise'.

Politicians don't go into politics because they want to make the world a better place; they go into politics because it is a good career. Politicians get paid extremely well. And they know they don't have to do anything.

Politicians don't have to deal with the horrors of the world because they know that people don't care enough.

***

In this book I intend to explain how you can regain your individuality and some, at least, of your freedom from a cruel world, and how you can begin to take back (at least some) control over your own life. I will explain how you can preserve your privacy, your dignity and your liberty until the revolution comes.

Freedom means different things to different people. But it is an essential prerequisite for happiness and a vital antidote if you hope to minimise the effects of toxic stress. Furthermore, it is only through acquiring and maintaining *personal* freedom that you will have the spiritual strength to combat and overcome the powerful establishment forces which want to limit individual rights and liberties and which are leading to a gradual increase in the powers of society.

***

During the last quarter of a century I have written over 75 books. It may not be obvious from a quick glance at the titles but the common theme, running through a majority of both my fiction and my non fiction books, has been 'freedom'.

Some of my medical books (from *The Medicine Men* and *Paper Doctors*, through *The Health Scandal* and *Betrayal of Trust* to *How To Stop Your Doctor Killing You*) were written to help readers understand how their freedom and their rights have been taken from them by an oppressive, dishonest and overbearing medical establishment. Books such as *Bodypower* and *Mindpower* were written to help readers take back their freedom through a greater understanding of their own innate powers. In novels such as *Mrs Caldicot's Cabbage War* the theme is clear: the heroine is fighting for her personal dignity and freedom. In my *Bilbury* novels the inhabitants of Bilbury are constantly battling against the forces of evil to preserve their idyllic rural lifestyle. Now, I hope that *Spiritpower* will be the ultimate 'freedom fighter's handbook'.

For decades I have been conscious of the fact that our freedom as individuals has been steadily disappearing; consistently eroded by a variety of potent forces. Politicians, the courts, large international companies and the professions have all taken away some of our freedom. Most alarming of all, however, has been the steady and unnoticed way in which the amorphous and almost indefinable beast known as 'society' has taken our freedom.

Little by little the established forces have taken more and more control over our lives. Today, we have far less power than at any other time in history.

We like to think of ourselves as 'free' but we are not. We congratulate ourselves on not having succumbed to the awfulness of Orwell's 1984. But the truth is that we *have* succumbed. The only difference between our modern world and the world which Orwell predicted is that those who control our lives have been rather more subtle than the power barons Orwell envisaged; they have disguised their takeover of our lives with hollow excuses, false explanations and unconvincing assurances that we are still in charge of our own lives.

The modern enemies of freedom do not arrive on our shores from landing craft; they do not fall from the skies with parachutes attached; and they do not arrive on earth in spacecraft. The modern enemies of freedom are here already; scattered widely in amongst us; they wear uniforms and white coats; they wear suits, clutch briefcases and carry coloured pens in their breast pockets. The modern enemies of freedom are the representatives of a society which no longer has any respect for the rights of the individual; the commercial and state bureaucrats, the car park attendants, the planning officers, the traffic wardens, the policemen, the politicians and the millions of others whose daily work on behalf of society gives them just a little bit of authority taken from the individuals who are society but who, as individuals, have no rights.

Independence and privacy are no longer yours by right; you must work hard to obtain and enjoy them. It used to be argued (not so many years ago) that an innocent man would have nothing to hide and would, therefore, be perfectly happy to allow the civil servants, the bureaucrats, the police and every other government or private agency to know whatever it wanted to know about him.

In an ideal world, where bureaucrats and others held to old fashioned values, that sort of attitude would have undoubtedly been healthy. In our modern world, where government officials, and, indeed, whole government departments, resolutely ignore the law, deceive and pressurise the innocent and exceed their authority for the sake of the mysterious force known as society (and, of course, of themselves and their careers) such an attitude shows an unhealthy level of innocence and naivety.

***

Don't let your life drift by.

You really can make a difference. Dust off your principles, drag your dreams back out of the attic and scream and shout and let the faceless men and women in grey suits know that you care, and that you will not let them win.

Every night, when you go to bed, ask yourself this simple question: 'What have I done today to make the world a better place?'

To survive and succeed in our modern world, to retain your independence, your freedom and your privacy and to allow your spirit, as well as your body and your mind, to flourish, you must know exactly what you want; you must be confident that you can succeed in getting it and you must set aside your fears. You must then plan and work towards your goals.

Spiritpower has been written to help you succeed in your journey's aim.

PART ONE

We Have Lost Our Freedom

'The mass of man serve the state not as men but as machines, with their bodies. They are the standing army and the jailers and the constables. In most cases there is no free exercise whatever of the judgement or of the moral sense; but they put themselves on a level with wood and earth and stones; and wooden men can perhaps be manufactured that will serve the purpose as well. Such command no more respect than men of straw or a lump of dirt.'

- Henry David Thoreau

CHAPTER ONE
Luddites, Factories And 'Society'

'We have not abolished slavery, we have nationalised it.'

- Herbert Spencer

We have fought two world wars in the twentieth century to protect our freedom. What went wrong? In today's society the ordinary citizen is in bondage.

From the days of the Renaissance we built up a civilisation that was, until the days of the Industrial Revolution, largely based upon the strengths and qualities of the individual. When originality and creativity and thought and progress and knowledge were stifled it was usually the Church which was at fault. And then came the Industrial Revolution – and the final end of the Church's great powers.

During the Industrial Revolution the English Luddites, who were protesting about the introduction of new machinery which they regarded as a threat to their livelihoods, forced machine owners to take the despised new equipment out of cottages and farm houses and put it into large warehouses where it could be protected.

Ned Ludd and his followers broke up stocking and lace making machines because they feared that the new machinery would put them out of work. Inventors, like all creative thinkers, are invariably regarded as a threat – as some sort of enemy. But the looms promised to create work instead of reducing it and, although they never knew the extent of their error, Ludd and his followers had made a huge mistake. The violence with which they opposed the new machinery had effectively created the factory system.

Up until this time people had worked in their own homes but the Luddites forced employers into building factories. And once factories had been built the erection of purpose built terraced housing (to house the workers) was an inevitable consequence. (In the section dealing with education I have explained how and why all this resulted in the building of schools.)

It is one of the great ironies of all time that the Luddites – who regarded themselves as revolutionaries, fighting for the survival of the individual – were the driving force behind the development of the factory and our modern, heavily structured and repressive 'society'. It was the Luddites who ensured that the industrial state would gradually become first the political state and then, finally, the police state.

By the start of the twentieth century post-Luddite man had, in general, reached a state of security and comfort which a century or two earlier would not have seemed possible.

It was at that point in the development of what he liked (and still likes) to call his 'civilisation' that western man started to turn towards regulating his life, with the development of something called 'society'.

In the end the very success of political liberalism, which grew out of public concern and some revolt against the uneven world which the Luddites had bequeathed to their successors, created its own decline as many citizens become increasingly unwilling to tolerate the social evils which they saw around them.

The liberal minded succumbed to the idea of a regimented life (and the loss of ordinary basic freedoms) because socialism promised freedom from want and need. It was, however, an impossible, idealistic dream.

The proposed new rights and freedoms, promised through socialism, were to include a brand new concept, a brand new type of freedom: the freedom from necessity.

The new socialist state promised to protect the individual and take on all his or her most onerous responsibilities. The theory was that by destroying the economic system which had evolved during the industrial revolution (and which had been created and built by individuals) the rights of the ordinary working citizen could be enhanced. The state would take power and responsibility from the employers and would use those powers and responsibilities to look after the people.

The big plan was to get rid of all physical needs, wants and privations; to redistribute wealth, eradicate the differences which were an integral part of a class system, and bring everyone down to the same level. The state took on the enormous task of giving the voters a new freedom: the freedom from want. Although it was not (and is still not) recognised as such this was a form of totalitarianism; something completely different to the gentle liberalism which had previously been concerned with protecting the rights of the poor. 'In a free society,' wrote Walter Lippman, 'the state does not administer the affairs of men. It administers justice among men who conduct their own affairs.'

Both at the time and afterwards there seemed to be little understanding of the fact that when a government takes total control of all economic life it must inevitably take away each individual's personal freedoms – and that the removal of those freedoms must lead to oppression and discrimination.

Because totalitarian leaders need an identifiable 'enemy' to motivate the people, to excuse the laws they make and to justify their style of government they frequently create friction and discord and build up an 'enemy'.

(The Conservative government in Britain benefited enormously from the Falkland conflict – a small war which gave the voters a cause to 'believe in' and provided an excuse for many of the things the government was doing. It is far easier for a government to get its citizens' support through hatred or envy or some other negative emotion than it is through some positive emotion. In Germany, prior to and during the Second World War, the Jews were targeted because the Nazis needed to attack success, freedom and independence if they were to ensure that their ideas were widely accepted. The Jews represented capitalism in the popular mind and so targeting the Jewish people gave the German leaders – who presented a potent but strange mixture of socialism and fascism – both a way of overcoming the principles of commercial freedom and a target which they knew could be used to inspire the envy and hatred which would bind the voters together.)

CHAPTER TWO
The Regimentation Of Economic Life

'The whole of society will have become a single office and a single factory with equality of work and equality of pay.'

- V.I. Lenin

As Adam Smith pointed out, governments which regiment economic life are put into a position where to support themselves they are obliged to be oppressive and tyrannical.

If you take control and direction of economic activity then you must suppress the freedom of individuals and true democracy becomes a genuine inconvenience. Modern governments do not like competition or freedom because where and when either exist it must inevitably mean that things are out of their control. Governments naturally prefer a directed economy.

Socialism meant – and means – the creation of a planned economy and the abolition of private ownership and private enterprise. It means the abolition of the entrepreneur and the development of a central planning body to oversee everything and everyone.

In principle this may sound vaguely attractive to those whose main driving forces are equality and egalitarianism rather than freedom and liberty, but in practice there are, inevitably, too many conflicting forces and pressure groups for any comfortable compromise agreement ever to be reached.

There will always be irresolvable conflicts in any community. Some people will want the countryside preserved at all costs. Others will want new factories, new housing estates and new roads. Every small group wants its own aims achieved, and believes that it is in the right. The end result is conflict.

The people want their government to run their lives (and to take on the responsibility for making all the decisions) but neither the people nor their political representatives can agree on a plan. The huge weakness in a democracy is that it produces indecisiveness and ineffectiveness which leave a power vacuum; everyone gets what no one wants.

The government cannot deal with the nitty gritty of life and certainly cannot satisfy the demands of all and so unless there is one group which is infinitely more powerful than all the others the end result is that power is handed over to the unelected 'authorities' (the bureaucrats) who then (anonymously) either simply bow down to the most powerful lobbyists or decide what they think will be best for everyone.

Under these circumstances the individual's freedom has been transmitted to the government and the government has passed it on to the unelected authorities, producing a dictatorship with a thousand small, invisible dictators.

Politicians are good at airing grievances and theory, but the nuts and bolts of daily administration usually end up in the hands of unnamed, unelected bureaucrats who are not bound by any rules nor subject to any appeals or controls, but have virtually unlimited discretion in regulating the activities of the electorate. And when a government delegates authority to the civil servants or bureaucrats it gives those bureaucrats authority with the force of law behind it. When the law says that a bureaucrat, or a group of bureaucrats, (worse still, a committee of bureaucrats – invariably a collection of pompous and unwise dictators pontificating about a business of which they know nothing) are backed by the authority of the law then anything that bureaucrat, or group of bureaucrats, chooses to do is legal and is sanctioned with the full authority of the law.

Today, the legal system is designed to protect the state and society rather than the individual. The end result is that the bureaucrats rule the world and the freedom and liberty of individuals is threatened more by the tyranny of the law than the actions of the lawless.

Virtually every day of every week there is news of yet another group of concerned citizens protesting because some government department or officially supported commercial enterprise wants to build a nuclear reactor, a toxic waste dump or some other nightmare in their neighbourhood.

Whenever this happens the authorities sneer at the protestors – describing them as part of the N.I.M.B.Y. syndrome (the acronym stands for Not In My Back Yard). The implication is that the protestors are in some way being unreasonably selfish in refusing to allow their local environment to be polluted.

And yet the evidence suggests that in many instances no one wants the nuclear reactor, the toxic waste dump or whatever it is that is being planned, to be built in *their* neighbourhood. And yet the authorities who want to build, or who authorise the building of, the unwanted whatever it is never ever withdraw, hold up their hands and say: 'Oh well, if no one wants it then we won't build it'.

Because the power given to the elected politicians has been distributed in great chunks to civil servants and bureaucrats the authorities no longer have any sense of responsibility to the electorate.

CHAPTER THREE
A Structured Society

---

*'Democracy and socialism have nothing in common but one word: equality.
But notice the difference: while democracy seeks equality in liberty, socialism
seeks equality in restraint and servitude.'*

- Alexis de Tocqueville

In a competitive, free society everyone has an opportunity to do whatever they
want. Even if you do not get the job you really want you have the knowledge
that you have a chance. In a free society anything is possible if we make the
effort. However unsuited you may be to a particular type of work you can get
there if you really want it enough.

But in a society where the selections are made according to fixed rules
decided by bureaucrats then strength of will and determination and individual
qualities do not count. State control doesn't lead to equality or universal fairness
for all but to inequality and universal unfairness for all.

In a competitive, free society anything can be bought – at a price. You
might feel that the price is too high. You might not be able to afford all the things
you would like to buy. But, in a free society, you have the choice. You can earn
the money you need. And you can spend it any way you wish. In a society run
by bureaucrats there is no freedom of choice – only orders, rules, restrictions
and prohibitions.

When a government controls 40% or more of national expenditure (as is
common these days throughout the 'developed' world) it effectively controls
everything. Individuals and companies get caught up in, and irretrievably tan-
gled in, the government's own all invasive bureaucracy.

During the last century or so people have learned to accept and even welcome an organised society. Society expects you to go to school, learn a great many things by rote (it doesn't really matter whether you are interested in them or understand them – society prefers you to be unquestioning and not to think too much), to marry and have a small family, to spend all that you earn (and preferably a little bit more – so that you can remain in debt and help the banks make a profit), to obtain and do a responsible, regular job (whether or not you find it of any interest), to pay your taxes regularly, to work until you are 65, carefully saving for your retirement, and then, when you retire and you are tired and weary, and all your ambitions and hopes and opportunities have gone, you can enjoy whatever minor hobbies or interests you have acquired and quietly prepare yourself for the grave.

Individualism today is associated with egotism and selfishness, and people who are prepared to have ideas and back them with their own mental, physical and financial resources are something of an anachronism; to be regarded with suspicion, resentment and disapproval.

The political development of our organised society has risen alongside a physically structured society in which we have all become increasingly dependent upon one another for lighting, food, heating, transport, communications and everything else. We are very vulnerable to society's whims. We live in homes and use equipment which makes us far more dependent than our ancestors ever were. They could light a paraffin lamp for light, put wood on the stove for heat or for cooking and walk or ride to the nearby market for any supplies which they could not grow or make themselves. We have created an infinitely more complex society in which true independence is difficult to achieve.

The mass of people welcome a structured society because it offers them several specific types of security.

First, through the provision of a police force, ostensibly hired to protect and represent citizens, it offers them security against crime and violence. Second, it offers security against physical privation. And third, it offers the security of a known and accepted standard of living. These are all reasonable and humane objectives.

But the original proposals have been dramatically enhanced. The security against physical privation and the security of a given standard of life have both been extended. The provision of security against physical privation (ensuring that every member of society has enough food, shelter against the elements and clothing to keep him warm, and is therefore able to preserve his health and his ability and capacity to work) can, as long as one assumes that this level of security is only offered to those who are genuinely in need, easily be provided through an ordinary 'free' society without in any way endangering the freedom of other individuals. But, in most modern societies, this original level of security has been superseded by a far broader level of social support. The result, today, is that the provision of a widespread, all encompassing social security service, designed to provide those who are not working, or who are for some other reason unable to look after themselves, with a standard of living which approximates to that enjoyed by those who are the lower end of the working population, has produced a considerable amount of dishonesty among those who want to take advantage of these 'free' benefits and an equal amount of resentment among those who are working and who are therefore supporting these individuals as well as themselves.

Protecting anyone's standard of living (or the standard of living they think they are entitled to) through artificial means results, inevitably, in the erosion of freedom and the disappearance of security for others.

The provision of a minimum income and a guaranteed standard of life for those who have no intention of working, or taking on the responsibility for themselves and their families, can only be provided by controlling a huge proportion of the wealth of those who are in work, and by establishing a socialist or communist system of government which takes control of much if not all of the ordinary person's life. And yet the freedom to make and control your own money (and your own life) is fundamental for human happiness and for true liberty.

***

Something else has happened to weaken the very structure of our society.

Traditionally, in any community, individuals have to choose between a safe, secure environment or a free and risky environment.

Those who choose to join the police force, the army or the civil service work within a safe, secure environment. In the army there is plenty of security but relatively little freedom. In nationalised industries (a safe, secure environment) the pressure is so small and the work so slow that anything and everything takes twice as long (and costs twice as much) as it would in the private sector. Around the world virtually every nationalised industry which has been privatised has become considerably more cost effective than it was before. This is simply because those who work within a nationalised industry are protected from the requirements of the real world.

In economic terms the relationship between freedom, security and reward has always been a relatively simple one. The soldier and the civil servant have sacrificed freedom for security and have always earned more than the unsuccessful businessman but less than the successful businessman. But in our modern society those who join the police force, the army or the civil service have succeeded in demanding and obtaining the same sort of economic reward as is obtained by the most successful businessmen. Civil servants, whose income and status are assigned and guaranteed by some unseen and unaccountable authority, want (and demand) total job security and index linked pensions (benefits which are denied those who are employed in ordinary businesses or who are self employed) but they obtain these securities at the expense of the ordinary non civil servant employee. After all, someone (the taxpayer) has to pay for those benefits. The result is that businesses and the self employed have less money and less freedom. The working community is guaranteeing to those who have the greatest amount of security a fixed part of a variable cake (the national Gross Domestic Product) and so the share left for the rest must fluctuate. Those who have willingly surrendered their freedom for security have taken freedom from those who do not have the security. This is, of course, an insidious, well disguised form of communism and yet it is a system which has grown and been sustained under allegedly 'right wing' governments.

Right wing politicians may have privatised former state industries but they have replaced state monopolies with private monopolies which are, generally speaking, pretty much as bad; they are more efficient and more profitable but they are still as large and impersonal and still in the hands of the new aristocracy: the bureaucrats.

Today's governments – whether left wing or right wing – are preoccupied and obsessed with the idea of managing the voters and regulating their every activity. In some countries you can now even be fined for not registering to vote! (Why? After all, you don't usually have to vote. The answer is that 'they' use the voting register as a way of checking up on the identities and whereabouts of all the citizens.)

Nothing, it seems, is now outside the remit of the government. Socialist Sidney Webb claimed that the future belonged to the great administrative nations, where the officials governed and the police kept order. His prediction has been proved accurate.

The great irony here is that modern socialism has been nurtured, to a large extent unknowingly and unthinkingly, by the very people who were originally the targets of socialism. Back in the 19th century Alexis de Tocqueville and Lord Acton both warned that socialism meant slavery. And they were right; modern socialism has meant that freedom, liberty and tolerance have all now pretty much lost their meanings.

It is easy to forget that the original founders of socialism wanted to create a dictatorial government, controlling the people, putting a stop to revolution and reorganising society on distinctly hierarchical lines. There was never any real difference between socialism, fascism and communism: these were all anti-democratic, anti-freedom concepts.

What, after all, is the difference between fascism and communism? To all those who follow these two beliefs it is the state and the machinery of the state which matters – rather than the individual. The concepts may sound different but the end results are the same. The freedom of the individual and freedom of thought have never played any part in socialism. It was the socialists, not the fascists, who first thought of encouraging children to join political organisations and organising sports, uniforms and special forms of address for the members of those organisations.

(As a side bar it is interesting to note that communism has always been just as elitist as any capitalist society ever devised. In the Soviet Union, under communist rule, the difference between the highest and the lowest salaries paid was about 50 to 1 – the same sort of magnitude that existed in countries such as the United States of America. In 1939 Leon Trotsky estimated that: 'the upper 11 or 12% of the Soviet population now receives approximately 50% of the national income. This differentiation is sharper than in the United States, where the upper 10% of the population receives approximately 35% of the national income.')

Socialists often complain that socialist parties have drifted noticeably to the right. In fact this isn't the case at all. It is the other way around. Steadily, and without anyone noticing, Conservative parties have drifted so far to the left that they have taken over the ground previously held by the socialists. They have initiated and approved a continuing growth in government control and state expenditure and they have steadfastly supported the continuing state interference in the lives of their citizens.

It was Lenin who introduced to Russia the twin question: 'Who, Whom?' when asking who dominated whom and who takes the decisions that affect whom. In a modern 'developed' and allegedly 'free' nation – even one allegedly run by 'right wing' politicians – it is the state and its servants who have become the 'Who?' and the citizens who have become the 'Whom?'.

CHAPTER FOUR
Great, And Even Greater, Expectations

'We put too much faith in systems and look too little to men.'
- Benjamin Disraeli

The big question raised by all this is a crucial one: why should young people take risks with their earning potential when they can get well paid pensioned jobs working for the state?

In recent years the privileges associated with state employment have multiplied along with the levels of security promised. Today's bureaucrats have taken the freedom of others and used it to enhance their own status and wealth. Today, a salaried and pensioned position gives security and power.

The likelihood of anyone choosing a 'high risk' career as an entrepreneur has been reduced still further by the fact that businessmen are constantly reviled as being rather nasty and in some ways unpalatable individuals by hypocrites whose own status and success is dependent upon the business success of others but who, nevertheless, maintain to sniff at profits as somehow immoral and disreputable, and who make it clear that they regard the very employment of others as synonymous with exploitation.

The successful businessman is sneered at and reviled by legions of talentless and unsuccessful pseudointellectuals and half witted academics (and, in particular, by second rate journalists on the broadsheet newspapers) for being successful, and the unsuccessful businessman is reviled for being unsuccessful.

The pseudointellectuals are too stupid to see that the very elements of society which they pretend to admire most wholeheartedly are at risk not because of businessmen but because of bureaucrats. The pseudointellectuals who think of money making as a low thing, and who believe that geniuses never go in for business are, in truth, so badly educated that they do not realise that Plato defrayed his travelling expenses by selling oil during his journeys, that Spinoza polished glasses to earn money, that Linnaeus the botanist earned his living making shoes and that Shakespeare took more pride from the fact that he was a successful theatre manager than from the plays he wrote. His main aim in working was not literary success but to acquire an honest independence.

The pseudointellectuals use the word 'popular' in a derogatory sense. ('He is just a 'popular' writer') because they are too poorly read to realise that Shakespeare was a popular playwright. Today, in pseudointellectual circles, the two prerequisites for 'literary' success are to be 'unpopular' and 'unreadable'.

**

Despite the shortsightedness of the pseudointellectual supporters of our bizarre and bureaucrat run society the power of a millionaire employer today may be less than that of a small, pen pushing clerk who has the discretion to make (or not make) petty decisions and who has the authority of the state behind him.

It is true that wealthy individuals do have some power. But the antithesis of a world in which the wealthy have power is a world in which only the powerful can attain wealth – and it is this sort of world which we are rapidly creating.

Minority groups are far freer in a capitalist system than in a state system for there is a much greater chance of a member of a minority gaining money and offering employment to his friends and associates in a capitalist system than there is of a state functionary offering work to members of an officially frowned upon or even forbidden minority.

If, instead of money we only had public honours and distinctions, special privileges, more servants (though not called 'servants' of course), a better class of travel, more luxurious accommodation and smarter cars (as was the case in many communist countries) then the person awarding these privileges would have the power normally associated with money – the only difference would be that he would be able to decide the format and extent of any reward. The recipient of this community largesse would have no choice in the matter. He would have no freedom to decide how to spend his 'value' to society.

Karl Marx himself noted that the evolution of private capitalism, with its free market, was an essential precondition for the formation and development and sustenance of all the freedoms we associate with democracy. Money may have its evils but there is no alternative. It is surprising, therefore, that Marx and his followers did not foresee that the freedoms we enjoy might disappear if the free market also disappeared. But then those with far left wing beliefs are often as blind to the truth as those who have far right wing beliefs.

**

People now expect society to protect them from hunger, poverty and every other possible threat to their wealth, health and general well-being. Investors expect society to reimburse them if they lose money through their own stupidity or greed. Patients expect society to get them better even if they have become ill through their own fault (by eating fatty food or smoking cigarettes and so on).

Those with jobs expect society to provide them with unemployment benefit even if the company which was employing them goes bankrupt as a result of their own demands for excessively high wages. This interference with the natural course of events has led to a population which demands more and more and expects more and more and to a society in which freedom is continually eroded.

Householders expect society to pay the bill if they lose their homes through some natural disaster. There may be no moral justification for their misfortune but once society starts to take on such a massive role it must inevitably make demands upon those who have not been so unfortunate. Every penny given to the unfortunate must be taken from those who have not been so unfortunate.

Farmers expect society to reimburse them if their crops fail to prove as profitable as expected, or if their own greed and stupidity has led to a crisis within their industry.

The culture of subsidy has become international, rather than just national or individual. Every country, every large company and every large group demands official government funding and support. Protection against failure of almost any kind is now demanded and expected even though this type of protection (and security) is irreconcilable with a free society.

In a free society it is inevitable that some skills will disappear as new inventions are developed. The invention of the motor car led to the demise of the coach building industry and the need for a constant supply of horses to pull the coaches. The people employed in those industries became unemployed. In today's society such developments are not allowed to take place unless those who have lost their livelihood (and those who have invested in the industries which have been put out of business) are compensated by society or promised alternative employment.

It is always sad when a skill or an industry is superseded and those involved may not be at fault (though in many cases a little foresight would have helped minimise the extent of the damage) but when society tries to take on such huge and endless responsibilities it must inevitably remove many freedoms from the ordinary citizen. Government handouts never made a man great.

***

People expect someone else to take the responsibility for everything. They prefer to take vitamin and mineral tablets recommended by others rather than make the effort to eat wisely, and they prefer to put their hopes on the lottery rather than put any effort into making their own fortunes.

And (and this has been one, if not the, major force in the development of inflation and the ensuing and continuing global economic chaos which has been such a feature of the twentieth century) everyone seems to consider it their right to have their standard of living raised annually. A sufficiency is no longer enough and the greed for more is seemingly inexhaustible. To make matters even worse some trade unions have exacerbated the situation by introducing restrictive practices designed to keep jobs for their own members. This, inevitably, has limited the opportunities available to those individuals whose own jobs have disappeared through the consequences of progress. And so, in yet another way, freedom has been eroded.

***

The masses even allow society to help them deal with their boredom by providing them with non stop television programmes. Taking over leisure is not a new function of the state. The official organisation of leisure activities has been done in both Italy and the Soviet Union and the Nazis even invented a word – 'freizeitgestaltung' – to describe the act of shaping the use of people's free time (rather a contradiction if you stop to think about it since the time can hardly be 'free' if it is spent doing things that the authorities want you to do).

What most citizens do not realise (largely, I suspect, because they never stop to think about it) is that they have paid a high price for the development of a structured, organised society. They have lost their freedom.

When the state takes new powers it is creating those new powers out of nothing – since such powers do not exist in a healthy, free, competitive society. And the state cannot take more power without the citizens giving up some of their own power over their own lives – in other words their freedom.

When support and security is provided for some it is a privilege paid for at the expense of others; and since our communal wealth is in the end finite the end result is that the security of those who have contributed to the protection of others will be diminished. When governments shelter the unfortunate and provide them with full compensation they are able to do so only because they have, at the same time, taken away the freedoms and the rights of others.

In order to pay those who have been unlucky society has to take more and more from those who have worked hard and not been unfortunate. The worker, the inventor and the investor must all pay a growing portion of their earnings to society in order to help fulfil society's responsibilities.

And yet how can these active parts of society function without reward? If the reward for working, inventing or investing becomes too small then everyone will simply sit back and let society look after them. There will be no incentive to work or to succeed. If you remove all potential risk from life then you also remove all possible reward. Unless there is a relationship between risk, usefulness and remuneration society cannot survive. Without incentives, and the economic discipline associated with success and failure, society is doomed.

It is possible to see what happens when the relationship between risk and reward disappears by looking at state run industries. The managers of state run enterprises should be as vulnerable as the managers of commercial businesses. They should be accountable. But although they demand equal pay they do not accept equal levels of responsibility. Managers of state run enterprises are well rewarded without taking risks and so there is no innovation and no development. Mistakes go unpunished, particularly when they are errors of omission rather than errors of commission – it is far harder to punish a manager for not taking a decision than it is to punish a manger who takes a decision which can be shown to have been the wrong one – and managers inevitably stick to the safe route and avoid anything innovative and therefore risky.

CHAPTER FIVE
Bureaucratic Totalitarianism

*'The worth of a State, in the long run, is the worth of the individuals compos-
ing it.'*

- J.S.Mill

The sweetener which has been used to make the loss of freedom palatable (or,
rather, unnoticeable) has been the promise of a far greater degree of security
than has ever been available before. In most developed societies citizens expect
to be protected not only against crime but also against poverty, hunger, cold and
all the privations which used to be regarded as personal responsibilities. Most
citizens have remained blissfully unaware that by accepting organisation and
security they have also accepted a bureaucratic totalitarianism.

The authorities have freed us from the responsibility and necessity of
solving our own problems. In doing this they have taken away our individual
freedom. The 'new' freedom, offered by our ostensibly kindly state organisations, is no freedom at all. In today's world it is society itself which has all the
rights and individuals who have all the responsibilities. The individual today is
simply used by society in the service of the community. The will of the invisible
masses, represented undemocratically by society, has been imposed on us all.

And in our society the masses are the least original and most dependent
force. However much people may talk about 'cockup' and 'conspiracy' theories the major driving force in our Society is apathy.

***

Some people believe that this steady but determined removal of all our
freedoms is part of some global plan; part of a conspiracy designed to lead to
world government, putting all the power into the hands of a tiny élite.

A more likely explanation is that the erosion of our freedoms, and the rise in the power of the bureaucracy is simply the result of a process which is no longer within anyone's control.

As I explained in my book *How To Overcome Toxic Stress*, we have created a monster ('society') over which we now have little or no control.

We tend to think of the word 'society' as referring in some vague sort of way to all of us. I think we would be wiser to regard 'society' as a malignant being with an identity and a force of its own.

To a large extent it no longer really matters very much whether the disappearance of personal freedom and the rise in state freedom is a result of a conspiracy or has simply happened. The only way in which the present system could be changed would be through a revolution; a popular and general uprising. It is a nice thought. And although it may seem unthinkable at the moment it will happen – just as there have been people's revolutions in the U.S.S.R., East Germany, Yugoslavia, South Africa and elsewhere in recent years, so there will be a worldwide people's revolution throughout the 'civilised, developed' west. But it is unlikely to happen for a while for the very simple reason that most people have no idea what has happened.

Voters may protest if taxes rise too high or if a particular freedom is removed but such protests are usually fairly short lived.

Occasional, very specific, protests against new roads or infringements of freedom may succeed. And, by succeeding, such small and very specific protests help to persuade us that we live in a democracy where the voices of the people can be heard. But all this is superficial and largely irrelevant. Most people are too comfortable, too cowed and too frightened to protest yet about the erosions in their freedom which really matter. For example, Britain (which currently has more electronic eyes per capita than any other nation on Earth, with the result that tens of thousands of powerful cameras connected directly to computer bases constantly spy on people and cars) has, in recent years, gradually become a police state without anyone noticing.

Apologists for our society frequently reassure us smugly with the thought that George Orwell's predictions for the future (as outlined in his novel '1984') have not come to pass. But the fact is that they *have*. The only difference between fiction and reality, the only thing that Orwell got wrong, is that the takeover has been much more subtle than expected – and most people haven't even noticed what has happened.

Most of today's citizens have become gullible and docile; they are far more interested in watching their television sets than they are in taking part in a revolution. The masses have no real convictions and are easily swayed by cheap promises. They can no longer tell the difference between political truths and political lies. And they aren't much interested. They feel that, generally speaking, things aren't too bad.

If they ever stop to think about it they accept that if there is a choice between liberty and a society which promises economic security they will choose the economic security (the fact that the security offered is a myth is irrelevant).

Those individuals who want to remain free, and in control of their own lives, have little choice. If the majority chooses economic security then everyone's liberty will be eroded and eventually imperilled.

Today, too many of the rich get rich through speculative gains on the financial markets and through simple greed – such as is often displayed when industrial executives whose work involves little more than administration pay themselves huge unearned salaries and fat bonuses. The lucky become rich through winning the lottery and those who are unwilling to work or make any effort on their own behalf survive and thrive through state benefits. Economic security, provided by an all encompassing, all knowing, all seeing, 'nanny' society can only be obtained at a price: and the price is a general loss of freedom and liberty. (The corollary is also true, of course. The price of personal freedom and liberty is the risk of personal failure and personal poverty. Freedom carries risks and responsibilities.)

* * *

Whether the erosion of our freedom and our privacy is the result of a global conspiracy, or a malignant and out of control bureaucracy, constantly expanding and acquiring new powers, is now to a large extent irrelevant.

The fact is that it is now up to every individual who wants to regain and retain some of his or her freedom and privacy to take charge of their own life.

This isn't easy – and it is getting harder every day – but it is the only way to retain freedom of choice, freedom from the arbitrary power of other men and freedom from coercion. The modern, developed, 'civilised' society is so organised that until there is a global revolution and a degree of anarchy previously unimagined nothing will happen to change things.

Is a global revolution ever possible?

I believe it is. Eventually, the citizens will wake up and shout 'enough'. The widespread availability of computer technology and fax machines will mean that the revolution will be global.

But, as I write this towards the end of the 20th century I cannot see a global revolution developing for at least another two or three decades.

Until then the ordinary citizen will remain relatively content. He will be slightly embittered about the level of taxes he has to pay, and when he turns away from his television set he will notice that the state seems to be taking more and more control over his life, but he will not respond to a call to revolution until the point is reached where the number of people working and contributing to society is smaller than the number of people who are dependent upon society for their income.

PART TWO

Where Did Your Freedom Go?
(To Find Out You Must Understand The Society In Which You Live)

'Men labour under a mistake. The better part of the man is soon ploughed into the soil for compost. By a seeming fate, commonly called necessity, they are employed laying up treasures which moth and rust will corrupt and thieves break through and steal. It is a fool's life.

- Henry David Thoreau

'Even despotism does not produce its worst effects as long as individuality exists under it; and whatever crushes individuality is despotism, by whatever name it be called.'

- John Stuart Mill

CHAPTER ONE
The Separation Of Authority From Responsibility

'Innumerable are these small and pitiable men; but raindrops and weeds have already brought about the destruction of many a proud building.'
                                                                    - Frederick Nietzsche

'Excuse me,' said the pregnant woman, climbing out of her car with considerable difficulty. She was holding a small child in her arms. 'Would it be all right if I left my car here for a moment while I popped into the pharmacy? I've got to pick up a prescription for my husband. He's at home, ill in bed.'

The traffic warden, to whom she had addressed this entirely reasonable request, stroked his moustache and glared at her. 'More than my job's worth,' he said gruffly. He pointed to a nearby post upon which were fastened several lines of instructions. 'You can park here after six o'clock, but not before.'

The woman looked at her watch. 'But it's five to six now,' she said. She looked around. 'And there's hardly any traffic. I'm not going to cause an obstruction.'

'I don't make the rules,' said the traffic warden, drawing himself up to his full height. He looked very smart in his expensive uniform. He would have made a good gestapo officer.

'And the pharmacy shuts at six!' the woman pointed out. 'If I drive to the car park I won't be able to get the prescription made out.'

'Not my responsibility,' sniffed the traffic warden. 'You should have come earlier and given yourself time to park.'

'I couldn't come earlier. The doctor has only just called.' said the woman. 'We've been waiting all day for him to arrive.'

The traffic warden shrugged his shoulders.

'Give me the prescription,' I said to the woman. 'You drive round the block once and I'll pop into the pharmacy and get your husband's pills.'

And so her husband got his prescription and the traffic warden was denied another victim.

(I repeatedly attack traffic wardens in my newspaper column. The traffic wardens sometimes complain and say that the attacks are unfair because they are simply 'doing their jobs'. However, I think that we need to attack them and to marginalise them. They are the visible tip of the cruel, uncaring, authoritarian iceberg which is threatening civilisation.)

***

If there is anything more frustrating than having responsibility without the necessary authority it must be coming face to face with people who have authority but no personal responsibility.

Responsibility is a burden, authority a weapon and it is just and right that a man prepared to accept the strains of one should enjoy the complementary power of the other.

However, it sometimes seems that no one wants to take responsibility for their own actions. And society no longer expects people to take responsibility for their own actions.

Traditionally, responsibility and authority have always been close. The man (or woman) who has responsibility has traditionally had the authority to back up that responsibility.

But, power, responsibility and authority have been split from one another in our society.

I believe that it is the artificial separation of responsibility and authority by those unwilling to accept the former but eager to enjoy the latter which causes much of the anger, dissatisfaction and jealousy in our society and which, therefore, indirectly causes more stress induced illness than anything else.

A factory foreman or junior manager may have the responsibility for ensuring that the output in his department remains high, but it is unlikely that he will have the authority to enable him to order the equipment or materials he needs. Nor will he have the necessary authority over the workers for whom he is theoretically responsible.

A hospital doctor who is morally and legally responsible for the health of the patients in his care does not have the authority to insist that the hospital is kept supplied with the staff or drugs he believes to be necessary. He cannot even insist that the heating is turned on when he thinks it is necessary. His responsibility extends far beyond the boundaries of his authority.

But the bureaucrat or administrator who does have authority will have no responsibility for the output of goods or for the health of patients. His responsibilities are defined and limited but his authority will be great.

Administrators, clerks and officials all have the authority of the rule book and of the people who drew up the rules, but they have no personal responsibility.

Try arguing with a ticket collector or with a traffic warden and you will see what I mean. There is plenty of authority there, but no willingness to accept personal responsibility.

And, of course, while the man with authority cannot lose, the man with responsibility cannot win. The man with authority has only to insist that the rules be obeyed but if anything goes wrong the man with responsibility carries the can.

It is hardly surprising, therefore, that it is the people with the responsibility who most frequently suffer from stress diseases; who commit suicide, who die young and who break down unable to cope.

But when the people with the responsibilities have all gone – defeated, dispirited or simply dead – what will we have left? What is a society with rules and regulations if there is no one to lead and direct, to take decisions and to accept personal responsibilities?

In any society it is those who are prepared to accept responsibility who make up the foundations upon which all else stands.

We must ensure that those who have authority accept personal responsibility for their work. No longer should the petty official be allowed to escape from responsibility simply by sticking to the rules. He should be responsible for his interpretation of the rules. When he interprets the rules in a cruel, inhumane or clearly stupid way he should be disciplined or even fired. He will then learn that authority and responsibility go together.

And we must ensure that those who have responsibility are entitled to the authority they need. Only when he himself takes the decisions which influence his own success or failure can a man be expected to assume full responsibility.

Until we have reunited responsibility and authority we will all be living in totalitarian states.

***

Those who play a practical role in the management of a totalitarian state must be prepared to ignore or break all moral rules in order to achieve the ends they consider appropriate and they must also accept specious justifications for whatever vile acts they may be called upon to perpetrate.

The administrators of the totalitarian machine must have no ideals of their own and no personal views on 'right' or 'wrong'. They must simply get on with their distasteful tasks in the daily search for power and in their daily obeisance to the party machine. Their pleasure is that of being obeyed by the 'peasants'; of being the servants of a large and powerful state machine and of knowing that everything that is not specifically permitted is prohibited. In any state organisation power drifts towards those who are unprincipled and unscrupulous; those who are honest and honourable have too many morals and scruples to survive in a harsh, unbending, unsympathetic bureaucratic world.

In any totalitarian society there is an almost endless demand for individuals who are prepared to be unthinking and who are willing to put the machine before their own individual feelings. ('It's more than my job's worth, mate.' 'I can't let you do that – it's against the rules.') At some levels the requirement is merely for a functionaries who do not question the rules but who obey them – and see that everyone else obeys them too. In return for this obedience they receive a regular wage, a smart uniform and far more power than they could have ever acquired through their own actions. At higher levels the need is for people who are prepared to be cruel, intimidating and deceptive on behalf of the state. The Nazi's SS Ministry of Propaganda has its counterparts in all modern societies.

The biggest mistake made by the well meaning and kind hearted is to underestimate the number of psychopathic individuals in our society who are prepared to do anything for a little regular money and a small degree of power. People in power – whether it is a small amount of power or a large amount of power – enjoy power. The possibility of a man in a position of power being there by mistake is slight indeed.

(It is also a mistake to underestimate the number of individuals in positions of power who obtain pleasure through causing pain, distress and unhappiness. It is surprising that we consistently underestimate the number of people who are prepared to act in a cruel way. And yet we should not really be surprised. After all, our newspapers and our radio and television stations frequently publish material which vilifies and subsequently destroys named individuals who have done little or nothing to deserve such opprobrium and public contempt. They publish this material because they know it is what a large number of their readers want. It is a worrying fact that many people obtain real pleasure from the discomfort of others. It is, therefore, hardly surprising that there are plenty of people around who are prepared to work as local government officers, prison officers, abattoir workers, traffic wardens and so on. People who work in positions of petty power – where there can be no self justification on the grounds that they have or even understand a feeling for the greater good of society – are inherently unprincipled people. None of these people take these jobs by accident or against their will.)

***

I loathe and despise the bureaucrats because of the harm they are doing to our world.

A friend of mine had a breakdown because he could not cope with the bureaucrats. He was brilliant at what he did. But he couldn't cope with the endless silly rules. He was for ever in trouble with the bureaucrats. He tried to argue with them. It was futile. In the end they broke his spirit. He is now dead.

Another talented friend set up a small business. She saved hard, studied hard and worked hard. She put everything she had into her business. But in the end the bureaucrats broke her. The bureaucrats drowned her in paperwork. They wouldn't listen when she asked for sense. They took months to make simple decisions which affected her life. In the end she gave up the struggle. A decade or two ago she would have been a huge success. But in today's society it is the bureaucrat who has the power and the authority. The entrepreneur has only the responsibility.

I sympathise with anyone whose life is made miserable by these petty horrors. They steadfastly refuse to take responsibility for their own actions. The bureaucrats are dedicated to obstruction, they are inescapable. They are everywhere.

And we must fight them!

There is, however, no point in trying to fight them by their rules. The bureaucrats have endless supplies of paper, time and money. They have your money and my money.

If you try to argue with the bureaucrats by using their rules you will lose. They know their rules well. They will suffocate you with paperwork.

If you try to plead with them to be sensible they will sneer at you. They have no hearts. Point out that their silly rules are threatening your job, your business, your family and your health and they will shrug their shoulders and wander off to sharpen another pencil.

The only way to challenge them is to complain about them to their superiors (for the one beauty in all this is that every bureaucrat has a superior, every bureaucrat must obey the rules and every bureaucrat is scared because he knows that if he loses his job, his place within the system, then he will be left as naked as you or I in a world for which he is quite unprepared).

And for those of us in the real world there is one final consolation.

If, in the end, we lose, if the bureaucrats win complete control of our lives, then there will still (for the rest of us at least) be a 'happy' ending.

For without the entrepreneurs, the businessmen and women, the people who are prepared to take risks, take chances, take responsibility, and risk their lives, their money and their health in the pursuit of a personal dream, the bureaucrats will have nothing. There will be no one earning any real money. There will be no one to pay for the offices, the fat salaries, the inflation linked pensions, the endless courses in expensive hotels, the comfortable offices, the long holidays and the empty weekends. The bureaucrats will be in charge of a society which will die and their final victory will be their own defeat.

CHAPTER TWO
Growing Dependency Upon The State

---

*'The effect of Socialist doctrine on Capitalist society is to produce a third
thing, different from either of its two begetters – to wit, the Servile State.'*
- Hilaire Belloc

There is an old Chinese proverb which says: 'If you give a man food you feed
him for a day. If you teach him to grow his own food you feed him for a lifetime.' This is the 'hand up' rather than the 'hand out' philosophy.

Charity workers trying to combat starvation in Africa have for some years
now followed this principle with some enthusiasm; recognising that it makes far
more sense to build roads and provide agricultural implements than merely to
fly in bags of food. Encouraging people to think and act and improve themselves, and to be free and to act independently, is true philanthropy.

However, there is no little irony in the fact that while charity workers in
the developing world are encouraging people to be more independent and to
think for themselves exactly the opposite is happening the 'developed' world.

Today, in the western world, the new standard state philosophy is based
upon the 'hand out' principle rather than the 'hand up' principle. An increasing
number of people are now dependent upon society for all their needs. And many
more are learning to turn to society when life gets tough. People are widely encouraged to expect and accept money from society rather than to do more to
look after themselves. There is now little sense of personal or public responsibility, little compassion and little feeling that it is each man's (and woman's) duty
to take his (or her) life into their own hands. People expect doctors, teachers,
civil servants, bureaucrats and the courts to take responsibility for *their* lives
(and then those same people complain (quietly) when they think the system is
being 'bossy', taking too much power and pushing them around).

Everyone, it seems, wants more and more public money – with no thought about where the public money will come from. Scientists want public funding for their experiments. Investors want to be given public money if their investments turn sour. The unemployed expect to be given public money in lieu of employment – with absolutely no regard for whether or not they actually need public money in order to provide themselves with food, clothing and shelter. There are now small armies of people who have grown up accustomed to the idea that society will look after them. They regard the funding provided by society as 'soft' or 'easy' money. Their constant demands for money are now leading to a great division not between the 'haves' and the 'have nots' but between the 'givers' and the 'receivers'. The receivers want more. The givers want to give less. The resulting tension provides the authorities with a constant excuse for more policing and less freedom and less independence.

Society worries endlessly about the 'have-nots' but the so called 'haves' are also under pressure. They have to fight to preserve the things they have worked hard to achieve, and because all around them they see people who are receiving but not giving their motivation is constantly being weakened. They have to struggle daily against personal and family anxieties and yet they receive no support or encouragement from society.

**

There is much talk about drug addiction in our society and yet all the evidence shows that drug addiction is, in statistical terms, a relatively small problem.

(The quantity and quality of health damage done by illegal drugs is minute compared to the type and extent of damage done by prescribed drugs and by freely and legally available substances such as alcohol and tobacco.)

The greatest dependency in the western world (and the most damaging and the most destructive) is dependency on state welfare support; dependency on society and an expectation that someone else will always take the responsibility.

The 'developed' world has created an almost universal 'dependency sickness'. 'I am broke – give me money.' 'I am unemployed. Find me a job or give me money.' 'I am sick. Make me better.' 'I'm old. Look after me.' 'I'm pregnant. Take care of me and my child.' State welfare has undermined the principles of self support and mutual aid. This sort of dependency stifles the imagination and destroys the urge to work and it will surely destroy our society.

There is a bizarre assumption among many who have made state support a way of life that the money comes from some surreal, inexhaustible source. We have created entirely false expectations about what governments can and should do. The expectations have grown to totally unsustainable levels and have weakened our ability to fend for ourselves.

The provision of all these funds is a constant and exhausting drain on those who work. We will now never be able to provide all the money that is needed – any more than health care systems will ever be able to find all the money that is needed to support and pay for complete health care for every citizen.

National progress has been, at least in part, defined as the sum of individual industry and energy, while national decay has been defined as including the sum of individual idleness and selfishness. A state which endorses dependence upon itself encourages the latter and discourages the former.

***

The dependency upon other people has, in some areas of life, reached bizarre depths. For example, for twenty years or so now it has been an increasingly common practice in some countries for surgeons to remove women's breasts so that they don't get breast cancer. We know that women can dramatically reduce their chances of developing breast cancer by changing their diet (briefly, by avoiding fatty food and meat – there is more detail in my book *Power over Cancer*) but many women prefer to have their breasts removed, rather than make the effort required to alter their diet.

Similarly, many people prefer to have heart surgery rather than deal with their heart disease by changing their diet and lifestyle (once again there is now evidence to show that it is possible to cure as well as prevent heart disease by making lifestyle changes of this type – this evidence is summarised in my book *How To Stop Your Doctor Killing You*).

I find these choices quite astonishing but largely symptomatic of a society in which it is now commonplace for people deliberately to choose to hand over responsibility for their health to the medical professionals.

It is this same principle which results in the widespread expectation that there will be a pill for every illness; that every health problem, be it sleeplessness, unhappiness, overweight or a double chin, can be dealt with in some way by someone else. Patients prefer pills and surgery (the easy solutions) to making lifestyle changes (the hard solutions). And doctors, not knowing what else to do, usually oblige.

Too many people want slick, quick solutions to all their problems – whether those problems are financial, health related or anything else. The need for support – and for a constant stream of 'hand outs' rather than an occasional 'hand up' – has been rising for decades and will continue to rise indefinitely. We will never be able to provide enough money or resources to satisfy all the demands.

CHAPTER THREE
Everyone Wants To Win The Lottery

'Anything acquired without effort and without cost is generally unappreci-ated.'

- Napoleon Hill

Gambling is one of the most basic instincts of all. Like the sexual urge it is there within us all – constantly waiting to be released. Gambling may have now equalled television as the most popular – and most dangerous – addiction in the world. The reason for this is simple: gambling – particularly through that now almost universal institution 'The Lottery' – offers something that not even television can match: the lottery offers wealth without work. The fact that gambling has become one of the most popular 'hobbies' in the 'developed' world is a symbol of the fact that everyone now wants a quick and easy solution to their financial problems.

The lottery is a perfect example of the 'something for nothing' philoso-phy which pervades our society; a perfect accompaniment to the welfare state. It is, indeed, more than an example: it is a beacon, leading millions astray with the faint and false hope of riches, and a symbol of the constant demand for a quick and slick solution to all of life's problems, an easy and quick escape from a humdrum life. The lottery offers a solution that does not involve any acceptance of responsibility or even, heaven forbid, anything as horrifying as work.

The people who buy lottery tickets are, by and large, the very people who can least afford them. Lotteries, by definition, take money from today's poor and give it to tomorrow's rich. A very small number of the poor become rich. But most of the poor are simply made poorer. The surprising fact is that if the poor or relatively poor people who gamble saved the money they spend on the lottery they could, within a remarkably short time, improve their own lives them-selves.

Lotteries undermine the principles of working and saving to achieve success but they have other serious faults too. Even in those countries where lotteries are run with the aim of raising money for the community the charitable contributions made hardly seem designed to improve the lives of the poor. Much of the money goes to subsidise branches of the arts, such as opera. Lottery money is, indeed, widely used to support predominantly upper and middle class culture and activities.

I have little doubt that as years go by the damage done by lotteries will rise steadily. A recent survey of children between the ages of 11 and 15 showed that two out of three had bought lottery tickets. In a strange, perverse sort of way buying a lottery ticket is now almost seen as being a 'good citizen'.

CHAPTER FOUR
When Black Isn't Black And White Isn't White

---

*'The socialists believe in two things which are absolutely different and per-
haps even contradictory: freedom and organisation.'*

- Elie Halevy

*'Failure in any good cause is ...honourable, whilst success in any bad cause is
merely infamous.'*

- Samuel Smiles

*'Obscene is not the picture of a naked woman but that of a fully clad general
who exposes his medals won in a war of aggression.'*

- Herbert Marcuse

We live in a world where superficiality rules over substance. Our standards are
reducing daily. Moral ideals are absent from our society. Our world is confused,
and confusing, because people have thrown over the old standards without acquiring any new ones.

From our very earliest days we are brought up to think of all sorts of
things as sinful. And yet, too often, it is difficult to see the logic in the arguments
we are encouraged to follow. For example, we are taught by teachers and parents that bad language is sinful. It is difficult to see just why this should be. Why
should one collection of letters be considered worse than another? Why should
we forfeit the love of our God and those close to us by using words which are
regarded for some arbitrary reason as offensive? We are taught that sex is sinful.
And yet sex is nothing more than physical loving and conception (though not
necessarily together). What is wrong with physical love? What is wrong with
conception? Why should talking about, thinking about or doing these things be

an offence against our parents, our teachers and God? The truth is that these are nothing more than superstitions.

We are told, when we are young, that lying is never justified. But is that true? Bertrand Russell, the eminent philosopher, mathematician and peace campaigner, told this story in his book *The Conquest of Happiness*: 'I once in the course of a country walk saw a tired fox at the last stages of exhaustion still forcing himself to run. A few minutes afterwards I saw the hunt. They asked me if I had seen the fox, and I said I had. They asked me which way he had gone, and I lied to them. I do not think I should have been a better man if I had told the truth.'

Russell is absolutely right, of course. He would most surely have been committing a far greater sin in those circumstances if he had told the truth.

What is black and what is white? What is sin? When is a sin really sinful? And, just as confusing, what about the apparently sinful things which are not officially regarded as sinful at all.

Violence, for example, is rarely regarded as quite as sinful as sex or even nudity. And yet surely the glorification of violence is more obscene than anything requiring nothing more than one or more healthy, naked human bodies.

***

Back in 1995 the whole of Britain seemed to be joining in public events designed to celebrate the 40th anniversary of victory over the Germans in the Second World War.

I found the whole idea of celebrating a victory obscene. It seemed to me that banners in the streets, balloons, street parties, cucumber sandwiches and crates of beer on trestle tables in the local church hall were not really the way to remember a war which killed so many millions.

I wasn't even sure what people were celebrating. Were all the parties being held to celebrate the fact the Allied bombs were bigger and better than German bombs and that the megalomaniacal leaders representing the forces of 'light' and 'good' were better, brighter and tougher than the megalomaniacal leaders representing the forces of 'darkness' and 'evil'?

Was the dancing in the streets somehow supposed to help us remember the men and women who died in this global bloodbath?

'Have a glass of sherry and a mince pie, Miss Blenkinsop. Let me just have one more look at the tear and blood stained letter your fiance wrote just two hours before he was blown up by a German landmine and then we'll dance down the street together popping balloons and singing Vera Lynn songs.'

Or were people just putting on their finery and decorating the streets to remind themselves of more glorious days?

'Have another cup of tea and a ham sandwich vicar, and look at these pictures of Dresden burning. If you look very carefully you can see German people in agony with their clothes on fire.'

On the one hand the British people were being told that they would soon all be part of a single European state. They would all sing the same anthem, offer their loyalty to the same flag and carry the same currency in their pockets.

And yet people were playing hopscotch in the streets to remember the last great European war.

Was the dancing in the streets supposed to help people remember the horrors of war? Were people supposed to collapse, exhausted and slightly drunk, at the end of the celebration parties and say: 'We must never, ever have another war again.'

Some of those organising and enjoying the street parties said they were celebrating because the Second World War stopped all wars.

Really?

While Britain's V.E. celebrations were going on there were no less than forty eight civil wars and revolutions going on in various parts of the world. Forty eight separate wars, all being fought by two lots of people who thought that they were in the right and who believed that their cause justified the death, the pain and the suffering that war entails.

As I write this today there are four million unexploded land mines in Bosnia and fifteen million unexploded land mines in Angola. Heaven knows how many unexploded land mines there are around the rest of the world. Land mine design and manufacture has become extremely sophisticated in recent years. Modern mines are designed to maim rather than to kill because the armaments manufacturers have realised that maiming an individual ties up hospital and medical services, causes social disruption, creates fear and distress and costs the enemy more than just killing people. Children seem to be the most common victims of many of these modern mine laying exercises. This is no accident.

***

The problem is that most of our feelings about sin are nonsensical Sunday school beliefs, infantile babblings taught to us as part of society's rules and regulations; based on a little religion and a little community spirit. A sense of traditional sin, and a respect for the definitions of sin which have been accepted for centuries, does not make a man good or happy. Indeed, such a distorted sense of sin will make him unhappy, permanently damage his self confidence and fill him with grudges and discontent.

We grow up in a world where the woman most men are taught to love most is a woman with whom any sort of sexual contact or talk is forbidden. The result is that many men feel that contact with women is wrong and that women should disapprove of sex because a woman who does not disapprove of sex cannot be respected. Society then rightly and understandably expresses surprise when the man whose wife is not interested in sex (or, at least, purports not to be interested in sex, or believes she is not interested in sex) finds satisfaction for his natural urges elsewhere. Society then expresses further surprise when the man feels guilty and hates the woman with whom he has had sex. Society then rightly and understandably expresses indignation, anger and astonishment when a man starts killing prostitutes. In the mysterious way in which our society works we are then told that the man has become a 'sex maniac' because he has read too many magazines showing pictures of naked women. No one thinks to blame the morally absurd teachings of a powerful and dominant religious force.

When contemplating sin we should replace our infantile, gloom and doom laden beliefs with real, substantial, and substantiated beliefs.

Too often, in our society, truly horrendous acts, showing a complete absence of compassion, kindness or thoughtfulness, go unpunished and uncriticised. Apparently respectable citizens say cruel things about their fellow citizens without a moment's thought or regret or guilt. Employers exploit their employees who, in turn, cheat their customers. There is widespread and apparently approved cruelty to people and to animals. The sick, the frail, the elderly and infirm and the young are all abused and pushed around, not just by cosh waving louts and thugs but also by pen toting bureaucrats working for and on behalf of society. Animals are tortured and killed for no good reason (other than financial ones) in the laboratories of vivisectors who are paid on our behalf.

Dishonesty and unkindness are, it seems, the norm rather than the exception. And yet none of these actions seem to attract retribution of any kind; none seem to be classified as sins; none seem to be regarded as in any way worthy of criticism. Our civilisation has been slowly and steadily destroyed by these cruel actions but the misery which has been created by the perpetrators seems to attract no ignominy at all.

Children are taught about sin without ever being taught the true meaning of the concept. Children are taught moral values which are based upon superstition and nonsense and quite irrational taboos. Children are taught little or nothing about the true meaning of any sort of honest or honourable relationship. Our modern values of sin were created centuries ago by priests who lived in a different world. Sin today is divorced from any real understanding of moral rights or wrongs. Respect and kindness mean nothing, but disrespect and unkindness are not regarded as sins in our world. We are surviving with concepts of sin which were learned by rote and created for society built upon different values and with a different work ethic.

We live in a prejudiced, cruel, wicked and dominantly immoral world.

CHAPTER FIVE
Women's Liberation – The Biggest Social Blunder Of The Twentieth Century

'When a woman behaves like a man, why doesn't she behave like a nice man?
- Dame Edith Evans

'He who would be a man must be a non conformist.'
- Ralph Waldo Emerson

The women's liberation movement has probably caused more fundamental stress and anxiety than any other social phenomenon for centuries.

Men have been put under stress because they no longer know how to act towards women. Men have been overtaken and overwhelmed by sexual politics. If they are strong and protective (as they were taught they should be) they are likely to be derided and dismissed as sexist. If they aren't strong or protective they are likely to be scorned as weak and wimpy. Most men are still not sure whether women expect them to be macho and chauvinistic (at the risk of being considered unacceptably aggressive) or soft, sensitive and understanding (at the risk of being considered wimpy and rather out of date). Some men are even worried that they should be bonding with their fellow men, though they probably aren't sure what all the sitting around the fire banging drums is really about. All this creates inadequacy and guilt. Most men are tortured by their relationships with the opposite sex.

Male uncertainty is summed up by the dilemma of a man sitting on a bus when a woman gets on. Whatever he does there is a good chance that he will be wrong. If he stands up and offers her his seat he may be attacked for being sexist. If he stays sitting down he is likely to be attacked for being rude and bad mannered. The man who puts his arm around a girl on a date may find himself in court on a charge of attempted assault. If he fails to put his arm around the girl he is likely to be dismissed as a cold hearted queer.

Women have been put under stress by the women's liberation movement too. They feel guilty if they do not fulfil their potential and carve out a successful career. But they also feel guilty if they do not care properly for their families. No one wins. The liberation of women has added to male stresses but, paradoxically, it has harmed women too.

There are, I believe, likely to be other, possibly even more damaging, long term consequences of the women's liberation movement. The aim of the original bra-burning proponents of the women's liberation movement was to close the gaps between the sexes: to remove inequalities by encouraging women to become stronger and more aggressive.

This was a mistake.

Instead of encouraging women to adopt damaging and destructive male qualities the bra-burners should have encouraged men to adopt more of the softer qualities normally associated with women. During the next few decades we will, I believe, see some of the disastrous consequences of this error.

For many years now women have, on average, lived around a decade longer than men. The life expectancy of the average white woman is currently nearly 80 years. The life expectancy of the average white man is just above 70 years. The life expectancy of the average black man is probably nearer to 65. Today men die earlier from all fifteen leading causes of death: including heart disease, cancer, accidents, violence and suicide. During this century, the incidence of stress related illness among men has risen dramatically when compared to the incidence of the same illnesses among women. Every significant stress related disease which is not physiologically unique to women is commoner among men. Nursing homes all over the 'developed' and 'civilised' world are now full of lonely old women who have outlived their male partners. There is no biological explanation for this. Women are not intrinsically healthier than men. Women do not naturally live longer than men. At the turn of the century women and men had an identical life expectancy.

I believe the explanation for the difference in life expectation is that while women have enlarged their role in society men have been pushed further and further into their destructive and damaging masculinity.

There are a few specific, simple explanations for what has happened.

One explanation for the difference in life expectation is that men, as a group, tend to work harder than women. If you include time spent gardening and dealing with chores around the house the average man works a 61 hour week whereas the average woman works a 56 hour week. And women get more health giving exercise than men – partly because their daily responsibilities include quite a lot of walking and partly because they have more free time for swimming, tennis, golf and other sports.

But these are trivial factors. It is social changes which are killing men and filling our hospitals and old people's homes with octogenarian widows. Women are in control in our society. From mothers to wives to daughters it is a woman's world. It is true that men, as a sex, often earn more than women. But although they earn more, men don't get to spend the money they make. And real power comes with the spending not the earning. Women control consumer spending in just about all areas. Stores devote seven times as much space to women's personal items as they do to men's personal items. Both sexes spend more on women than on men. Only in restaurants do men pay the bills and control the spending. It is because women do the spending that most advertising is aimed at women. And it is because most advertising is aimed at women that there are far more magazines and TV programmes aimed to please women than are aimed at men.

We live in a woman's world – and we have done for decades. Many women with two small children will admit that they think of themselves as having three children. They regard their husband as another child. It is not by accident that many men call their wife 'mother'. Men are still subordinated by their mothers and their wives. Men look for maternal comfort, love and solace from their partners and this weakens them and hands power over to the women in their lives.

The main reason why women now live so much longer than men is because their softer, gentler natures mean that they were better at coping with modern twentieth century stresses than men; they are less susceptible to feelings of frustration and less likely to be overcome with anger. It is their soft, natural feminine qualities which protects women from killers such as heart disease.

Although men are, fundamentally, just as emotional as women most men spend a great deal of effort on hiding their emotions. They don't show their sadness or their happiness or their anger. They suppress their tears. They hide everything inside them. They respond emotionally but they do not show those emotions. The damage done by this suppression is phenomenal: it is this suppression of emotional responses which is largely responsible for the pandemic of stress related diseases in our society. Thousands of men are dying of heart disease in their fifties, forties and even thirties because they do not feel able to express what they are feeling. Those locked away fears and anxieties do a massive amount of damage.

***

The whole women's liberation movement was a massive social blunder – probably one of the most important mistakes of the twentieth century. If the proponents of female equality had thought things through a little better, and decided to encourage men to be more like women instead of encouraging women to be more like men, male life expectancy would have increased and female life expectancy would have stayed high.

However, if society continues as it is at the moment male life expectation will continue to fall as the pressure and stress on men continues to grow. But female life expectation will start to fall as more and more women allow and encourage the aggressive, masculine aspects of their own personalities to emerge.

In the future, life expectation for women is going to fall because today's women are being widely encouraged to think and behave like men. They are encouraged to think of 'performance' and 'achievement' rather than 'love' and 'concern'.

The true tragedy of the liberation of women is the fact that instead of merely adding aspects of masculinity to their lives many women have allowed their new found masculinity to take over completely. Instead of adding aggression, power, ambition, exploitation, domination, prestige, control and other masculine manifestations of life to tenderness, playfulness, peacefulness, sensitivity, gentleness, understanding, love, concern and compassion many women seem to have replaced the latter group of qualities almost entirely with the former.

The result is that we are going to see more international confrontations and more wars. When women were allowed to think and behave like women they were a restraining influence on men. But too many of today's women are just as belligerent as men: often welcoming confrontation and war.

CHAPTER SIX
Don't Believe Everything You Read, See Or Hear

'Of all writings I love only that which is written with blood. Write with blood: and you will discover that blood is spirit.'

- Frederick Nietzsche

'Just look at these superfluous people. They vomit their bile and call it a newspaper.'

- Frederick Nietzsche

History is not necessarily what happened. History is, to a very large extent, simply what has been reported as having happened. History – and the 'truth' – are what people believe and remember. History – whether it be personal, national or international – is made up memories, interpretations, feelings and prejudices rather than the original facts. We do not remember what happened so much as what we think happened and how we responded to what we think happened.

All this is important because it means that our knowledge and understanding of our personal, national and global history depends very much upon the way we appreciate and respond to the facts of our personal, national and global experiences.

Since the way we 'see' and 'hear' the news depends very much upon our knowledge and our past experiences it is clear that if we are to form a clear view of the world (in all its aspects) we need to be presented with reliable, trustworthy information.

This does not happen. It is now almost impossible to get hold of trustworthy news about significant events through the normal media. Most people think they get the truth by reading, listening to and watching newspapers and radio and television news programmes. They don't get the truth: they get what the editors want them to read. If you buy all the newspapers and news magazines available on any one day you will see different stories, different emphasis, different facts and different interpretations – within the stories which are supposed to be 'news' stories. A story which hits the headlines in one paper might not appear in any other papers at all.

The problem is that the truth is far too complex. We are, in practice, fed a rich diet of lies, half truths and propaganda. Newspapers, radio stations and television stations are all commercial businesses; they are usually either government controlled or dependent upon advertisers. Many are little more than parts of show business. In order to stay in business they have to sell their product. If they don't attract readers, listeners and viewers by making sure that their presentation of the news is exciting and 'sexy' they will lose money and go out of business.

Crowds either destroy or worship the object of their attention. And they can turn on a whim. The individual who is, at one moment, a hero can easily become a villain. Newspapers are much like crowds. They can turn a villain into a hero or a hero into a villain in the printing of a page. A friend, a journalist, once told me a story which illustrated this fact well. Late one day the newspaper for which he worked received a story about an ordinary man who had done something to attract public attention. The details of the story are irrelevant. The newspaper's first inclination was to turn the man into a hero. They planned to publish a photograph and a story drawing the attention of their readers to the wonderful thing this man had done. But as they planned their story another story came into the newsroom. And the individual who was at the centre of this story was even more of a hero than the first person. And so, because the newspaper did not want to have two heroes on its pages, the editors turned the first man into a villain. A man who had, a moment or two earlier, been a hero in waiting now became a villain in waiting. He was attacked and vilified for doing the very same things for which, a moment or two earlier, they had been planning to praise him. And a man's life was ruined simply so that the newspaper editors could 'balance' the stories on their pages. Remember this next time you read any newspaper story. Depending upon the way in which it is written virtually any individual can be described as both a hero and a villain. Today's newspapers are merely comics for grown-ups.

All around the world those who read broadsheet (as opposed to tabloid) newspapers are generally rather naively convinced that they are getting the real facts. Sadly, this simply isn't true. The broadsheets publish exactly the same gossip and pre-packaged public relations fodder as everyone else. Indeed, the tabloids usually offer a more honest approach to most issues. There are two reasons for this. First, the journalists working for tabloid newspapers are of an infinitely higher quality. It is quite common for broadsheet journalists, columnists and contributors to 'graduate' to writing for a tabloid – where the pay is invariably much better – but almost unheard of for a tabloid journalist, columnist or contributor to take the step down to a broadsheet. Second, because tabloid newspapers tend to sell far more copies than broadsheets – and earn a considerable part of their income from the cover price – the publishers are usually less susceptible to pressure from advertisers than are the proprietors of broadsheet newspapers. Broadsheet publishers are less likely than tabloid editors to be prepared to annoy any large, powerful, rich companies. Finally, because they have acres of space to fill and are therefore more likely to end up reprinting news releases and information handouts, broadsheets are, like television news programmes, a lobbyists dream.

***

Most mass market news reporting, whether published in tabloid newspapers, broadsheet newspapers or magazines or broadcast on the wireless or on television is now biased and prejudiced. That wouldn't matter so much if the bias was open and the prejudice was visible. But the bias is frequently covert and the prejudice is rarely open. Those with vested interests to support (for example, the food industry and the drug industry) construct theories to support what they do and systematically and deliberately stimulate and encourage existing fears and prejudices which are to their advantage. Journalists then obediently and politely regurgitate these prejudices as though they were fact.

The almost universal support of vivisection among broadsheet newspapers (and the deliberate 'rubbishing' of any opposition, however well founded) is a perfect example of global broadsheet support for the established forces.

Today, all mechanisms for spreading information are used almost exclusively to spread views which, true or false, will strengthen a belief in the rightness of decisions taken by those in authority. Information that could cause doubt is withheld or suppressed. Every time you read a story in a newspaper or see a news programme on television you should ask yourself 'Who did that story benefit?' 'Why did they tell me that?' Acquire and nurture a healthy respect for the news media.

Those who write and speak on behalf of the totalitarians ensure that language is perverted. Words are changed so that meanings are hidden.

For example, consider the ways in which vivisectors (and their apologists in the media) distort the language in order to disguise what is done in laboratories.

Those who perform and support animal experiment are so embarrassed and ashamed of what they do that they frequently use euphemisms to disguise their activities. It is quite common, for example, for experimenters to talk of animals 'taking part' in experiments and 'helping us with our research'. The word 'experiment' has been replaced by the word 'procedure', which is less evocative. Experimenters (and the journalists who write sympathetically about what they do) have their own language. Here are just a few choice phrases they use (and their meanings):

vocal response = crying
major airway embarrassment = choking
reacting to adverse stimulation with vigorous motor responses = trying
        to escape
binocular deprivation = sewing the eyes up
decapitation = head removal
exhibiting lethal behaviour = dying
startle reflex = flinching
aversive electrical stimulation = electric shocks
thermal injury = burn or scald

The startling and rather frightening fact is not that vivisectors use these words and phrases (that is understandable) but that journalists use these words and phrases too. The vivisectors and their supporters regard facts as flexible resources for propaganda and they have persuaded politicians and journalists to accept their view.

Totalitarian propaganda destroys the morals of the people because it undermines the basic foundation of all moral values – the truth. And the sad end result is that people in totalitarian countries often do not feel oppressed because they are thinking as they were taught to think – they do not see anything wrong in the world around them. They do not think for themselves because they have not been taught to think for themselves and it is does not occur to them that they are entitled to think for themselves.

* * *

There are many influences which determine the extent, depth and direction of bias and prejudice in the media.

Some, such as the influence from advertisers ('If you publish/broadcast that story we will pull our advertising') is often direct, simple in operation and easy to understand.

Some, such as the influence from proprietors, shareholders and owners is rather more subtle but just as dangerous and certainly just as (if not more) effective. The proprietor or company chairman who has a global operation and who is hoping to do a deal with a government in one part of the world is unlikely to be pleased if one of his newspapers or television stations elsewhere in the world publishes an attack on that same government. Wise editors and producers make it their business to know the deals their proprietors and company bosses are involved in – the hidden agendas which they must take care to respect – for they know that if they are too 'independent' they will simply find themselves being replaced. (In order to avoid a public outcry this is usually done by promoting the individual who has transgressed to some superior position which sounds impressive and carries a large salary but has no editorial power. Within a few months the individual concerned can be eased out into the cold.)

**

Television is almost certainly the weakest and most unreliable source of information – and yet it is to television that most people turn when they want the facts. People feel comfortable with the television. They trust it because they can look at the pictures and think that they are seeing what is happening. And yet television is, generally speaking, pretentious, precious, self congratulatory and superficial. An ability to smile and banter, bouffant hair, capped teeth and a certain sexual chemistry with a colleague are infinitely more important than irrelevant old fashioned nonsenses such as truth, justice and passion. Like radio, television is constrained by the fact that every story must be read out aloud. This means that a fifteen minute bulletin is unlikely to contain more than around 1,000 words of text. And that means compacting and summarising world events in a way which inevitably distorts. A television or radio news programme will contain far fewer words than a page or two in a tabloid newspaper.

But it is its very dependence upon pictures which is television's main weakness. Because there are often no pictures of major news items (there clearly cannot possibly be a camera crew on hand whenever an embassy is stormed, a riot starts, an aeroplane crashes or a road accident occurs) the television team in the studio usually have two alternatives: either to use film and pictures taken from their library (often without saying that the film is stock footage taken some time earlier) or to adapt the news priorities to fit the available pictures – demoting in the running order the story of the demonstration in China or the earthquake in India and leading the news bulletin with the pre-arranged event of which they have got fresh, new film.

Most of the film television stations show will, of course, have been arranged in advance. If the TV crew is there and filming it is almost certainly because their editor sent them there. And he or she sent them there because the news team received an invitation. Television is the public relations officer's dream, the lobbyists perfect medium. A television news programme can be played like a piano. The lobbyist or public relations officer thinks up a good film opportunity, invites the TV crews and sits back and waits for the little bit of luck which is needed to ensure that his item gets a good showing on the programme.

People who work in television do their very best to hide all the truth about their own shortcomings from the public. They will frequently run stories complaining about the way in which newspapers (particularly the tabloid newspapers) have dealt with a story when in practice their own method of dealing with the story has been every bit as intrusive, one sided and unfair as the tabloid treatment. I have seen television programmes complaining about press intrusion which have shown a crowd of press photographers and described them as ghouls. Neither the television news teams nor the viewers seem to have identified the television cameraman, sound man and the rest of the film crew as being part of the rabble.

It is much easier to distort the truth on television than in just about any other medium. By holding the camera on an interviewee for a long period of time or by switching the camera to the interviewee in an unguarded moment it is possible to give a totally misleading impression of the interviewee. And if all else fails it is easy enough to edit out the interviewee's wise, sound, sensible or witty retorts and keep in only the dull, inarticulate or stumbling remarks. If that still doesn't satisfy the requirements of the editor or producer or the vanity of the presenter it is quite easy to cut in some sharp, cutting or incisive remarks from the interviewer at a later stage. Anyone who appears on a recorded television programme must inevitably trust the integrity of the television team.

Viewers tend to forget that television is primarily an entertainment medium.

***

In order to influence journalists and editors a public relations agency will often set up an allegedly non profit, non partisan research organisation which can then 'study' a particular subject and issue regular 'independent' research bulletins to the press. Surprisingly, the only research which ever gets promoted aids the financial aspirations of the companies which are funding the research group. Newspaper and television journalists swallow up all this 'independent' research with enthusiasm and rarely bother to try and find out who is funding the high sounding research groups whose press releases land regularly on their desks.

When news items break and the studio-based news editors are looking for guests they usually turn first to the experts they know can be trusted to turn up at short notice, talk coherently and not expect a fee. They frequently obtain those guests from public relationships companies or representatives. In order to disguise the true origin of some speakers there are now hundreds of Foundations, Bureaus, Research Institutes and Information Offices in existence. These organisations, which appear on the surface to be simply public spirited, independent offices, gathering information or even conducting what sounds on the surface like genuine research, are frequently simply 'fronts' for the industries or political parties which fund them.

The highly paid employees of these organisations are extraordinarily adept at manipulating the news in a way which will benefit their paymasters. For example, around the world drug companies enthusiastically encourage health and medical writers working for newspapers or magazines to publish information extolling the virtues and advantages of particular, named prescription drugs. This public campaigning to promote particular drugs is designed to encourage patients to buy and take the drug (if it is available without a prescription) or to ask their doctor to prescribe the drug for them (if it is only available with a prescription). And it works so well that expenditure on this sort of promotion is growing rapidly.

***

Sometimes, drug companies can be very subtle. For example, some have used a rather clever approach to try and influence writers of columns which are based on the Question and Answer format. I noticed that a few years ago. I would receive a press handout for a new treatment for a common complaint and a day or so before or after the handout I would receive a 'letter' from a 'reader' asking me a question which would lead directly to the product being promoted. So, for example, I might receive a press pack on Tuesday telling me about a wonderful new treatment for left handed, 46 year old women suffering from headaches. And, lo and behold, on Wednesday I would receive a letter from a left handed, 46 year old woman telling me that she was suffering from headaches and asking if I could recommend a remedy.

***

The public relations experts and spin doctors have also used their skills to throw doubt on real risks and to protect existing commercial interests. For example, while writing this book I saw American newspaper reports announcing the 'good news' that there is 'no hard evidence linking power lines and cancer'. The key here lies in those words 'hard evidence'. Just what does that impressive sounding phrase really mean?

Well, 'hard evidence' usually means laboratory tests – commonly animal experiments. (Scientists are still in denial over animal experimentation. Despite the fact that it is now crystal clear to anyone with two neurones to rub together that animal experiments are of absolutely no relevance to human beings, scientists still persist in doing animal lab tests in preference to studying relevant and significant epidemiological results involving human patients.)

If pushed to define 'hard evidence' without using animal experiments the white coated scientists would in these circumstances probably claim that 'hard evidence' proving a definite link between electricity and cancer could only be obtained by performing a double blind clinical trial. This would mean that one group of volunteer patients would have to stand directly under a power line for ten, twenty or thirty years while a second group of matched volunteer patients would have to stand directly under what looked like a power line (but wasn't) for exactly the same length of time. For the trial to be 'double blind' none of the volunteers or the scientists conducting the experiment would know which of the two possible power lines was really 'live'.

At the end of the trial the researchers would simply count up the number of volunteers in each group who had developed cancer. And if a statistically significantly greater number of volunteers in the first group had developed cancer then that would be regarded as pretty 'hard evidence' that power lines cause cancer. (Although even then I have no doubt that companies around the world involved in the electricity industry would think of all sorts of reasons why the research results should be ignored).

You will not be surprised to hear that no such trial has been performed. And so there is no 'hard evidence' proving a link between electricity and cancer.

A similar defence (no 'hard evidence') was used when I first pointed out that eating meat causes cancer. Various defenders of farmers, butchers and the huge international meat industry quickly pointed out that there is no 'hard evidence' proving such a link. I assume that they meant by this that no double blind trial had been conducted to show that volunteers who eat nothing but meat for thirty years are more likely to get cancer than volunteers who eat something that looks, tastes and smells like meat but isn't. (The volunteers would not be allowed to eat vegetables – or indeed any other foods – with their meat since these might interfere with the trial.)

For reasons which I can understand, but not accept or condone, the meat industry doesn't seem keen to accept the overwhelming epidemiological evidence linking meat eating to cancer. (My book *Power over Cancer* gives details of the research providing this evidence.)

The same eternally useful phrase ('hard evidence') is sometimes used by those who struggle to defend the tobacco industry.

'There is no hard evidence linking tobacco to cancer,' some will claim. And they are right. To get hard evidence linking the smoking of tobacco to cancer scientists would have to persuade one group of volunteers to smoke cigarettes containing tobacco for a lengthy period of time (say thirty years) and another, matching group of volunteers to smoke cigarettes containing no tobacco for an equal length of time. At the end of the thirty years the two groups would be compared. If there was evidence that there were more cases of cancer in one group than in the other then that would be 'hard evidence'.

Finally, it is also sometimes argued that there is no 'hard evidence' linking drunken driving to road traffic accidents. Once again, to obtain 'hard evidence' of such an association scientists would have to... well, I'm sure you can guess the rest.

The fact is, of course, that there is overwhelming epidemiological evidence to support all these links. I firmly believe that there is plenty of available evidence to show that drunken driving leads to more accidents, smoking tobacco increases your chances of developing lung cancer and eating meat causes cancer. And I also believe that living under – or working close to – a power line, increases your chances of developing cancer too. However, generations of spin doctors have, over the years, persuaded doctors and journalists not to regard epidemiological research as 'hard evidence'.

The one thing that all these health threats have in common is that they are strongly protected by large, powerful and profitable industries with plenty of money to spend on public relations companies and journalists. There is a good deal of money at stake. The electricity industry, the meat industry, the tobacco industry and the alcohol industry are each understandably keen to delay the day when a link can be shown between their highly profitable product and cancer (or, indeed, any illness).

***

The growing number of genuinely independent newsletters which are now published and distributed throughout the world are by far the best source of independent and reliable information about world, business and commercial affairs. The editors (often also the publishers and owners) of these newsletters usually have no paymasters other than their subscribers. They have no advertisers and no corporate responsibilities. They are frequently passionate and prejudiced but their passions and prejudices show and are not hidden. By subscribing to more than one of these newsletters it is possible to obtain a much greater insight into what is going on in the world than by reading daily newspapers or watching the television news.

CHAPTER SEVEN
When Progress Isn't Really Progress At All

'We were the first to assert that the more complicated the forms of civilisation, the more restricted the freedom of the individual must become.'
- Benito Mussolini

My computer printer broke down. I wanted it repaired. But the dealer told me that it was two years old and out of date. Is that progress?

My portable telephone needed new batteries. The company from which I bought the telephone just over a year ago told me that the telephone is no longer being manufactured. And they have also stopped manufacturing the batteries. This means that the telephone is useless and will have to be thrown away. Is that progress?

I wanted to listen to some old fashioned vinyl records. I tried to buy a record player. The assistants in local shops laughed at me when I told them what I wanted. Is that progress?

The glass in the wing mirror on my car cracked. A few years ago the garage would have simply replaced the glass. It would have taken a few minutes and cost very little. But the garage couldn't obtain a replacement glass. They had to send away for a sealed unit. The whole operation took weeks and cost a small fortune. Is that progress?

When I dare to ask what the hell is so terrific about progress, and why we have to bow down before it as though it were the God of our times, folk 'tut tut' and look at me as though I'm an alien from another planet.

'You can't stand in the way of progress!' they say, implying that it would be improper, unpatriotic, immoral and probably illegal even to try.

Well, I've had enough of progress. Without progress everyone would still be in work. Without progress the workshops of the world would still be alive, men would still be making things they were proud of and it would be possible to buy things on a Wednesday and expect them still to be capable of doing whatever it was they were bought to do on Saturday.

There is a myth that progress means automatically 'better'. It doesn't. In reality, progress means that more and more people have to exchange a rich, varied, wholesome, healthy lifestyle for one which is hollow and filled with despair and loneliness. Progress means deprivation for people but strength for our social structures. Progress means that the jobs people do become more boring and less satisfying. Progress means more power to machines. Progress means that things are more likely to go wrong. Progress means more destruction, more misery and more tedium. Progress means more damage to our planet.

Those who worship at the altar of progress make two simple but vital errors. They assume that man must take full advantage of every new development and invention. And they assume that he must always search for a better way of tackling everything he does.

Neither of these two assumptions is soundly based.

Just because man invents computers, supersonic jets and atomic bombs he doesn't have to use these things. Those who believe implicitly in progress believe that we must always endeavour to use every new nugget of information we obtain. They believe that if man invents a quicker and more effective way to kill people then we must use this quicker and more effective weapon of destruction.

Progress lovers believe that if it is possible to make a machine which manufactures identical galumps at the rate of 6,000 an hour then we must have that machine. And that those galumps will be better than galumps which have been hand carved by craftsmen.

The lovers of progress are so keen to embrace the future and eradicate the past that they will introduce new laws ensuring that only the new computer made identical galumps can be sold. The market for the old fashioned galumps will disappear.

The progress lovers don't care about the fact that their galump making machine will put thousands of craftsmen out of work.

Progress for the sake of progress often simply means change for the sake of change. But (and this is probably heresy and will undoubtedly get me into trouble with whichever masturbatory authority is in business to protect progress) change is not always for the better.

The problem lies largely with the definition of the word 'better'.

What, exactly, does it mean?

Is a television set better than a radio or a good book?

Is a motor car better than a bicycle?

Is an aeroplane better than a yacht?

Are modern motor cars, equipped with electric windows and air conditioning, better than ancient Rolls Royce motor cars equipped with neither of these facilities?

Is artificial turf better than real grass?

Is a poorly written, badly acted television situation comedy which is in colour better than movies such as Citizen Kane and Duck Soup which were made in black and white?

Are artificial flowers better than the real thing?

Too often progress simply means more frustration and more unhappiness. It means that we become more dependent on one another and less capable of coping with the crises in our lives.

Progress means that when something goes wrong with the electricity supply your central heating boiler won't work. Progress means that it has become nigh on impossible to mend anything around the home without calling in an expert with a van full of tools. Even then he will probably tell you that he's got to send away for another part.

Progress means that when your windscreen wiper blade needs replacing you have to buy a new windscreen wiper system.

Progress means that when you want to buy a niplet you have to buy a blister pack of five which can only be opened with a kitchen knife, a screwdriver and a blowlamp.

What the hell is going on? What are we doing to our world? Will people be wiser, happier and more contented when nuclear powered, seven speed nose hair clippers are finally available?

It would be stupid to claim that all progress is bad. Progress is neither good nor bad unless we make it so. Progress is good when we use it rather than when we allow it to rule our lives. But no longer are we allowed to choose between those aspects of progress which we think can be to our benefit and those which we suspect may be harmful. Our society wants constant progress and that is what it gets.

CHAPTER EIGHT
Let Down By Science

'When trouble is sensed well in advance it can easily be remedied; if you wait for it to show itself any medicine will be too late because the disease will have become incurable. As the doctors say of a wasting disease, to start with it is easy to cure but difficult to diagnose; after a time, unless it has been diagnosed and treated at the outset, it becomes easy to diagnose but difficult to cure.'

- Niccolo Machiavelli

If you fall ill and visit your doctor you probably imagine that you will be given a treatment which has been tested, examined and proven by reliable, responsible, honest scientists.

Wrong.

Only about 15% of medical interventions are supported by solid scientific evidence and only 1% of the articles in medical journals are scientifically sound.

What sort of science is that?

The modern clinician does not put his treatments to the test and does not want to put his treatments to the test. He will argue that his treatments do not need to be tested because he knows that they work.

That is science?

Today's medical training is based upon pronouncement and opinion rather than on investigation and scientific experience. In medical schools students are bombarded with information but denied the time or the opportunity to question the ex cathedra statements which are made from an archaic medical culture.

If medicine was a science then when a patient visited a doctor complaining of a symptom he would be given the best, proven treatment, a treatment that was quite specific for the disease. Treatments for specific symptoms would be predictable and diagnostic skills would, because they would be based on scientific techniques, be reliable within certain acknowledged limits.

But that is not what happens. Doctors still make decisions about treatments according to their personal beliefs, instincts and hunches rather than according to any scientific principles.

Time and time again new treatments and new techniques are introduced on a massive scale without any scientific support and without doctors knowing what the long term consequences are likely to be. Medicine doesn't anticipate disasters – it simply reacts to them. Men in white coats never seem to blush when they utter phrases such as: 'Nothing can go wrong'; 'It's perfectly safe' and 'We never thought that would happen'. And yet, despite the constantly lengthening sequence of disasters which have marked twentieth century medicine most people will still argue that *their* doctor knows what he is doing, is trustworthy and reliable. They say this because they *want* and *need* their doctor to be trustworthy and reliable. People are quite prepared to believe that most doctors are incompetent and dangerous buffoons, educated by the pharmaceutical industry and free of moral or ethical standards. But they are not prepared to believe that about the physician into whose hands they have chosen to put their own life.

In the preface to *The Doctor's Dilemma* playwright George Bernard Shaw points out that during the first great epidemic of influenza which developed towards the end of the 19th century, a London evening newspaper sent a journalist posing as a patient to all the great consultants of the day. The newspaper then published details of the advice and prescriptions offered by the consultants.

The whole proceeding was, almost inevitably, passionately denounced as an unforgivable breach of confidence, but the result was nevertheless fascinating. Despite the fact that the journalist had complained of exactly the same symptoms to the many different physicians, the advice and the prescriptions that were offered were all different.

Nothing has changed.

Even in these days of apparently high technology medicine there are almost endless variations in the treatments preferred by different doctors.

Doctors offer different prescriptions for exactly the same symptoms; they keep patients in hospital for vastly different lengths of time, and they perform different operations on patients with apparently identical problems.

Going to a doctor is something of a lottery, and treatments vary not because patients are different, but because doctors are different!

Despite all these variations in the types of treatment offered, most doctors seem to be convinced that their treatment methods are beyond question. Many doctors announce their decisions as though they are carved in stone.

But most decisions about how patients should be treated are based on nothing more scientific than guesswork, personal experience, intuition and prejudice.

Tragically, worthless and dangerous treatments are often administered for many, many years. When pressed for an explanation or for supporting evidence doctors will usually defend their activities by claiming that they are using 'clinical judgement'. This sounds as if it is a professional decision but what it really means is that the doctor has strong opinions and is not prepared to listen to anyone else.

Even when techniques are assessed doctors will frequently ignore the results if the scientific evidence does not fit in with their own personal prejudiced beliefs. New treatments are tried until they kill too many people and have to be abandoned, or until something more exciting comes along.

Research has shown that the wrong diagnosis is made in more than half of all patients. This presumably also means that in more than half the patients the wrong treatment is given. And since modern treatments are undeniably powerful it also presumably means that many patients die not because of their disease but because of their treatment.

Doctors go to great lengths to disguise the fact that they are practising a black art rather than a science. The medical profession has created a 'pseudoscience' of mammoth proportions and today's doctors rely on a vast variety of instruments and tests and pieces of equipment with which to explain and dignify their interventions. This, of course, is nothing new. The alchemists of the middle ages and the witch doctors of Africa recognised the need to impress their patients with their knowledge and so they created a secret and impenetrable structure of herbs, songs, dances, rattling of special bones, chants and ceremonial incantations. Today's clinicians have much more sophisticated mumbo jumbo to offer. But it is still mumbo jumbo.

***

A doctor recently rang me up and asked me to go and visit him in his wonderful new health centre.

'You're a pretty forceful critic of modern medicine,' he said, and I knew immediately that he felt that he was not one of the doctors who should be included in my criticisms. 'You should come along and take a look around the new 'state of the art' place we've had built.'

Always anxious to keep up with what is going on in the world of medicine I readily accepted his invitation. And so a few days later I found myself tottering through huge plate glass doors and into a magnificently built medical centre. White walls, white floor, white ceiling. A team of immaculately coiffed smart young receptionists in spotless white coats stood waiting behind glass partitions. I had to pinch myself to make sure that I hadn't died and gone to heaven.

It all seemed such a very long way from the simple and rather homely surgeries in which medicine used to be practised in the primitive, bad old days. I remembered one very dear, former friend who practised in a tiny and rather cold conservatory built onto the side of his house. Patients sat waiting in his dining room where tattered, well thumbed magazines laid out on the dining table provided the entertainment. The entertainment was needed for patients might have to wait anything up to four hours to be seen.

From time to time the doctor's stern and stout wife would potter into the room to check that no one was smoking, spitting or talking and to tidy the magazines up into neat piles.

When my dear old chum was ready for his next patient he would shout 'Next!' It was a simple technique but it worked and there was no reliance on wiring, electricity or other fallible consequences of the twentieth century.

When a consultation was over the patient, probably still buttoning up her dress or his trousers, would leave through the conservatory door, along the garden path and out through the side gate. This rather efficient system meant that there was never any congestion at the key point: the door between the dining room and the conservatory.

Those days are, I suspect, gone for ever.

The doctor who had invited me to visit him proudly escorted me around the new building. There were, he explained, surgeries and examination rooms for all the doctors, consulting rooms for two nurses and a small but well equipped operating theatre for minor surgery.

But he seemed proudest of the pharmacy – an extremely impressive and extraordinarily well stocked drug shop. It was the centre point of the whole building; a sort of pharmaceutical shrine at which all were expected to worship.

'Patients are processed in three simple stages,' he explained, rather like a tour guide at a stately home. 'First they are seen by the one of receptionists, who gives them a consultation number. Second, one of the doctors sees them. And then, finally, they visit the pharmacy to collect their prescription which will have been automatically ordered when the doctor completed his computerised record of the consultation. When collecting the prescription the patient is automatically given the date and time of their next appointment.'

'What about patients who don't need a prescription?' I asked.

The doctor stared at me. 'What do you mean?' he asked.

I tried to redesign the question. 'What happens to patients who need another appointment but don't need treatment with drugs?'

The doctor continued to stare at me. 'All patients need treatment,' he said. 'Why else would someone visit us if they didn't need treatment?'

'Well, I think the idea that all patients need treatment is arguable,' I said, feeling rather like the small boy declaring that the Emperor was wearing no clothes. 'But what about those patients who need treatment but don't need drugs?'

'How else would we treat them?' asked the doctor.

'I don't know,' I shrugged. 'It rather depends on what is wrong with them. Osteopathy, acupuncture, dietary advice, relaxation exercises, meditation training...'

I stopped talking because I was aware that the doctor was looking rather alarmed.

'I hadn't realised that you were one of those nutters,' he said, pulling his white coat around him, as though it were a suit of armour which would protect him from contamination. He instinctively backed away a few inches.

'Surely some patients might just need someone to talk to?' I suggested, rather lamely.

'It's obviously been a little while since you practised,' said the doctor, rather coldly.

I left there feeling rather sad and even depressed; convinced, more than ever, that medicine has been taken over by the hugely powerful and immensely profitable pharmaceutical industries.

Doctors are no longer in the business of caring for patients. They are in the much simpler business of dishing out pills.

***

Annette (not her real name) woke up one morning a few months ago, looked out of her flat window and saw that the front passenger window of her car had been smashed. She went downstairs and found that vandals had broken into her car and stolen the cassette player. It was the third time in a month that her car had been vandalised.

She was so upset about the incident that while preparing her breakfast she cut her hand badly with the breadknife. She couldn't see what she was doing because she was crying. Her boyfriend washed the wound and took her to the local surgery.

The doctor who put a stitch into the wound noticed that she had been crying and asked her why. Annette told him about the damage that had been done to her car. She said she felt really depressed about the amount of crime where she lived. When the doctor had finished attending to her wound he wrote out a prescription for some pills.

A few days later Annette started to complain of a ringing in her ears. She told her boyfriend about the ringing noise. He suggested that she visit the doctor again. He told her to ask if the new symptom could be a side effect of the drug she was taking.

The doctor dismissed Annette's question about side effects with a laugh. He told her that she had a condition called tinnitus and he prescribed some pills which he said would help. He told her that the pills might not make the condition disappear completely and he warned her that tinnitus sometimes lasts for years.

After another week the tinnitus was still present and Annette had also begun to feel edgy, anxious and rather irritable. She went back to see the doctor and told him how she felt. She said that she was also having difficulty in sleeping. The doctor increased the dose of the original drug and also prescribed a sleeping pill.

When Annette asked the doctor what the original drug was for the doctor told her that it was an anti-depressant. She asked him if he really thought she needed the drug. He said he had given it to her because she had told him that she was depressed. He said that it was important that she continue with the drug since there can sometimes be unpleasant withdrawal effects if drug therapy is stopped suddenly.

A week later Annette was feeling so ill that she did not want to get out of bed. She felt dizzy, nauseous and edgy and the tinnitus was worse. She could not concentrate to read, listen to the radio or watch television. She had lost all interest in sex. Her boyfriend telephoned her doctor's surgery and insisted that a doctor visit her at home.

The doctor who had seen Annette in the surgery was not available and another doctor called at the flat. He looked at the pills that Annette was taking and announced that he was going to increase the dose and add another drug. He said that Annette should get out of bed and try to go out for long walks.

Annette tried to get up and go out but she was so dizzy that she had to keep on sitting down. The tinnitus was now so bad that she cried almost continuously. She was also complaining of indigestion and a skin rash. The persistent nausea meant that she wasn't interested in food and that she was losing weight. Worst of all she started having difficulty in speaking. Her boyfriend called the doctor again.

Another different doctor arrived. He said he didn't know what was wrong but he prescribed yet another drug and increased the dosage of the original anti-depressant. Because Annette's skin rash had become infected he prescribed an antibiotic. He said he thought that Annette needed plenty of rest. Annette cried throughout his visit and when he was about to leave she grabbed at his coat lapel and shouted at him. No one could understand what she said. The doctor, who seemed shaken, said that he thought that perhaps Annette needed to be in hospital. He said he would talk to his colleagues about this.

Three days later the first doctor, the one who had treated Annette when she had cut her hand, visited the flat. Annette was in the lavatory when he arrived. She had bad diarrhoea and was also suffering from stomach cramps. She couldn't stop crying.

The doctor was clearly shocked at Annette's appearance. He admitted to Annette's boyfriend that he didn't know what was wrong. He said he thought that the main problem was depression and that Annette had obviously had what used to be called a nervous breakdown but added that there might be some hormonal problem or perhaps an immune system disorder as well. He said he wondered whether Annette might have had a small stroke. He took her blood pressure and said that it was raised.

The doctor said he would arrange for Annette to go into hospital. Annette's boyfriend said he thought that this was a good idea since he was having great difficulty in coping.

Two days later, when they had heard nothing from the doctor about a hospital bed, the boyfriend rang the surgery. A receptionist told him that since Annette's problem was non-urgent they were having to wait for a bed to become vacant. The receptionist promised that someone would ring when they had any news.

That evening, while her boyfriend was at work, Annette took an overdose. She swallowed just about every drug in the flat. When her boyfriend arrived back home he telephoned for an ambulance and Annette was taken to a nearby casualty department. The hospital was crowded and Annette, who was unconscious, was left lying on a stretcher in a corridor. She vomited, inhaled her own vomit and choked to death.

All the symptoms from which Annette suffered were side effects of the drugs which had been prescribed for her.

I leave it to you to decide the moral of this tragic story.

***

Doctors aren't the only scientists to have let us down; to have lost touch with the real needs of the community. For example, consider the world of research – now almost devoid of morals. Tobacco companies, drug companies and other industrial giants sponsor research to show that their products are safe and that other peoples alternative products are not as safe. The research is designed to look for whatever the sponsor hopes to find and if negative results are obtained the chances are that they will be ignored or certainly not given the same sort of promotional exposure that they will be given if some way can be found to make them commercially valuable to the sponsor.

One of the biggest fears I have for the future concerns the whole area of genetic research.

It is twenty years since researchers first started splicing together genes from different organisms and for several years now the food industry has been excited by the possibilities offered by genetic engineering.

Scientists working for or on behalf of the food industry have been busy messing around with foods in an attempt to make them look or taste 'better' or make them last longer. Researchers have created tobacco plants designed to be more resistant to disease, a hybrid animal that is half sheep and half goat and a cuboid tomato that will be easier to use when making sandwiches. There have even been reports that scientists have put human genes into plants in order to produce more acceptable food products. (How many human genes do there have to be in a tomato before the tomato can complain if you dare to threaten it with a knife?)

In an attempt to keep up with the world's distorted requirements for food, scientists and farmers are busy messing around with genes in an attempt to grow bigger crops. Modern, laboratory bred crops help boost yields and profits.

But there is a risk because new crop varieties are identical: each ear of wheat, each potato, each tomato is the same as the one next to it. And each farmer grows the same crop variety in order to maximise his profits. This is all very well when everything goes fine. But when a bug comes along which affects one plant every plant will be affected. And the result will be a wipeout.

About 150 years ago a fungus caused the Irish potato famine. Today, we are far more vulnerable than the Irish were. One new fungus or other infection which affects the latest laboratory engineered crop could cause a worldwide shortage of wheat or potatoes and a worldwide famine.

I have no doubt that it will happen soon. And when it does the farmers whose crops have been destroyed will demand cash so that they don't suffer financially. No one in the food industry will give a damn about the fact that deaths from starvation will rocket – as a direct result of their greedy, selfish, short sighted policies. Thanks to the farmers and the food industry the long term future for the world is hunger, growing food shortages and wars as the starving fight for food.

The clock is ticking. Before long it will be too late to stop scientists doing irreversible damage to our food. I am convinced that genetic engineering is one of the biggest threats any of us face. But no one seems to care. Journalists seem besotted with the idea of genetics and the politicians certainly won't stop the scientists because the lobbyists who represent the world's food companies are working hard to suppress fears and allay any suspicions.

CHAPTER NINE
What Do They Do With Your Money?

'It is every day becoming more clearly understood that the function of Government is negative and restrictive, rather than positive and active.'
- Samuel Smiles

I don't know about you but when I hand over a chunk of my hard earned cash I like to think I'm buying value for money. Whatever it is I'm buying – car insurance or a bottle of something smooth and pleasantly toxic – I want to know that the person who is getting my money is doing something for me in return. If I feel that I'm being consistently short-changed then I take my business (and my wallet) elsewhere.

By far the biggest bills I pay are to the government. Taxes everywhere are rising inexorably. Most taxpayers assume that the hard earned money they hand over to their government will be used to improve the world in which they live. But in practise most of the money raised by governments is used to subsidise an ever expanding bureaucratic machinery.

If you pay 25% of your income in tax then you are working for other people for 15 minutes out of every hour. You are, quite literally, a slave for a quarter of your working life. If you pay 40% income tax and work 40 hours a week then you are a slave in chains for 16 hours every week.

Taxes are a relatively new invention and have risen dramatically for the last few decades as politicians and civil servants have discovered the power that comes with having lots of other peoples money to spend.

The theory is that the government will use your money to look after you when you are sick, to feed you and your family if you are unable to find work, to give you a pension when you are old and to provide you with a complete range of personal and social services. But if you take a hard look at what you get for your money you will find that the practice falls rather short of the theory.

The following details relate to life in just about any civilised, developed country in the world.

* Health care: even if 'free' health care is available you probably either pay cash for decent care when you need it or pay premiums to a private insurer so that you can get medical and dental care from the doctor or dentist of your choice. If you need an operation or any other type of treatment you will have to pay – unless you are prepared to risk dying on the waiting list. If your general practitioner gives you a prescription you may have to pay a prescription charge which is higher than the value of the drug.

* Insurance: if you want to carry on eating and doing all the other things to which you have grown accustomed then you probably pay insurance premiums so that you receive cash if you are injured, fall sick or unable to work. The government may claim to offer support to individuals who fall into these categories but you probably realise that you would be wise not to rely upon the government's generosity. When you pay insurance premiums you will probably pay an additional tax.

* Pension: You may have been paying money to the government in the hope that they will eventually give you a pension. But if you are wise you will not expect to be able to survive on any pension the government may pay you. If you don't wish to spend your declining years living in a cardboard box you probably pay regular sums into a private pension scheme.

* Transport: The government builds roads so that you can drive around in your car. But as a motorist you pay additional sums of money to cover the building of roads. You probably pay money to get a licence to put your car on the road. And you give the government even more money when you buy petrol. You will also give the government extra money if you buy a new car or have an old car repaired or serviced.

* Services/utilities: You probably pay a full commercial rate for your gas, electricity and water. And you probably pay the local authority additional money for local facilities such as street lighting. If you have your rubbish collected then there will be a service charge for that. And if you want to have your children educated you probably have to pay for the teacher and the school. You will pay more money into the central kitty if you want to park your car, if you are caught parking on a yellow line or caught speeding.

You hand over more money when you buy a house, a share or a bottle of whisky. You give the government money every time you buy clothes or make a telephone call. So what the hell is the government doing with the money you give it? What other useful services are you getting for your money?

Well, your government will be hiring armies of bureaucrats to smother small businesses with paperwork and to remove as much of your freedom as it possibly can. And it will be using your money to subsidise a massive, international arms industry which you may not want to subsidise.

You may be tempted to suspect that the government is not giving you value for money. But don't be tempted to stop handing over money to the government as a protest because if you do that they'll send you to prison.

And maybe that is the explanation. Maybe that is where your money goes. Maybe you are giving nearly half of your working life to pay for the prison service.

CHAPTER TEN
The Twentieth Century Addiction

'Literary coteries have no vital contact with the life of the community, and such contact is necessary if men's feelings are to have the seriousness and depth within which both tragedy and true happiness proceed.'
- Bertrand Russell

I see dozens of surveys every week. Public relations companies send them to me in smart folders. Most of them are about as stimulating and as exciting as a compromising photograph of a politician.

I just can't get moved about the fact that 33% of housewives believe that carrots are an essential ingredient when preparing a Sunday lunch.

But although I saw it some time ago I can't get the results of one survey out of my head. It keeps popping into my consciousness – rather like a tune that won't go away.

The survey that won't go away showed that when small children aged between four and six years old were asked to say which they liked best – television or daddy – around half voted for television. And if that doesn't frighten you then it damned well should.

Exciting, quick, instant pleasures requiring no real effort are now essential and commonplace – and television is both the best example and the source of this new attitude to life. Children's thoughts are always directed to the next instant fix rather than any long term sense of achievement or true fulfilment. Ask a child today what he or she wants to do with his or her life and he or she will probably answer: 'Win the lottery!'. That is hope not ambition. Today's generation is constantly on the run, rushing from one instant pleasure to the next. Thanks to television there is no time for taking pleasure from a beautiful scene, a walk enjoyed, a book read or a piece of music listened.

We are, it seems, creating a new generation with an even lower tolerance to boredom and low capability for sticking at things. Modern food is junk food. Instant food. There is no effort involved in preparing or eating food. You just stuff it into your mouth, chew and swallow and then get on to the next momentary thrill. We can thank television for that. Children are not encouraged to extract any pleasure from life in their own way. They are not taught to use their imaginations or their hands. We can thank television for that. Tomorrow's creators will, I suspect, all come from the third world or from deprived homes. The future of the world is Muslim.

Of course, it isn't just kids who are hooked on television. The average adult in most so called developed countries watches five hours of television a day. (In America the average adult watches television for a literarily mind numbing seven hours a day.) Five hours a day is 35 hours a week and nearly 2,000 hours a year. (Seven hours a day is 49 hours a week and over 2,500 hours a year.)

What a terrible way to waste your life! Watching TV for five hours a day is like giving away a third of your waking life to someone else.

I wouldn't mind if the stuff on television was good. But the vast majority of the programmes now being made for television are superficial, trivialising nonsense put together by untalented nonentities with an average IQ lower than the daily temperature in Reykjavik. You can't even wrap chips in old television programmes.

When I was young and innocent I used to do a lot of television. But no more.

I banned myself from one channel when a producer told me that he wasn't going to broadcast an interview in which I had revealed the truth about a laboratory experiment for which a number of dogs had died because he had been reliably informed by the researchers that they hadn't used any animals at all.

'But I've got the evidence!' I protested. 'They published a research paper describing what they'd done.'

'But they didn't use any animals,' argued the producer. 'They only used animal tissue.'

What could I say to that? I'm proud of the fact that I managed to put the telephone receiver down without breaking it.

I was banned by the other side after I swore at someone on a late night chat show. Genuinely angered by the other guests I used a word rhyming with 'duck' but beginning with a letter coming a little later in the alphabet.

The word is heard constantly in films shown much earlier in the evening and it first appeared in The Times over a century ago, but the television company concerned was dismayed because I'd used it in anger.

I received a great deal of mail in support of my choice of language and as far as I know the TV company didn't receive any complaints, but the producer demanded a public apology which I refused to give. I rather think that what upset them was not the use of the word itself (it is, as I've explained used regularly in movies), but that I'd used it in anger. I'd meant it. I'd spoken with passion and feeling. After years of appearing on TV programmes I honestly feel that television producers don't feel entirely comfortable with passion. They don't really know how to deal with it. And it frightens them.

* * *

I turned on my television set the other morning to check the results of a sporting event in which I had been interested. Instead, by accident, I found myself watching a programme which appeared to be set in a supermarket. A woman was frantically running up and down the aisles looking at the available products. Judging from the picture on my screen it appeared that a man with a camera was running around with her, filming her as she darted hither and thither.

I discovered, by listening to a subsequent conversation between her and an amiable sort of fellow in a suit, that she had been trying to find out where the poppadoms had been stored. She had failed in this onerous task and seemed disproportionately disappointed. I turned off the set and so did not find out whether she was to be given a second chance to demonstrate her poppadom searching skills. Nor did I discover whether or not the programme was intended to be educational ('how to find poppadoms when visiting your local supermarket'); entertainment ('watch a woman running around a supermarket'); sport ('let's see how quickly this woman can run around a supermarket and find the poppadoms'); suspense drama ('let's see if this woman can find out where the poppadoms are hidden in this supermarket'); or just plain news of the local TV variety ('woman searches for poppadoms in supermarket').

In many ways the poppadom hunt seem typical of the sort of stuff that television companies seem to like these days; undemanding mass market viewing, cheap to produce and unlikely to offend any viewers or upset the advertisers.

It has for years been easy to dismiss television as a medium which has never truly found its way, an opportunity which has been lost – given over for commercial reasons to froth and undemanding trivia. In a way this is true. Television is a medium that has lost its way; it's half show business, half advertising billboard and half propaganda vehicle for politicians. Television promised much but has failed to deliver.

But for some time I have thought it rather dangerous to regard television in such a simple way. Television is far a more sinister medium than the poppadom hunt might suggest. It is a propaganda tool for the establishment, designed constantly to reinforce the message that authority is never wrong.

For years television has exerted a powerful and disturbing influence on society – through the drip drip drip influence of the weekly soap operas, the popular drama series, the quiz shows, the advertisements and even the news.

The essential message television has given out has inevitably been in support of the status quo: the materialistic, conservative (with a small c) society. Programmes about video cameras in our streets and buildings tell us how useful these devices are at helping to prevent crime. They never bother to question whether or not having video cameras everywhere could be an infringement of our privacy. Programmes about the police have taught us to respect the forces of law and order and programmes about hospitals and doctors have taught us to respect the wisdom and integrity of the medical profession.

It has been the way that television has sanctified violence which has worried me most of all. The sanctification of violence began in the cowboy movies – where the cowboys in white hats (the good guys) were allowed to beat up and kill the cowboys in black hats (the bad guys) or the Indians (also the bad guys). It continued in spy thrillers – where the hero working for our side was allowed to beat up and kill his opposite numbers working for their side. And, most alarming of all in my view, it carried on in police programmes. The rules on television have always been simple: the police are the good guys and anyone they don't approve of is a bad guy. It is, say the unwritten television rules, perfectly all right for the police to be violent. After all they are only beating up bad guys who deserve to be beaten. Television does not show us the reality: that ordinary, law abiding citizens are frequently beaten up by the police, either because the police have made a mistake and burst into the wrong house, or because they have arrested the wrong pedestrian or motorist, or simply for the hell of it. We never see the way power is abused.

For years television has taught us that violence is acceptable as long as it is perpetrated by the established and accepted forces of light and aimed at those who represent evil.

Not that the glorification and justification of violence is the only important legacy television has given us. At the same time television has constantly shown us – and held up for our admiration – the many material goods we can acquire if we are prepared to work hard and play the rules according to the requirements of society. Every evening, when the viewer returns home tired and bored, the advertisers and the quiz show hosts tantalise him by showing him the things and the experiences which can be his if he continues to work hard and pay homage to the social structure.

The end result of all this insidious propaganda has been the creation of generation after generation of television viewers who are quietly prepared to support the status quo. Viewers have been taught to respect the police and the medical profession and to endorse violence when it is used by any representative of the establishment in the defence of the status quo; and they have been taught to worship the pursuit of money and material goods.

The average viewer's life, thoughts, ambitions, fears and respects have all been defined by television.

***

Every year or two there are serious discussions among politicians about whether or not violence on television could be a cause of the rising amount of violence in our society. These 'new' discussions always give me an uncomfortable feeling of 'déjà vu'.

It was way back in 1983 that I forecast that by the mid 1990s our society would be overrun by violent young adults. I pointed out that according to knowledge available at that time 40% of all children over the age of six years had seen one or more video nasties. And I warned that: 'If their viewing habits remain unchanged, thousands upon thousands of them will have become violent, aggressive and virtually uncontrollable. We will have successfully bred a race of super thugs.'

Sadly, tragically, it looks as though I was right. We have bred a scarred generation. We live in a violent world where crazed men and women obtain pleasure from causing pain, from killing and maiming complete strangers.

The numbing effect violent videos can have on children is terrifying.

Just read these three quotes which I reported back in 1983:

Child No 1 (female): 'I like scaring myself and I like looking at blood.'

Child No 2 (male): 'I like all the blood coming out.'

Child No 3 (male): 'I like the bit in Driller Killer where he puts a man up on sticks and then he gets the drill and puts it through his stomach and he screams for ages. Then he dies.'

Those three children were nine years old when I quoted them. And there are thousands more just like them.

The link between television or film violence and real in-the-streets violence is no mystery. Psychologists first noticed the link over thirty years ago. It has long been known that children (and some adults) find it difficult to differentiate between the violence in movies and television programmes and the violence they see in news footage. It all merges together in one great blood bath.

In 1964 it was reported that by the time the average American child had celebrated his 14th birthday he would have witnessed on television the deaths of 13,000 people. By 1971, the figure had risen to 18,000 and observers were getting very worried. The American Government was so concerned that it set up a commission to study the problem. After careful deliberation the commission concluded that: 'Violence on television encourages violent forms of behaviour and fosters moral and social values about violence in family life which are unacceptable in a civilised society.'

Read that again.

Read it out loud.

Read it to your friends, your neighbours, your partner and your children.

It isn't pornography which turns children into dangerous citizens. It is violence.

Showing naked bodies doesn't do any harm. Breasts don't kill people. You can't bludgeon someone to death with a penis – erect or limp. Showing naked individuals having sex doesn't do any harm either. But showing films of wild, unlimited violence causes a great deal of harm.

Every time someone is murdered 'Concerned' parents and 'Anxious' politicians join together to try to put pressure on the authorities to take some action – though no one ever seems sure what sort of action they think will be most appropriate. The usual cry is for censorship, although all the evidence suggests that censorship has never solved any problem. If violence is banned from television then, as long as there is a demand, the people who make and sell portrayals of violence will find a way to reach their markets. Creating a new law will simply result in the creation of yet another breed of law-breakers.

Back in 1983, when I first pointed out that the problem created by violence on television was coming, I argued that the responsibility lay fair and square on the shoulders of parents. I felt then, and I feel now that it is, after all, the responsibility of parents to make sure that their children do not watch material which might have a damaging effect on the way they develop. 'Our apathy could be breeding a scarred generation,' I warned.

But parents prefer to blame everyone else. They do not want to take any responsibility. They put some of the blame on the people who make these violent programmes. And the rest they reserve for 'society'. They blame the politicians and the amorphous 'them'.

It is parents who could and should have stopped their young children watching programmes which were destined to turn them into thugs and killers. But yesterday's generation of parents has clearly failed and it does not seem likely that today's generation of parents will do any better.

CHAPTER ELEVEN
The Tyranny Of The Law And The Disappearance Of Justice

'The value of legislation as an agent in human advancement has usually been much over-estimated.'

- Samuel Smiles

'Must the citizen ever for a moment, or in the least degree, resign his conscience to the legislator? Why has every man a conscience then? I think that we should be men first, and subjects afterwards. It is not desirable to cultivate a respect for the law, so much as for the right. The only obligation which I have the right to assume, is to do at any time what I think right. Law never made men a whit more just; and by means of their respect for it, even the well disposed are daily made the agents of injustice.'

– Henry David Thoreau

'No laws, however stringent, can make the idle industrious, the thriftless provident or the drunken sober.'

- Samuel Smiles

It is important to understand that the law is not on your side.

During the last few generations, as a direct result of the fact that it has changed its priority from the protection of the individual to the protection of society, justice has turned from the protection of the individual to the oppression of the individual.

We like to think that the Germans who worked in the concentration camps were exceptionally evil individuals. But every nation contains thousands of people who will obey orders as long as they're paid well, given lots of authority and provided with smart uniforms. If your government decided to exterminate beggars or Jews they would, I have no doubt, find it easy to recruit the necessary staff.

Most of those who satisfy the requirements for gas chamber attendants are currently working as lawyers, policemen and traffic wardens. And in their hands each nation is rapidly becoming a police state.

For years politicians and lawyers (two words which, I feel, go together like 'vomit' and 'floor-cloth') have been doing their efficient best to take away all your rights. Now the greatest threat to your liberty comes not from criminals but from the legal system. Recent governments have passed endless oppressive and unjust laws and all around the 'civilised' world new laws mean that you're guilty if the police say you're guilty. Human rights have been replaced by police rights.

Those paid to run the legal system have forgotten that the law was invented to protect the ordinary citizen. Consequently, the prison population is rising so fast that it won't be long before prisoners will have to come outside and law abiding citizens will have to go inside.

No society has ever had as many laws as we have. And few societies can ever have had less justice. Ring up and complain that you've been robbed, mugged or raped and a snotty, supercilious, patronising, overpaid employee with an 'I'm-far-too-busy-and-important-to-be-dealing-with-your-piddling-little-problem' voice will reluctantly take down your details before explaining that they're far too busy to do anything. But leave your car outside the police station to complain that you've been assaulted and when you get back to it you'll find that someone has found the time to give you a ticket.

Motorists are easy targets. Most have an in-built fear of authority and a long established respect for the law. And it is far easier to make the crime statistics look good by catching a few, generally law abiding, middle class motorists than it is to try and catch potentially troublesome criminals. The modern police patrol the streets as though they own them. They interrogate citizens as though they are unwelcome intruders. Once, when lost, I remember stopping my car to ask a policeman the way. I was told rudely that I couldn't stop where I was. I repeated my question, politely explaining that I simply wanted to know whether to turn left or right at the next junction. There was no traffic behind me and my car was not causing an obstruction. The policeman, turning very aggressive, demanded my driving licence and insurance and threatened to arrest me – though I know not what for. On another occasion, when I stopped at the scene of an accident on a motorway I was rudely told to move off. I explained that I was a doctor and asked if there was anything I could do to help. The traffic policeman angrily repeated his command that I drive on.

There is an overriding tendency among those employed to defend the law to treat ordinary citizens without respect. The individual is of no significance. The policeman regards his duty and responsibility as being towards society.

(Although, there is, of course, an exception to the rule that policemen and others involved with maintaining the law tend to treat ordinary citizens without respect. Policemen and traffic wardens are quick to grovel if they think they're dealing with someone whom they regard as important. A year or two ago I acquired a large and impressive looking Buckingham Palace car park pass for the windscreen of my car. I quickly discovered that once they saw the sticker traffic wardens treated me very reverentially. When I parked *inside* a shopping arcade I found a traffic warden waiting for me. But he didn't give me a ticket. Instead he stopped the traffic while I reversed out of the arcade. He then saluted while I drove away, leaving him enveloped in blue exhaust smoke.)

***

Sadly, it is now a mistake to confuse the law with justice, liberty, freedom and equality. Today's law has very little to do with these fundamental moral principles. The law (man's inadequate attempt to turn justice into practical reality) is inspired more by the self interest of the lawmakers than by respect or concern for human rights.

This is why protest with a purpose attracts far more attention than mindless vandalism. If animal rights activists do a relatively small amount of damage to a building where evil scientists are doing indefensible and unspeakable things to animals the whole area will turn blue with policemen looking for clues. The damage is considered to be a threat to society. But if an individual complains that he or she has been the victim of a similar crime the police will show very little interest in it.

The law was originally introduced to protect individuals but the law has itself become one of modern society's greatest tyrants. The law now oppresses the weak, the poor and the powerless and sustains itself and the powers which preserve it. The cost of litigation means that there is one law for the rich and no law for the poor. The law threatens and reduces the rights of the weak and strengthens and augments the rights of the powerful.

As political parties come and go so we accumulate layer after layer of new laws. And as the oppression of individuals continues, lawlessness grows among officials and those in power. Brutality, arrogance, corruption and hypocrisy have all damaged public faith in the law but the only response from the establishment has been to create new laws to outlaw disapproval. The primary interest of the legal establishment is to protect itself. The establishment is not concerned with justice, freedom or equality since those are values which give strength to you and me.

***

Traditional laws are fairly simple to understand. Murder is not allowed and we must all drive on one, specified, side of the road.

But in recent years a new type of law has developed under which the authorities (namely the unelected bureaucrats) have the power to do whatever they like – without any controls. Decisions (which effectively have the power of law) are taken according to the whims and fancies of the adjudicators.

Today, we have far too many laws which fit into the second category; vague, general, oppressive laws which take away our freedom but give us no rights. Anyone who has ever run a business will know that the bureaucrats seem to delight in creating pointless and confusing new rules and regulations. The result is that it is extremely hard for a small business to stay solvent in the current regulatory environment.

In an honest country the laws are designed to restrain (and constrain) the government as well as the citizens. The citizens know how the government will use its powers because the laws are all written down. Under those circumstances it is possible to plan your life according to the law.

But we have created a society in which the laws are so complex that no one really understands them any more. The law has become devalued because there is so much law that no one can recognise it any more and no one knows whether a law is a good law or a bad law. Governments have become arbitrary, decision makers have endless discretion and basic freedoms (such as the freedom to remain silent) have gone. Only the bureaucrats (when operating as bureaucrats) are above and beyond the law.

As a result, trust and faith in justice have been steadily disappearing for decades. A recent survey showed that in 'developed' countries two thirds of the population feel that they will get no justice from their courts.

In a free society the laws have to be applied evenly and fairly – otherwise people simply lose all faith in the law. In modern societies, however, the laws are not applied evenly or fairly. There is ample evidence to confirm that punishments vary according to the whims and caprices of those responsible for handing them out – and according to the skills of those who represent the defendants.

Governments never pass laws designed to give people more freedom, and they never repeal laws which take away freedom, and so, every year, numerous new layers of law are laid down on top of the old ones. The result is that no one – not the politicians or the judges or the lawyers – knows what all the laws are.

The absurdity here is, of course, that according to the law, ignorance of the law is no excuse for breaking the law. And yet the law is now so complex that no lawyer or judge in the world would claim to know precisely what is and is not legal. Indeed, in many cases those laws which are not created by unelected bureaucrats, operating under the authority given to them by politicians, are often created in the courtroom when a judge, aided by counsel and shelves of legal textbooks containing precedents, hands down a new ruling.

Does this not sound like something out of a novel by Kafka?

There can be no liberty without law but the wrong kind of law – or law that is administered unfairly – can take away liberty from those whom the law is supposed to protect.

CHAPTER TWELVE
Affirmative Action

'The finest opportunity ever given to the world was thrown away because the passion for equality made vain the hope for freedom.'

- Lord Acton

'All the complaints which are made of the world are unjust; I never knew a man of merit neglected; it was generally by his own fault that he failed of success.'

- Dr Samuel Johnson

'I recently applied for a job I really wanted,' wrote a reader of mine. 'I had all the necessary qualifications and exactly the sort of experience the advertisers said they were looking for. I was short-listed for the job. But I didn't get it. The advertisers gave the post to a black woman. She had only basic qualifications and didn't have my experience. One of the people on the interviewing panel told me afterwards that they hadn't been able to give me the job because I am male and white. What is going on? I thought that discrimination was illegal.'

This reader is half right in his assumption that discrimination is illegal. Some types of discrimination are illegal. For example, discrimination against black people is illegal. Anyone who refuses to give someone a job because they are black could end up in big trouble. And I think that's quite right. Colour prejudice is wrong. And discrimination against women is, quite rightly, illegal too. I support that as well. Discrimination on the grounds of sex is totally unfair and indefensible.

But discrimination against white men is, it seems, never illegal. It is called 'positive discrimination' or 'affirmative action' and many people (black and white) regard it as a 'good thing'. This new form of apartheid was created by, and is sustained by, those who believe that the rights of the individual have to be subjugated to the needs of society.

My reader's experience is by no means unusual.

Discrimination against white men is now commonplace, and middle class, white men have, strangely and unpredictably, become today's new oppressed minority. The theory behind this bizarre activity is that because black people and women have been discriminated against in the past, discriminating against white men will somehow put things right.

Those organisations which deliberately choose to give jobs, houses or whatever else to people of a particular colour or sex are practising racism or sexism just as clearly as they would be if they were deliberately giving jobs to white males. I can see absolutely no difference between 'affirmative action' and 'apartheid'. Attempting to satisfy preordained quotas of black people or women is both absurd and unfair.

It seems clear to me that there are only two possible long term consequences of 'affirmative action'. The first is that organisations will become less efficient and less capable of doing whatever it is they are supposed to do. If 'affirmative action' is allowed to spread it won't be long before every organisation in the world will have poorly trained or inadequately qualified individuals in key jobs. And the second long term consequence is that a huge amount of anger and resentment will build up.

In South Africa, where 'affirmative action' seems to have its deepest roots, it has been suggested that at least half the employees in management posts within public sector departments should be black. That's a fine theory. If all the good candidates were black I would suggest that all the employees in management posts within public sector departments ought to be black. But surely the important word should be 'good' not 'black'? Surely, in a fair society the best candidate should get the job.

But in practice what happens if there aren't enough good black candidates to fill all the allocated posts? The simple answer is that incompetent and not very good black candidates will still get the jobs.

What a patronising, disempowering, insulting way this is to try to right the wrongs of past generations. The real danger is that if 'affirmative action' is allowed to continue everyone will suffer. Some black people and some women might feel that they are getting a good deal. And there is no doubt that some blacks and some women will get jobs that they wouldn't have got in a fair, just world. But the blacks and the women who have jobs they can't do properly will end up feeling miserable, unhappy and incompetent. The organisations they are working for will become inefficient and they will crumble. If they are commercial organisations they will go bankrupt. And the white males who were qualified to do those jobs will eventually rise up, rebel and fight for their forgotten rights. Within decades, embittered white men will be campaigning for this new variety of discrimination to be abolished. History will simply repeat itself.

The only real answer to the problems, injustices and unfairnesses created by past discriminatory policies is through education. We must make sure that black children get exactly the same opportunities as white children. We must make sure that girls get the same opportunities as boys. Introducing a new, late twentieth century version of apartheid into society is no way to deal with the problem; it is, rather, a patronising way of simply ensuring that freedom and liberty are further eroded. 'Affirmative action' is typical of the sort of slick, short term solution favoured by those who put the rights and needs of society above the rights and needs of individuals.

CHAPTER THIRTEEN
The Demographic Threat

'Life is a checkerboard and the player opposite you is time...you are playing against a partner who will not tolerate indecision.'
- Napoleon Hill

The average age of citizens in the 'developed' and so called 'civilised' world has been rising steadily for years. This is not because people are living longer (they aren't) but because birth rates and infant mortality rates have both fallen dramatically during the last century or so. As a result of poor eating habits, chemically polluted foods and environmental pollution today's elderly population is also more prone to sickness than previous generations. The result of all this is that governments constantly need to increase taxes in order to support this large, dependant population.

***

One of the principle themes of my book *The Health Scandal* (published in 1988) was the argument that by the year 2020 western civilisation would have reached crisis point, with more than half the population being financially dependent on the remainder of the population. By the year 2020 one third of the population in the developed world will be over the age of 65, and for every home where there are two healthy parents and two healthy children there will be four disabled or dependent individuals needing constant care.

Diseases such as schizophrenia and diabetes (which are genetically transmitted) and blindness (which is ten times as common among the over-65s and thirty times as common among the over-75s) will be as common as indigestion and hay fever are today, unemployment and stress related diseases will be endemic and developed countries around the world will face bankruptcy as they struggle to find the cash to pay pensions, sick pay and unemployment benefits.

Tragically and unfairly, resentment, bitterness and anger will divide the young and the old, the able bodied and the dependent, the employed and the unemployed; there will be, within 20 years of the start of the 21st century, anarchy, despair and civil war with ghettoes of elderly and disabled citizens abandoned to care for themselves.

For years those who have forecast the end of the human race have talked of nuclear war, starvation in the third world and pollution as being the major threats to our survival. But the decline of the developed world will be triggered not by any of these forces but by much simpler and entirely predictable developments. We are heading for a medical and social catastrophe. And every day that goes by makes that catastrophe increasingly inevitable. Everyone will suffer: today's elderly, tomorrow's elderly and tomorrow's young too.

When I first published this forecast in the 1980s the medical and political establishments refused to take my warning seriously. I was dismissed as a scaremonger. No one would broadcast the TV series I wanted to make and the book I wrote about the whole issue was studiously ignored.

It now looks as if my calculations were accurate. If anything they were rather conservative. There seems to me to be little doubt that in the next thirty years age will have a far more divisive effect on our society than race, sex or class have ever had. Recent figures from Italy show that country now has 20 million workers and 21 million pensioners. It seems that in Italy, at least, the horrific scenario I outlined has already arrived. The number of individuals who are dependent on the state for their income now exceeds the number of individuals who are creating wealth. The consequences are terrifying. And with the ratio of births to deaths now down to one to one in Italy (to give you an idea of the enormity of the demographic change which has taken place, as recently as 1968 there were two births to every death in Italy) to say that the future seems bleak is an understatement of heroic proportions.

In developed countries total populations are increasing very slowly but the size of the ageing populations are increasing at a dramatic rate. For example, during one recent decade the total population of Britain increased by less than one per cent. But in the same period the pensionable population rose by ten per cent. In many westernised nations one person in five is already a pensioner. By the year 2020 a third of the population in most developed countries will be pensioners.

Several things make this explosion in the size of the elderly population particularly significant.

First, there is the fact that among older populations there is inevitably a higher proportion of disabled and dependent individuals. The incidence of chronic disease rises rapidly among older age groups.

* Among 16 to 44 year olds 20% of the population suffer from chronic

illness.

* Among 45 to 64 year olds 40% of the population suffer from chronic illness.
* Among 65 to 74 year olds 50% of the population suffer from chronic illness.
* And among people aged 75 or over 65% of the population suffer from chronic, long term illness.

In many developed countries it is common to find that half the beds in hospitals are occupied by patients suffering from some sort of stroke. Stroke patients generally need to stay in hospital for long periods of time and they need intensive nursing care.

The incidence of diabetes is doubling every decade. In 1984 just 2% of the population in the average sort of developed, westernised country was diabetic. If the increase continues at the same rate then by the year 2020 (less than half a lifetime away) one in four people will be diabetic.

There is also ample evidence to show that mental disease is on the increase. The number of patients with mental illness needing to be admitted to hospital is rising by 10% every decade. Today, between 10% and 15% of the population will, at some stage in their lives, suffer from mental illness severe enough to warrant their admission to a mental hospital. Once again it is the increase in the size of our elderly population which is at least partly responsible.

One side effect of all this will be that more and more of our hospital beds will be blocked and unavailable for emergencies. All this will inevitably mean that waiting lists for non urgent surgery will get longer and longer, and the number of people in our community suffering from disabling and untreated problems such as arthritic hips will grow even faster. The steady increase in our elderly population will mean that the quality of health care for everyone will steadily deteriorate.

The second reason why the explosion in the size of the elderly population is dangerous is that the number of young people is falling. And the result will be that in the future a smaller and smaller working population will have to support a larger and larger dependent population.

That takes us neatly into the third reason why the explosion in the size of our over-60 population is likely to produce real problems: money.

Most workers who are currently paying pension contributions assume that the money they are paying will be invested and repaid to them when they reach pensionable age. But that is not the case. The pension contributions paid by today's workers are used to pay the pensions of yesterday's workers – today's pensioners. If pension programmes were being organised by private individuals they would be described as pyramid or Ponzi schemes and the organisers would be in prison.

The pensions that today's workers will receive when they retire will be paid by the regular contributions made by tomorrow's workers. But the working population is getting smaller and smaller. And the retired population is getting bigger and bigger. Thousands of people are now demanding to be allowed to retire earlier and earlier. A decade or two ago anyone who retired under the age of 60 or 65 was considered rather odd. Today it is not at all unusual for men and women to retire at the age of 50 or 55.

(What do all these retirees do with the rest of their lives? Many of them die early for they have no purpose in their lives. Their work may have been dull but it at least gave them a sense of importance and purpose, and a sense of camaraderie. Most of them will just sit at home, their minds and bodies decaying, as they eat, smoke and drink themselves into an early grave – watching television and clutching their lottery tickets in the hope that tomorrow might bring something better. What a miserable, pointless way to live and die.)

You don't have to be a genius to see the disaster we are heading for. By the end of the century the size of our elderly population will have begun to concern politicians. By then it will be too late.

This is a problem that we should be worrying about *now*. It is, without a doubt, one of the biggest problems our society must face. It is something I've been writing about – and warning about – for over a decade but our politicians still don't seem to have noticed it and very few members of the public seem to understand it.

***

The easy and often voiced explanation for both the increase in the size of the developed world's elderly population, and the increase in the number of disabled and financially dependent individuals, is that modern medical miracles, produced by the medical profession and the pharmaceutical industry, have produced the change by enabling people to live longer.

Doctors and drug companies have for some time excused their errors and successfully distracted attention away from their incompetence by arguing that their efforts have resulted in a consistent and impressive improvement in life expectancy during the last century or so. The increasing size of our elderly (and disabled) population is, say the industry's supporters, a direct consequence of medical progress.

The truth, however, is rather different and the medical profession and the drug companies are guilty of a confidence trick of gargantuan proportions.

The fact is that during the last century doctors and drug companies have become louder, more aggressive, a good deal richer and far more powerful but life expectancy has not gone up.

Improved sanitation facilities have meant that the number of babies dying – and the number of women dying in childbirth – have fallen dramatically, but for adults life expectation has not been rising.

To prove my point I prepared a list of 111 famous individuals – all of whom lived and died before the start of this century. I then checked to see how old these individuals were when they died.

I found that the average age at death was 72.39 years.

The conclusion is simple: despite all the expensive razzmatazz of mod-. ern medicine life expectation has simply not increased in the last century or so. The biblical promise of three score years and ten has been fairly steady for centuries.

There are two reasons for what has happened. First there has for many decades been a steady reduction in the number of children being born in the developed world. Terrified by what was originally described as the 'birth explosion time bomb' millions of couples decided to limit the size of their families – or not to have children at all. The development and introduction of the contraceptive pill and of sterilisation techniques for both men and women made this easy.

(In contrast this has definitely not been the case in the developing world and the global political consequences are far reaching. In Muslim countries birth rates are extremely high and the average age in those populations is inevitably much younger. A society which is predominantly composed of young, healthy individuals obviously has a very different outlook to a society which is dominated by older, often unhealthy individuals. The future is Muslim. Our ageing, western, largely Christian society has very little future.)

As the number of elderly people as a percentage of the overall population has been steadily increasing so also the incidence of disability among the elderly has been increasing steadily too. Today's elderly are nowhere near as fit as their ancestors were. Our fat and toxin rich diet is just one factor which has led to a steady increase in the incidence of cancer, obesity, heart disease, arthritis and many other causes of long term disability. Mental illness such as chronic anxiety and depression, caused by the unavoidable 'toxic stresses' created by the structured society in which we live (and which I described in detail in my book 'How to Overcome Toxic Stress') are now endemic – as are the myriad illnesses caused by the powerful drugs frequently prescribed by doctors with such carelessness.

***

Nothing has happened about any of this because politicians don't like to act quickly if at all. Politicians everywhere tend to think in four or five year terms at the most. They are concerned only with the now – rather than with the future – because what happens now decides whether or not they get re-elected. And professional politicians care about nothing as much as they care about political power.

Nevertheless, it is now to a large extent too late. Whether the politicians ever act or not this problem exists and it is going to affect all our lives in a very real and dramatic way. The incidence of illness and disability is going to rise and rise and the availability of public resources is going to fall and fall.

If you are currently over the age of 35 then the chances are that by the time you reach the sort of age at which you might hope to retire you will discover that any publicly funded pension you might receive will either be very small or non-existent and the availability of sheltered or nursing home accommodation will be extremely limited.

If you are currently under the age of 35 then you are going to have to pay a steadily increasing percentage of your earnings in income tax and national insurance deductions. You can safely ignore anything politicians say about cutting taxes. The fact is that taxes are probably never going to be lower than they are at the moment.

The young are, I suppose, in the very worst position of all. Throughout their working lives they are going to have to struggle to pay towards the care of a larger and larger elderly population. When they themselves reach retirement age they will be in even bigger trouble for they will probably not have been able to save anything to look after themselves.

The whole concept of retirement is a bizarre one – and a relatively recent innovation, introduced simply to satisfy political needs and create higher employment levels. It was also introduced to provide a carrot for people who do jobs they hate doing. The carrot is simple: work hard for 40 or 50 years and at the end of that time – assuming that the stress of doing a job you dislike has not killed you, which in all honesty we won't mind terribly much because when you have finished working you won't have any further value to society – we will allow you to do what *you* want to do. We will even give you some money so that you can eat and keep yourself warm and sheltered.

Why should a perfectly healthy man who reaches the age of 65 be forced to suddenly stop working? Politicians, who introduce all the laws relating to retirement frequently carry on working well into their 70s and 80s. When I was a general practitioner I had a patient who was still working even though he was in his 90s. His son and his grandson – both eminent local businessman – wanted him to retire. They said it was because they were worried about him injuring himself but I rather suspected that they didn't like the idea of their father and grandfather mowing lawns and weeding vegetable patches. Eventually, they forced him to retire and even though he was mentally and physically fit they put him into a retirement home. He was dead within two months. They had taken away his very purpose for living and killed him just as surely as if they had put a bullet in his brain.

CHAPTER FOURTEEN
The Suppression Of Creativity And Innovation

'In a country where the sole employer is the State, opposition means death by slow starvation. The old principle: who does not work shall not eat, has been replaced by a new one: who does not obey shall not eat.'

- Leon Trotsky

A symptom of any society which is crumbling and relatively close to the end of an era (as I believe ours is) is a reluctance, or even a total inability, to accept anyone who is unconventional.

Our society has numerous prejudices against individuals who behave in any way which is perceived to be outside the 'norm', and against activities which are either not accepted or not understood, however harmless they may be. These prejudices are so powerful that individuals who have jobs which require the authorised respect and approval of their employers or their neighbours may have to keep any idiosyncrasies secret if they wish to succeed or even survive. Intolerance and standardisation are key words in our modern society; the mediocre are now dominant and keen to destroy anything which could be described as different or 'better than average'.

And yet most of the great developments which have changed human life (and the world) for the better have come from outside the official channels (political, business, educational or scientific) and have, in their time, been opposed and sneered at by those within the establishment.

Ordinary, conventional people, for whom there is little more to life than regular bowel movements, a slowly growing pension entitlement and an intimate knowledge of the characters in their favourite television soap opera, loathe those who depart from convention. I suspect that this may, at least in part, be because they do not feel it fair that they should have to be conventional in order to survive while someone else should get away with living his or her life freely and without restraint.

(It is the same sort of jealousy which drives literary and dramatic critics to bitterness. Most of them hate authors or playwrights who are successful. They hate them because they know that they are making money doing something which they would love to do if only they had the courage and the talent.)

And, in a way, the ordinary citizen hates unconventional behaviour because he regards it as a criticism of the society to which he has paid his dues by behaving in the 'proper' fashion.

***

When I wrote an article about crossdressing (also known as transvestism) in my newspaper column I received a vast number of letters from male readers who had never before dared admit to anyone that they liked dressing in the sort of clothes normally worn by women. They had kept an important part of their lives entirely secret because they were frightened of what would happen to them, their families and their lives if they dared allow their secrets out into the harsh light of our unsympathetic and cruel world.

One man wrote to tell me that he had been crossdressing for many years. He apologised for not signing his letter but said that he was terrified of anyone discovering his identity. Indeed, he was so frightened of being found out that although his communication to me was anonymous he had driven to another town some distance away in order to post his letter.

What sort of world do we live in where dressing in clothes considered socially inappropriate carries such opprobrium that a man has to take such precautions against discovery?

***

One of the fundamental problems with our society is the fact that too many people are paid to suppress innovation, to avoid taking positive decisions and to stop other people taking positive decisions. It is frequently far safer to say 'No' if you are an employee or a bureaucrat. In large organisations hardly anyone ever gets into trouble for not authorising something and so more and more things are, if not actually forbidden, suppressed through not actually being authorised.

Society wants you to go to school and learn a great deal of dull and probably inconsequential information by rote in order to train your mind to soak up information and not ask questions. (The aim of a modern education is to train the individual for work and to produce unquestioning and unthinking graduates). After leaving school the perfect citizen will marry and start a family (thereby taking on responsibilities which will stop him from wasting time dreaming and also stop him rebelling), buy a house which he can only just afford (thereby increasing the wealth of the 'system' and tying himself up with a large mortgage), train for, find and keep a responsible, regular job (whether or not he finds it of interest), work until he is 65 and carefully save for his retirement from the employment he has loathed for so long. Finally, when he is tired and weary and all his ambitions and hopes and opportunities have gone he can retire quietly, enjoy his insignificant hobbies and quietly prepare himself for the grave.

***

You should not be afraid to be different and to make enemies. You will be far more likely to succeed if you dare to make enemies. Lewis Carroll once said: 'If you limit your actions in life to the things that no one can possibly find fault with you will not do much.' Ben Graham, American writer and investment guru, once said that he hoped every day to do: 'something foolish, something creative and something generous.' It isn't a bad aim.

Imaginative, thoughtful and creative individuals have always had a hard time. The 'system' has to be defended. The questioning individual is a threat and must be ridiculed, isolated and silenced. Look back in history and you will find countless examples of citizens who were harassed or persecuted simply because they dared to think for themselves – and tried to share their thoughts with others.

Our world has never welcomed the original, the challenging, the inspirational or the passionate and has always preferred the characterless to the thought provoking.

The unconventional are the creators of our society. They may seem odd (that is, after all, why they are unconventional) and their choice of clothes, cars, homes and so on may not fit comfortably with what society expects, but their originality drives society and is the basis for all that we create.

And yet the immediate future will lie firmly in the hands of the mediocre and the incompetent for today far too much power has been put into the hands of the unelected, who are therefore above and beyond public control and criticism. The democratic process may allocate power (in theory) but it does not guarantee that the distribution of power will remain equitable. It is only the limitation of power which stops it from becoming cruel and arbitrary and in our society there are no limits on the amount of power to which the bureaucrats can help themselves.

CHAPTER FIFTEEN
Society Takes The Responsibility For People Who Make Themselves Ill

'Half the useful work in the world consists of combating the harmful work.'
- Bertrand Russell

The heavy drinking, heavy smoking, heroin-using, overweight, promiscuous homosexual man who never uses condoms and who has a penchant for motor car racing and hang gliding will probably have to pay over the odds for his life insurance. The underwriters know that his chances of living long enough to enable them to make a profit out of an ordinary premium are pretty slim.

Similarly, the driver who is involved in a road accident and who is shown afterwards to have had far too much to drink, to have driven on bald tyres and to have left his seat belt dangling on its hook could find that his chances of getting massive damages are low.

Those are just two of the ways in which people who ignore expert advice are penalised. And rightly so. They have been given the opportunity to accept the same advice that everyone else has been given and they have rejected it. Indeed, there are many other specific ways in which the foolish may be penalised for ignoring good advice. There are, for example, now many companies which prefer not to employ smokers on the very good grounds that a smoker is more likely to need time off work during the winter months than a non smoker. His mild chest infections are more likely to become serious. This seems to me to be an excellent philosophy. The individual has a choice. If he wants to smoke, hang glide, ski off piste down steep mountains, race motor cars or do any one of a thousand dangerous things that's fine. It's his choice. But he should be prepared to take responsibility, and pay the price, for his decision. Society should not prevent people from doing what they want to do but nor should it (or can it) subsidise those who deliberately choose to risk their health and their lives.

After all, because there is always going to be a shortage of medical equipment and medical personnel those who are ill through no fault of their own will, when resources are spent on those who have deliberately chosen to take a chance with their health, frequently end up suffering and paying a high price for the selfish stupidity of others. People who recklessly play 'catch me if you can' with cancer by eating meat or smoking cigarettes are creating longer waiting lists for everyone. Hospitals everywhere are so desperately short of funds, equipment and staff that every year thousands of people who need treatment and who could be saved are left to die. Many thousands more die before they can be properly investigated. Is this fair when hospital departments and hospital beds are frequently filled with patients who have only themselves to blame for their ill health?

In our modern society the individual is no longer expected to take responsibility for his own health – or to pay the physical or economic consequences. Those who pay tax or health insurance premiums are subsidising the recklessness of those who drink too much, smoke too much, allow themselves to remain overweight or eat meat.

Why should the man who regularly smokes 30 cigarettes a day expect the nation to pay for treatment for his bronchitis, his lung cancer, his heart disease and his gastritis? Why should the woman who refuses to diet expect others to help pay when her obesity causes medical problems? Why should the man who persists in drinking too much get free treatment when his liver finally fails to cope? Why should the meat eater expect to receive free medical care when he or she develops colon cancer, breast cancer, prostate cancer, endometrial cancer, rectal cancer, pancreatic cancer or kidney cancer? There is, after all, plenty of research available proving that those cancers are linked to eating meat. Indeed, we now know what causes 80% of all cancers and so cancer is, to a large extent, optional.

Why should society insist that individuals who have deliberately exposed themselves to disease receive free care while others, less selfish and more sensible, are left untreated?

Why should the drunken driver have his injuries treated free of charge? Why should the climber who sets off in bad weather expect the nation to pay the cost of his rescue and subsequent treatment?

These people have chosen to take the risk of damaging their health and they should pay for the treatment they need. They should take responsibility for their own actions instead of expecting society to take on that responsibility. Without this proper allocation of responsibility all our freedoms will continue to be diminished.

CHAPTER SIXTEEN
The Drugs War

'Those who would give up essential liberty to purchase a little temporary safety deserve neither liberty nor safety.'

- Benjamin Franklin

The extent to which we have lost our freedom cannot be overestimated. Everything has to be planned these days. Like it or not, we are living in a police state and there are forms to be filled in for just about everything you want to do. Anything spontaneous is disliked and disapproved of in our highly structured and regimented society, particularly if the results cannot be foreseen in advance.

If you want to open a bank account of move money from one account to another you must be prepared to produce your passport and a series of solid explanations as to why you want a new bank account and why you want to move your own money around. When governments introduce new banking rules which take away your privacy and decimate confidentiality they persuade ordinary people to support them by claiming that the new rules are designed to stop drug barons laundering money. Really? How many drug barons do you think have bank accounts at your local bank? The drug barons use sophisticated banking techniques to move money around. They don't toddle into your local bank clutching a small bag of mixed notes and coins. Our streets and shopping malls are watched by video cameras. We are constantly encouraged to believe that this is a Good Thing since it will help to reduce crime. Governments claim that they are trying to spot drug smugglers. Does anyone really believe that? The video cameras are there because politicians and administrators like to keep an eye on us at all times. They want to know where we all are and what we are doing. When governments get tough and make it harder for ordinary people to move between countries they say that they are doing it in order to stop drug trafficking. What nonsense. Do you really think that the drug barons are going to worry about a few new restrictive laws? The drug barons buy planes and ships and move their drugs in bulk and in secret. They take no notice of national boundaries.

When governments talk about introducing identity cards they claim that they are doing so to counteract drug smugglers. The same, constant excuse is used to explain and excuse giving the forces of law and order greater resources.

Governments and law enforcement agencies explain away all this loss of privacy by claiming that it is all being done so that they can stop the drugs war. This is, of course, absolute nonsense. The drug smugglers don't worry about law restricting freedom or the movement of money around the world any more than bank robbers and getaway drivers worry about speed restrictions on the roads. Governments want to take away our privacy because by doing so they give themselves more power over us. Privacy, liberty and freedom are all interlinked.

The drugs war, though ineffective and pointless, has become a great excuse for totalinarianism: a twentieth-century tyranny masquerading as a moral crusade; an excuse for the plan to deprive ordinary people of as much freedom as possible.

The drugs war has given the establishment a wonderful excuse to end banking and personal secrecy with blanket legislation originating with the excuse that it will help further the aims of the drugs war but inspired in practice by much more sinister motives. The drugs war is, to be blunt, designed to reduce civil liberties. The authorities know that they will never stop drug use (any more than they will ever stop prostitution).

As I explained at some length in my book *The Drugs Myth* legalisation or decriminalisation would make far more sense. But legalising or decriminalising drug abuse would not enable the politicians to erode our liberties with quite so much freedom. It does not surprise me that politicians in the rest of Europe constantly attack Holland for its decriminalisation policy – even though Holland has fewer drug addicts than other countries, and its policy has clearly worked. Politicians outside Holland are terrified that if the public find out about this the drugs war will have to be abandoned and the best and most enduring twentieth century excuse for totalitarianism will have disappeared.

No leading politician today seems prepared to suggest that drugs such as cannabis should be decriminalised. Even newspapers seem frightened to air the debate without making it clear that they are firmly opposed to decriminalisation.

* * *

Despite the almost hysterical support for the drugs war, the facts show that legalising – or at least decriminalising – drugs makes total sense. Those who oppose the legalisation or decriminalisation are, in practise, supporting the status quo; they are supporting drug use and supporting the state's continuing and expanding interference in our lives.

The global drugs war has been a total failure. Despite the expenditure of untold billions of dollars it has changed absolutely nothing. The drugs war has not stopped people selling drugs such as cannabis, cocaine and heroin. Occasional arrests of a few people here and a few folk there make no real difference to the major drug barons. They remain safe, secure and aloof from the day-to-day hazards of arrest and their businesses remain untouched by the phoney war.

And the drugs war has not stopped people taking these drugs. Putting people into prison for taking a drug does no good at all. Turning drug users into criminals merely makes them more vulnerable and alienated – and increases the likelihood that they will continue to take drugs.

The evidence shows clearly that if the drugs war were stopped there would be less drug taking and far fewer drug related deaths. The real irony is that those who support the drugs war – and who claim that drug pushers and users must be arrested and imprisoned at all cost – are directly responsible for many deaths.

There is a hidden agenda here. The drugs war is not about drugs at all. It is about power. The politicians love the drugs war because it gives them an excuse to exercise power over the rest of the community. The drugs war is used as an excuse for just about every new piece of legislation which takes away our freedom.

***

New rules which remove your civil rights are introduced because the politicians don't want you to have any civil rights. New rules which remove your freedom are introduced because politicians (among whom dishonesty is now the norm rather than the exception) don't want you to have any freedom.

The drugs war is a convenient excuse for these constant infringements of your liberty.

Every new restriction and infringement of your liberty is blamed on the drugs war. That is absolute nonsense and the politicians know it.

The well meaning do gooders who believe that by supporting the drugs war they are helping to stamp out drug use and drug addiction are doing nothing of the kind: they are in fact merely supporting governments around the world in their determination to take total control of the lives of their citizens.

If you want the state to control your life then you should support the drugs war. If you do not want your freedom then support the drugs war. But you should not support the drugs war if you want to help stamp out drug addiction. That is just about the last thing it will do.

Since the drugs war started the number of drug addicts has risen steadily and governments have made no realistic move to stop this; the fact is that governments do not want the number of drug addicts to go down because if that happens then the excuse for the drugs war will disappear.

For as long as the drugs war lasts it will enable our politicians to pass more and more new laws, which add more and more restrictions to our lives. The threat of increasing drug abuse provides a permanent good excuse for the erosion of our remaining freedoms. The drugs war is nothing other than an excuse for a steady and constant erosion of our freedoms and our privacy.

CHAPTER SEVENTEEN
The Dangers Of Envy

'What people fear when they engage in the struggle is not that they will fail to get their breakfast next morning, but that they will fail to outshine their neighbours.'

- Bertrand Russell

'Talk about modest merit being neglected, is too often a cant by which indolent and irresolute men seek to lay their want of success at the door of the public.'
- Washington Irving

Bertrand Russell, the philosopher, once wrote that 'Envy is the basis of democracy'. There was much truth in that apparently pessimistic thought. The two are inextricably linked. The oppressive moralists who believe in democracy above all else have created a sad, sad world.

In a true democracy no one is allowed to achieve or own more than anyone else. In a true democracy the rules and the laws are devised by the incompetent to satisfy the incompetent, greedy, unsuccessful and envious.

Envy in our society creates much hatred and fear. Attempts to create a uni-dimensional, totally democratic society, based on a single level of achievement and possession, have led to absurd social legislation.

Envy and malevolence are closely linked. The envious, themselves often living miserable lives, seem to obtain their greatest pleasure from seeing or inflicting pain or misfortune on others. Envy and malevolence are twin emotions; both driven by a love of scandal and shame and sustained by hypocrisy. The result is that any story told against another individual has a better than average chance of being believed if it says something against that individual.

Nasty, unpleasant gossip is instantly accepted as the truth by many simply because they want to hear evil of others. The propaganda which is most successful and most likely to be believed is the propaganda which stirs up contempt and hatred.

People who have done little or nothing with their lives love putting someone down and 'in their place'. And they particularly enjoy seeing someone suffer if the person doing the suffering seems previously to have achieved something out of the ordinary. It is this love of unpleasant gossip which explains the unique success of many newspapers these days. The broadsheet (or so called 'quality') newspapers are just as bad at this as the much maligned tabloid newspapers. In fact the hypocrisy of the broadsheets (which generally pretend to be above gossip but then print just as much of it as the tabloids) makes them particularly unpalatable.

In a fair world you might imagine that if someone saw another individual driving a Rolls Royce motor car he would be likely to say: 'That's a lovely car. I'd like a car like that one day'. But many people, when they see someone driving a Rolls Royce, are likely to sneer and, when they are sure that no one is looking, put a deep scratch into the paintwork.

(I have personal experience of this peculiarity of human nature. Envious, spiteful vandals once used a penknife or a key to carve a deep scratch around a classic Bentley which I owned. Because it was old the car wasn't particularly valuable and at the time I considered that it was far better for the environment to keep an old car on the road rather than to buy a new car but the damage to the paintwork cost a small fortune to repair.)

Our capacity for envy sometimes seems to be infinite. There are some in our society who even envy those who have the courage to do as they will. And envy is exhibited against those who dare to sin against our false morality values. The price we demand for forgiveness is punishment, debasement and chastisement.

The child who feels that he or she didn't get a fair crack of the whip when young will often go through life carrying imagined injustices. He or she will often seem to wallow in unhappiness. Friends (often few) frequently get fed up of trying to avoid saying anything which could possibly be falsely construed as a slight. The child who feels that he or she didn't receive enough love when small will sometimes go through life feeling hated and feeling like an outsider. Many of those who express constant bitterness and resentment and who seem constantly twisted into a position of anger are driven by envy at the love and happiness enjoyed by others.

Most bizarrely of all perhaps, some are envious even when they are doing well and seem to have everything to be grateful for. They see someone doing better than them but instead of saying 'I am doing well' they say 'He is doing better' and feel aggrieved.

Curiously, many people envy most those whom they regard as closest to them in social status. So, the corner shop owner will reserve his greatest envy for the man who has two corner shops rather than for the man who has a whole chain of shops and the man with a small house will feel the greatest envy for the man with a slightly larger small house rather than for the man with the huge mansion.

There is, of course, always someone in history or legend who is more successful than you can ever be and so it is always possible to make a comparison. 'If you desire glory you may envy Napoleon,' wrote Bertrand Russell. 'But Napoleon envied Caesar, Caesar envied Alexander, and Alexander, I dare say, envied Hercules who never existed.'

Envy means seeing things not for themselves but only in relation to others. How sad it is that the gambler who wins a small sum of money on the lottery is likely to feel envious towards the individual who has a bigger win.

CHAPTER EIGHTEEN
Learning Shouldn't Stop When Education Ends

'The best part of every man's education, is that which he gives to himself.'
                                                            - Sir Walter Scott

'One needs only to know the letters of the alphabet in order to learn everything that one wishes.'
                                                            Edmund Stone

'I learned grammar when I was a private soldier on the pay of sixpence a day. The edge of my berth, or that of my guard bed was my seat to study in; my knapsack was my bookcase; a bit of board lying on my lap was my writing table; and the task did not demand anything like a year of my life. I had no money to purchase candle or oil; in winter time it was rarely that I could get any evening light but that of the fire, and only my turn even of that. And if I, under such circumstances, and without parent or friend to advise or encourage me, accomplished this undertaking, what excuse can there be for any youth, however poor, however pressed with business, or however circumstanced as to room or other conveniences?'
                                                            - William Cobbett

Regular, mass market schooling for everyone was originally a by product of the industrial revolution. Prior to the industrial revolution most people lived in villages and hamlets and only a relatively small percentage of the population lived in towns and cities.

The first factories and industrial towns developed in England when industrial machinery such as spinning wheels which had been installed in cottages, barns and village halls were smashed by the Luddites; rebellious workers

122

who believed that the introduction of machinery threatened their livelihoods.

As a direct result of the Luddite activities the machine owners put their replacement equipment into specially built 'factories' so that they could be protected against vandalism.

Since public transport did not exist this, inevitably, meant that the people who were going to work in those factories had to be housed nearby. In this way the first new, purpose built industrial towns developed.

The first schools were built not to educate or to inform but because unless some provision was made for looking after children factory owners could not employ women as well as men. The development of the first towns had meant that family units had been splintered and it was no longer possible for young parents to turn to their own parents for help and support.

Either by purpose, design or simple good fortune it was quickly discovered that the development of formal schooling had an additional benefit. Employers found that children who got into the habit of attending a school for regular hours during the day adapted more readily to work in a factory. Many of their parents, who had been brought up working as farm labourers, found factory work, hours and discipline difficult to get used to. Children who were accustomed to school work, hours and discipline had no such problems.

***

Today, a formal education is still primarily designed to occupy pupils, to keep them busy and out of mischief and to prepare them for an ordinary working life. Very little of the tedious by rote learning which goes on in schools has any practical purpose. Children are taught algebra, trigonometry and Latin – and then subjected to examinations designed to find out how well they have absorbed the entirely useless material they have been taught. The aim is to not to teach or impart learning but to produce school leavers who will feel comfortable with the standard working ritual of modern life.

Schooling is a disciplinary activity rather than an educational one (although the latest and most fashionable educational methods – those which are designed to educate without work, study, labour or pain – fail even to instil discipline into pupils). Students are certainly not being given information which would enable them to live independent lives. They are being taught to fit into society's demands for them, rather than taught how to think.

Why, after all, would society want to teach young people how to think for themselves? People who can think for themselves are likely to be a nuisance rather than an asset to a closely structured society which depends more on discipline and routine than on innovation or imagination.

Students, at schools, colleges and universities, are trained to do as they are told. Is it is for this reason that rules play such a crucial part in all educational establishments. Learning to obey the rules and do as you are told is a more important part of any educational establishment than learning to create or to question. Most education and training is designed to make sure that people do not maximise or optimise their own skills but that they accept whatever life or fate offers.

The society which we have created, which now has a purpose and an agenda of its own, does not want thinking citizens. People who think are likely to threaten the status quo.

* * *

And yet there are many citizens in our society who believe (with apparent sincerity) that once their formal education is over they can stop learning. They assume that when they leave school, college or university they do so as educationally complete individuals, and that they can, from that point in their lives onwards, stop expanding, exploring and discovering.

This is no accident.

It is exactly what society wants.

When graduating students believe that they no longer need to learn they inevitably become content and stable cogs in society's complex machinery.

The truth, of course, is very different.

The truth is that even a genuine education, one which encouraged original and creative thinking, would be merely a beginning.

* * *

The word 'educate' is derived from the word 'educo' which means to draw out and develop. Education should not be about learning and remembering dates and mathematical formulae. An educated man is one who has developed his mind to take advantage of his skills and talents and to get where he wants to be without hurting the innocent. It is perfectly possible to be both ignorant and yet well educated.

An ignorant man who has been taught to think can get hold of all the knowledge he needs in order to deal with his ignorance – either from a library or from people who have the knowledge.

But a man who is merely educated, and who may wrongly think he is knowledgeable, will remain in an intellectual rut.

The truth is that a modern, formal education is irrelevant to life. How many of the great thinkers of the past do you think were school or college graduates?

All of which explains why so many people do so well without any formal education and why so many modern employers prefer to hire intelligent and enthusiastic staff who do not have any formal (and often stifling) education.

* * *

You probably have far more knowledge than you think you have. And

knowledge is only valuable when it is used. The knowledge you have stored −
but which you do not use − is of no value to you or anyone else. Knowledge
does not have a use or a value unless you do something with it. Knowledge is
potential power and potential wealth. But knowledge and wisdom, unlike money,
only really show their value when you put them to use. And knowledge and
wisdom can, unlike money, be spent more than once. A good formal education
should (in theory) show you how to acquire knowledge and how to use knowledge when you have acquired it. Sadly, however, very little modern formal education teaches people where or how to acquire more knowledge for themselves
and hardly any formal education is designed to show people how to use what
they have learned.

CHAPTER NINETEEN
Too Little Love And Not Enough Kindness

'Not only is love a source of delight, but its absence is a source of pain. Love is to be valued because it enhances all the best pleasures, such as music, and sunrise in mountains, and the sea under the full moon. A man who has never enjoyed beautiful things in the company of a woman whom he loved has not experienced to the full the magic power of which such things are capable.'

- Bertrand Russell

I was standing behind a young woman in a bookshop. At her behest the assistant was searching through several huge reference books looking for details of a book in which she said she was interested. I had a single paperback in my hand, together with the exact amount of money needed to pay for the book, and was standing behind the customer waiting with what I thought was pretty commendable patience.

After waiting for a minute or two (it seemed like an hour but probably wasn't more than a few minutes) my attention was caught by an advertisement for a concert in the woman's folded newspaper which lay on the counter in front of her. I was interested in the concert and started to read the advertisement in that rather cautious way one uses when reading someone else's newspaper.

I must have leant forward slightly in order to read the smaller print towards the bottom of the advertisement for suddenly the woman turned round, realised that I was reading her newspaper and in one swift and rather aggressive movement turned the paper over. Her sole and clear intention was to stop me reading her newspaper. She then glowered at me as though she had caught me trying to steal her purse out of her handbag and carried on with her interminable (and it has to be said rather boring) conversation with the assistant. A simple, everyday, deliberate act of unkindness.

126

Friends of mine had a much worse experience when they moved house. On moving in day they found that the vendors had removed the lawn (they had rolled it up and taken it away to put down in their own new garden), all the doors and the skirting boards.

Simple, everyday, deliberate, random acts of unkindness.

CHAPTER TWENTY
An Epidemic Of Depression

'The mass of men lead lives of quiet desperation.'

- Henry David Thoreau

Look around at the people you know. Many of them will be constantly consumed by anxiety, living well beyond their emotional means. They will have little personal time or creative energy for anything but the struggle to survive. One of the most awful unique human burdens is the one which forces us to worry so much about the past and the future that we do not have time for the present.

***

People suffer from stress in many different ways.

Some are simply besieged by anxiety. For them life is filled with threats around every corner. They are filled with dread and a sense of doom and danger. They give up, cannot cope and become depressed.

Some become too competitive, too hostile, too impatient and too pressured by time. They are determined to achieve and they push themselves constantly and without quarter. The pressure they put on themselves means that they become angry with co-workers who make mistakes. As a result they have difficulty working with people.

Some feel that they must constantly be on the move; changing their jobs, their homes, their lifestyle, their friends and even their nationality.

Many people believe that simply by working harder they can regulate every outcome. To a certain extent this is true. Hard work is, theoretically at least, one of the integral secrets of some kinds of success. If effort were always justly rewarded this theory would work well. But our society functions with numerous layers and levels of prejudice and many people will find that their opportunities are limited by prejudice. They can, consequently, be at a great disadvantage and suffer enormously.

Some people like to conform, like everyone around them to conform and like their lives to be neatly planned. They like absolutes and certainties. They are either angry or sad but never a little bit of both. They like to know what they will be wearing and eating and doing (and even thinking) in a fortnight's time. They do not like surprises. They live structured lives, they feel comfortable with rules. This type of individual tends to set up a black and white world. They like to go to the same place on holiday. They belong to clubs and sit on rule making committees. They know clearly what sort of behaviour is acceptable and what is unacceptable. They are stoic, hardworking, solid people. They will never achieve any level of greatness (and their very solidity may mean that in some circles they stand out as rather 'odd'). They hold everything deep inside them; determinedly suppressing their own true feelings. These people tend to suffer greatly when they discover that life is not quite as neat or as reliable as they have always hoped.

***

Most people do not have the time to relax or to fully enjoy their lives. And most suffer one or more stress related illnesses: irritable bowel syndrome, eczema, high blood pressure, indigestion, asthma and a thousand and one other physical and mental problems. Long term stress can cause heart disease, adult onset diabetes and insomnia, and can even damage the nerve cells in the hippocampus – the part of the brain which is a key to learning and memory.

There is an epidemic of depression and unhappiness in our rich and gadget ridden society. Mental illness of all kinds is becoming commoner and commoner. So widespread is the despair that many people actually feel bad if they feel good. There are many who need to get drunk in order to excuse themselves for having a good time. Millions regularly rely upon psychoactive prescription drugs and although there is less guilt and considerably less social opposition with prescription drugs the damage to the body and the mind can be greater than the damage done by illegal drugs.

Much of this unhappiness is due to frustration and pressure which is not within our control – the sort of stress which I describe as 'toxic' (and which is commonly produced by the psychopathic antics of bureaucrats and administrators).

In my book *How To Overcome Toxic Stress* (originally titled *Toxic Stress And The Twentieth Century Blues*) I argued that many of the most potent, destructive and stressful forces in our society are outside our personal control; they are a result of our living in a sophisticated and so called civilised community.

These external stresses, which cannot be alleviated by learning how to deal with stress or by making an effort to live a less stressful life, are most damaging because the frustration, anger and sense of impotence they produce cannot be countered by any logical means.

***

Finally, one of the great injustices of this life is that those who are compassionate and who care, suffer for the crimes of those who are neither compassionate nor who care. The hunter and the vivisector do not suffer any pangs of conscience. The caring, compassionate human being suffers on their behalf.

***

Anger and distress that isn't expressed turns into frustration, then into stress and finally into depression. Our natural zest for life and our natural ability to enjoy living has been destroyed by the abstract concept which we call society. In our modern world physical fatigue (a healthy type of fatigue which can be 'cured' by nothing more complicated than rest) has to a large extent been replaced by nervous fatigue – often to the point of nervous exhaustion. Escaping from stress and pressure becomes ever more difficult. Life isn't getting physically harder but it is getting psychologically harder – and we are still trying to deal with our new stresses in old fashioned ways. The truth is that thinking – like water or electricity – can be good or bad for you.

CHAPTER TWENTY ONE
The Coming Revolution

'The longest journey starts with the first step.'

- Confucius

The best thing a government or an institution can do for a man is to leave him alone, free to develop his mind and his skills and to improve his individual condition and the conditions of those around him.

In order to achieve this sort of world we need a society in which there is freedom for revolutionaries and reformers to think and constantly to improve and adapt society.

But our present society does not approve of the idea of either revolution or reform and there is a widespread fatalistic acceptance of the inevitability and unavoidability of our powerlessness.

Probably the most fundamental mistake we have made has been to assume that society's needs are the same as any individual's needs. This is, of course, an absolute nonsense. Every individual has different aims and needs and the community tends to reflect the needs not of the majority, nor even of the most vocal minority, but of the anonymous and unelected bureaucracy which 'runs' the community and which is, effectively, the voice of society.

The fact is that the community as an entity cannot and does not care about individuals. The needs of the two are diametrically opposed. The community can do whatever it wants to protect its interests. But what are the interests of the community? Who decides what the punishments should be when the community is offended in some way?

George Orwell's predictions in his novel 1984 have come true – but hardly anyone has noticed. We no longer rule our own lives but live in a world where discipline is imposed upon as though we were all monks, nuns or soldiers.

Society has taken over and the pseudointellectual chattering classes and the shirkers are its only supporters.

In modern society the individual has no rights – just duties. Traditionally, people have always loved a winner. No more. This is the era for losers. The modern and universal weakness is a lack of ambition – fuelled and lit by the fact that the state will provide the necessities of life and do its best to take away any extra you might make.

Self help is now despised. And yet it is through self help that every man and woman can grow to their full potential. Help from outside is often enfeebling and disempowering. Helping a child or an infirm person to do something that they can perfectly well do themselves is not helping them – it is taking away their freedom, their rights and their power over their own lives. Whatever is done *for* people takes away some of the stimulus and necessity for doing things for themselves. Too much guidance and too much government creates helplessness.

The sneerers also forget that the man who helps himself will invariably also end up by helping others. The man who drags himself up by his bootstraps will create work and wealth for many others.

***

If *you* hit hard times the community won't lend you a helping hand; the government is not going to smile and say: 'That's OK – just pay us when you've got the money' if you admit that you don't have enough cash to pay your income tax. It is sometimes said that a true democracy cannot possibly tolerate capitalism but it is only with a truly capitalist system (where there is freedom of ownership and freedom of choice) that a true democracy is possible.

There is a subtle but important difference between 'opportunities' and 'chances'. In our society there are plenty of chances (hand over your money and you may win the lottery) but the opportunities are becoming rare. A gloomy sense of powerlessness has made most people feel that much of life is pointless. Material comfort simply makes the pointlessness endurable and creates an even greater feeling of cynicism.

Citizens must be encouraged to reinfranchise themselves through campaigning; they must come to understand that freedom of thought and freedom of action create the circumstances for individual success. And, collectively, individual success means that society as a whole creates the wealth which enables it to care for the genuinely needy.

The creation of a formal structure designed to care has taken away freedom. We have created a philosophy of interference and control which is excused by the fact that the state constantly needs to raise more money (in taxes of various kinds) to pay for and manage the distribution of benefits. And we have created a society in which more and more people do not take any responsibility for their own health or wealth but have an attitude of 'Why should I work? Let *them* worry about me.'

The revolution which will help revive the western, 'developed' world will be led (probably in the second or third decade of the twenty first century) by those few individuals who have managed to retain their physical, mental and spiritual freedom; who have realised that the sum of small rights offered by the state do not go anywhere near to balancing the loss of big rights taken away from them by the state, and who are prepared to make an effort and take action whatever the cost may be to themselves – even though what they do may not be of direct benefit to themselves.

There will always be injustices and inequalities in any society. When those injustices and inequalities arise through fate it is bad enough. But when those injustices and inequalities arise deliberately, in an organised society, then even the apathetic, television and lottery addicted masses will sit up, take notice, become suspicious, become angry and eventually become rebellious.

Tomorrow's revolution will need leaders who realise that political and economic freedom go together and are inter-dependant and that true freedom means that individuals can decide whether or not the risks and benefits of a particular occupation or activity are worthwhile.

The leaders of tomorrow's revolution will come exclusively from those who have retained their freedom, liberty and independence.

Tomorrow's leaders will not be able to act unless and until the apathetic masses realise that liberty is not a means to an end, a price worth paying for state protection, but is ultimately, the purpose and the goal of life itself and that they have to rise up and demand back the freedom which has been stolen from them.

The next revolution will come when enough men and women believe that their happiness and well-being will not be secured through the pursuit of whatever values happen to be convenient to existing institutions and a ubiquitous bureaucracy but through individual responsibilities and individual freedoms.

Tomorrow's revolution will come when ordinary citizens realise that we need a revolution because our society does not approve of the idea of revolution.

PART THREE

How To Recover Your Freedom
(And Get What You Want Out Of Life)

A New Paradigm For Living: How to Regain Your Freedom And Survive And Prosper In An Increasingly Bureaucratic And Unfriendly World

'We make walls, floor, roof, doors and windows for a room;
But it is the empty space within that makes the room liveable.
Thus, while the tangible have advantages,
It is the intangible that makes it useful.'

- Tao Te Jing by Lao Tsu

'I have made as much out of myself as could be made of the stuff, and no man
should require more.'

- Jean Paul Richter

CHAPTER ONE
Who Are You? (And What Do You Want?)

'Between him who in battle has conquered thousands upon thousands of men, and him who has conquered himself, it is the latter who is the greater conqueror.'

- Buddha

'Opportunity has hair in front, behind she is bald; if you seize her by the forelock you may hold her, but, if suffered to escape, not Jupiter himself can catch her again.'

- Latin proverb

If you are going to liberate yourself you must first of all find out a number of basic truths about yourself.

You must, for example, know what you want to be free of. What are the great tyrannies in your life? Fear? Boredom? What else?

Where are you now and where do you want to be? What do you want out of life? What steps forward do you want to take? (Remember: there are no limits, other than those which you yourself set. But if you are going to get there you must know where you want to be in a month, a year and a decade. You must set yourself goals which mean something to you.)

Who do you consider to be the most successful: the individual who acquires the most money, honours, fame or power? What do *you* really want out of life: money, love, power, friendship or immortality?

Which do you value more: loyalty or honesty? If you had to choose between betraying a friend or betraying your country which would you choose?

What drives you? The desire for money, power, fame, sex, love or companionship?

What are your prejudices?

You must know what you want − otherwise you'll never get it. The more you know about yourself the greater use you will be able to make of your talents and skills and virtues. If you are going to develop your strength as an individual and carve out your own freedom then you must know yourself. And you must know your weaknesses as well as your strengths. Before you begin to reach your potential, free yourself from the constraints of our society and achieve a real sense of freedom, you must know what you are good at and, just as important, you must know what you are not good at.

You must know who you are. Many people spend their entire lives trying to be someone they are not. This causes great unhappiness. You must know what you want and what you are capable of (probably far more than you normally think you are capable of).

What are your most personal, most private, most precious dreams? Do you want to change the world? Do you simply want fun? Do you want a hedonistic life − full of sex, sunshine and toys or do you have artistic ambitions?

How far have you come in the last five years − financially, physically, mentally, spiritually? How far have you come in the last ten years − financially, physically, mentally, spiritually? How far do you want to travel − financially, physically, mentally and spiritually − in the next five and ten years?

Does your daily work provide you with all the hope and inspiration that you need in life?

Do you spend too much of your life helping other people and taking on their worries and anxieties?

Do you feel that your spirit is sufficiently strong and self contained?

Do you have enough determination to finish the things you start − assuming that you remain convinced that they are worth doing?

Do you learn from the people you respect?

Do you ever find yourself catering to the whims of people who are richer or of a higher social standing than yourself − and if you do, do you feel happy about it?

Do you worry so much about what other people say about you that your worries about what they might or might not say influence the way you act?

How much of your life do you spend trying to get what you really want?

Do any of your friends depress you? Are you conscious that any of the people who are close to you are holding you back through their negativity?

Do you have enough friends?

Do you deal with problems which make you unhappy − or do you allow them to drag on and on?

Do you allow your views and opinions about life and other people to be too easily influenced by strangers?

Do you always believe what people tell you?

Do you help people if they come to you for support and encouragement?

Do you use your body's natural healing skills?

Do you use all your mind's protective powers?

Do you allow your life to be influenced by worry about material possessions?

Do you spend too much time thinking about failure?

Which is most important to you: personal freedom or material success?

Do you learn something about yourself every day?

Does your life have a real purpose? Do you have a plan for your life?

Do you get nagged by people who are close to you? (If so, why do you let them?)

Do you learn something useful every day?

Do you get more or less self confident as you age?

Whom do you envy – and why?

Does your life seem full or empty of hope?

Is your daily life too full of stress and do you suffer from a lot of stress related disorders?

Do you often suffer from boredom?

Do you have to use drugs, tobacco or alcohol to get through the day?

Do you allow other people to make important decisions for you?

***

Only when you have discovered what you really want out of life will you be able to make sure that you acquire what you really want; and that you turn your hopes and dreams into reality.

Only when you know what you want will you be able to focus your attention and energies in the right direction – and stop wasting time, energy, effort and money.

The sad truth is that most people meander through life with no real sense of purpose or direction.

As children they have dreams, hopes and ambitions. Those dreams, hopes and ambitions may survive, and even grow, in their teenage years. But gradually the dreams and the hopes and the ambitions are smothered by society's expectations. Long term hopes are overwhelmed by what are seen as short term needs. Too often things happen by accident. Life progresses in a series of unplanned steps – often resulting in an unplanned, unwanted journey.

Life is there to be grasped and lived but most people live a life of frustration, desperation and mediocrity.

We may not think it but we are, in the end, in control of our lives.

No one does what they don't want to do.

Remember that your own motives aren't always as altruistic as you think them to be.

Don't overestimate your own merits and don't forget that you have faults (you should know your own faults as well as you know your merits).

Never expect other people to take as much interest in you – and your life – as you do.

Try not to worry too much about being persecuted. The more successful you become the more you will be subject to malignant gossip, but most effective people are far too busy with their own lives to spend too much effort persecuting other people. Any serious persecution you face will come from corporations and pressure groups – and will only arise if you become a threat to some status quo – rather than to individuals.

Remember that most of us make our own limitations. We refuse to take chances, we pass up opportunities, we take the safe route and we accept the small 'profits' that are there to be taken out of life instead of taking chances and going for the big 'profits'.

***

It is never too late to recapture those lost dreams, or to develop new ones.

But most people's lives are too full of petty responsibilities for dreams to survive.

Once the hopes and dreams have gone there is no chance at all of them ever being turned into reality.

***

You cannot possibly begin to use your natural talents and skills, or to take full advantage of them, until you know the precise nature of the talents and skills you have got at your disposal. Only when you know your true value, appreciate it and use it to its full extent, will you be able to take out of life what you are truly worth. We all have different assets. But we also all have enormous opportunities.

***

You must be able to promote your good qualities and defend yourself against those who will surely try to take advantage of you in those areas where you are weakest.

You must constantly be prepared to change your perception of yourself and your skills. Try to see yourself in others' eyes. What is your reputation? How do others see you? How do you think your friends would describe you? And how do you think your enemies would describe you? What are the nicest things people say about you? And what are the nastiest things people say about you? What sort of reputation do you have within your chosen sphere of work? How would your former school teachers describe you? If you could see the 'official' files on you what do you think they would say? If your obituary appeared in your local newspaper what would it say?

140

How would you like to be remembered and how do you think you will be remembered? What do like about your publicly perceived identity? What do you dislike? Is there something you could or should change? (It doesn't really matter how you are remembered – you will, after all, be dead then – but how you are remembered does, to a certain extent, reflect upon how you have lived your life.) Is there anything about your reputation which you would like to change? Is there anything you can or should change?

Don't assume that you have nothing extraordinary to offer. Everything about you is extraordinary, powerful and unique. Do not minimise or ignore the value of what you know, who you know and what you have already accomplished. Never, ever sell yourself short. Remember that if you expect yourself to fail then others will also expect you to fail and consequently failure will be almost inevitable. Success breeds success and failure breeds failure.

You must learn not to be frustrated by any absence of specific skills or specific chunks of knowledge. Learned skills and knowledge are important but these are assets which you can find through other people.

**

You must be careful not to let yourself be too easily influenced by other people's opinions. Nearly everyone in the world has a whole raft of opinions. Most of them pretty useless and poorly based. And most people with opinions are eager to share them with anyone who will listen.

Whenever you try to achieve something new or worthwhile you will find that there are many people around who will happily and enthusiastically tell you that your plans are futile, that your project is doomed and that you will fail. Those around you who have never dared break free themselves will be eager to warn you that you will fail because they want you to fail.

Be brave and determined: use your own mind and trust your own opinions, hopes and instincts.

**

You must use your various (and previously uncatalogued) assets to free yourself from the tyranny of slavery. Your assets – in the broadest sense of the word – will determine your best options and the ways in which you can most readily go about recovering your lost freedom. Never take your assets for granted. Don't undervalue them. Make an inventory of them and value them fully.

Be aware that your intangible assets – assets which you may not have been taught to appreciate – may have tremendous value to other people. You already know many things and have many skills which will be of value to other people.

Before you can successfully and thoroughly harvest your own assets you need to identify them. By this I mean anything (not necessarily material) that has value. Your greatest assets are probably not tangible. Material assets can rot, deteriorate or be stolen. They are vulnerable and, as I will show in another section of this book, can be a burden. But intangible assets are of lasting value.

Your assets are the stepping stones you will use to get you where you want to go in life and to help you achieve what you want to achieve. You can't achieve freedom without the proper use of your assets. Your skills are valuable to you because they are valuable to other people. The more other people want – or need – what you have got to offer the more valuable you become.

Most people in this world who are stuck in dull, repetitive, boring, unsatisfying jobs are stuck because they don't use their assets properly. And most people don't use their assets properly because they don't even know what their assets are.

And yet your assets are your raw materials. It is with the aid of your assets that you can build your life into whatever you want – and acquire and retain your freedom. Remember too that your asset base can grow steadily and you can turn your intangible assets (your skills) into tangible assets (lovely homes, fine motor cars and whatever else helps to make your life comfortable).

Once you know exactly what your assets are then you can start looking for ways to take the greatest advantage of them. How can you possibly utilise skills or knowledge unless you are aware of them and think of them as usable, valuable assets?

Begin, simply because it is probably easiest, by making a list of your tangible assets: your belongings. Your home, car and all your physical possessions. You may be surprised to discover that you have more tangible assets than you thought you had. And the more you think about this the more you may come to realise that you do have physical belongings for which you no longer have any real purpose or need. Maybe you could turn those unwanted physical assets into cash. Selling the bits and pieces from your attic, spare room and garage will liberate space as well as cash. Within days you could find yourself considerably richer (in cash terms) than you thought you were. And since this is 'extra' money, an unexpected cash bonus, you may feel better able to take a chance with it: to use it to fund an imaginative and possibly risky venture.

Next, make a list of your talents and abilities. Here is a brief list of possible talents to get you started:

* Meeting and befriending people (are you a good listener? do people like you?).

* Writing (you may not have written anything for money in the past but if people always congratulate you on your letter writing skills maybe you could).

* Public speaking (either to small or large groups of people or both).

* Leadership (are you good at persuading other people to do what you want them to do).

* Management (are you good at persuading other people to do what you

think they ought to do).

* Selling (if you can sell raffle tickets better than anyone else you know you can probably sell almost anything better than most people).

* Organisation, administration and planning (do you always plan the family holiday?).

* Negotiating (are you the best person you know at getting a good price when you go shopping?) .

* Languages (do you pick up foreign languages quickly and comparatively easily?).

* Problem solving (do other people turn to you to help them solve their problems?).

* Decision making (are you able to make a quick decision while others are trying to make up their minds) .

Third, try making a list of the things you know. And don't limit yourself to only those forms of knowledge which you have used professionally in the past. You may have information acquired in the pursuit of a hobby which could well be of value to other people.

You should list:

* Academic qualifications .

* Academic skills.

* Practical qualifications.

* Practical skills (if you enjoy and are good at performing simple household repairs you almost certainly have skills which other people would value highly).

* Knowledge of languages (what foreign languages can you speak – even if you only know enough words to order a cup of coffee that is a start – it's an asset).

* Knowledge about computers and computing.

* Understanding of people and psychology.

* Knowledge about collectibles (do you have knowledge about stamps, classic cars, books, coins or other objects which people collect – and pay money for).

* Knowledge about sports , literature, painting and music.

***

Your next task in understanding yourself is to decide on the priorities in your life. What are the values by which you will live the rest of your life?

(Remember that money is not a value. Money is not even a purpose for living. And the acquisition of wealth is not an adequate ambition. The only reason for acquiring and accumulating money is to use it to buy something. Money is a means to an end. Money can buy you fine possessions. It can buy you comfortable travel. And it can buy you power. Most important of all, however, is the fact that money can buy you freedom.)

Look at this general list and put all the items on it in order of importance (if you think of something which isn't on the list then add it):

* Health   * Love
* Security   * Freedom
* Fame   * Adventure
* Fun   * Success
* Knowledge   * Comfort
* Passion   * Power
* Wealth   * Respect
* Eradicating cruelty to humans   * Eradicating cruelty to animals
* Protecting the environment

When you have written out the list in the order which is most important to you (you can leave off your list any of the items which you do not consider important) you can work your way down the list adding detail and deciding how you can best ensure that you achieve your ambitions.

For example, do you want to be a success at a particular sport, at one of the creative arts or simply in the eyes of the people you know.

You can also decide which, if any of these items you feel passionate enough about to die for. You will notice that some of these passions are selfless – in that they concern other people, animals or the environment.

Do not limit yourself when working on this list. Do not curtail your ambitions or hold back in any way. When you are dreaming you should reach for the stars. If you reach only for the rooftops you are putting unnecessarily stringent limits on your own ambition.

Try to decide with some degree of precision what you want out of life – and in what order. Remember that you have absolutely no chance of getting what you want out of life until you know exactly *what* it is that you want.

***

When you know what you want out of life you should be able to work out what additional assets you need to acquire in order to achieve what you want.

Your ambitions need to be specific. There is little point in simply saying 'I want to be successful'. That is far too vague. You must decide precisely what you want to achieve. And then you must decide precisely how you are going to get there.

And you must then ask yourself what you have to do in order to turn your ambitions, your hopes and your dreams into reality.

And remember never to ask yourself negative questions. If you ask yourself 'Why am I so ugly? Why did God do this to me? Why can I never achieve what I want? Why I am doomed to be poor? Why do I feel so bad about everything?' the chances are that the only answers you will receive will substantiate and strengthen those negative views of yourself. You should ask yourself positive questions such as: 'How can I improve? How can I do this better?'

In order to achieve your dreams you must be positive, (to get respect you must respect yourself and treat yourself with respect) you must be focused, and you must be aware.

You must keep asking yourself: 'What do I want out of life?' And keep questioning yourself so that you can find the real truths. For example, if you want a bigger house or a smarter, newer car then ask yourself: Why?

That single word: 'Why?' will tell you a great deal about yourself. Ask it yourself often. ('Why am I doing this?' 'Why did I say that?' 'Why do I want to buy this?' 'Why did I agree to do that?')

Are you buying a holiday villa in a sunny Mediterranean resort because you will spend a great deal of your life there or because it will impress the neighbours. Would a hotel or rented villa be cheaper, less stressful and more suitable?

Once you understand yourself, and you know what you really want, you will have enormous power over your life. You will find this a liberating and exhilarating feeling. It is such a powerful feeling that you may also find it frightening.

To gain the full power of your spirit you must know your aims, your objectives, your goals, your proposed strategies and tactics and your role in the world.

Once you understand, and know yourself then you can concentrate your mind on where you want to go, what you want to do and what you can do to change the world.

Most people have no idea what they want out of life. They have no big plans. They have long since forgotten any of the dreams they may have had in childhood. They have vague aspirations and they somehow feel that it might be nice to have money, fame and power. They would like to be happy. But they don't know what they *really* want.

And until you know what you *really* want you don't stand a chance of ever getting it. Ask yourself what you want to do – today, tomorrow and for the rest of your life.

Then, when you have decided what you want to do ask yourself what you want to do it for.

And, finally, ask yourself what sacrifices you are prepared to make.

CHAPTER TWO
What Do Other People Really Want?

'Certain things are indispensable to the happiness of most men, but these are simple things: food and shelter, health, love, successful work and the respect of one's own herd.'

- Bertrand Russell

In addition to understanding yourself – and your own fears, ambitions, hopes, wants and needs – you must also know and understand what other people really want out of life. And you must find out what they want from their relationship with you.

Not surprisingly, most people's fears and needs are much the same as yours. Most people want health, wealth, respect, independence and peace.

If you try to present people with what they really want out of life then they will be far more likely to love, respect and honour you. If someone you know suffers because they don't feel loved, then provide them with what they want and your relationship with them will boom. If you provide a lonely person with companionship then you will make them happy. Only when you know what other people really want will you be able to satisfy their needs.

CHAPTER THREE
Three Words That Can Change Your Life

'It is not enough to be busy. The question is: what are you busy about?'
- Henry David Thoreau

Why do you work so hard? Why are you trying to make money? Why do you buy the things you buy? Why do you do what you do? Why does any of it matter? Why do you seek power? Why do you want this or that experience?

Most people ask themselves 'Why?' far too infrequently.

We live in a workaholic culture where most of us take on far too many commitments – many of which have no real value – simply because we feel we should.

For example, many car owners wash their motor vehicles once a week. They devote several hours of a weekend morning to this task. I wonder how many of them ever ask themselves why they are doing this – and whether the price they are paying (in terms of time) is worth the dividend.

I can think of several possible reasons (other than the fact that it is merely a long-established habit).

(a) Because if a car is washed regularly it will fetch a better price when it is sold

(b) Because a clean and shiny car is more likely to impress people

(c) Because it is fun

Now, if a man gets pleasure from washing his car then that is fine. It is rather sad but I wouldn't dream of discouraging him. In fact, I would be happy for him to pop round on Sunday morning and wash my car too if it would give him pleasure.

But, if he chooses either of the other two reasons then I would encourage him to think hard about the way he is spending his time.

Let's concentrate on answer a) to begin with: the hope that by washing his car regularly he will be able to get a better price for it when he comes to sell it.

If he washes the car once a week and spends three hours on the task that is approximately 150 hours a year. In three years (the average time for which a car is likely to be kept) that is 450 hours.

Now, work out much more you think a regularly washed car is likely to fetch when it is sold and subtract the cost of washing and polishing materials. This is figure A.

Then add up the total number of hours spent on cleaning the car in between purchasing it and selling it. This is figure B.

Finally, divide figure A by figure B to obtain the hourly rate you are effectively paying yourself for car cleaning.

You will, I suspect, be horrified to discover just how little it is.

Now, let's turn to answer b).

What is the point of spending hours every week washing a car simply so that people you don't know and will probably never meet will be impressed.

Is this really the best use of your time?

***

It is possible to apply this simple questioning to just about everything you do.

It is even possible to apply it to work itself.

Many men (and a growing number of women) do not seem to realise that they are caught on a treadmill which is taking them absolutely nowhere.

They could completely or partly retire and live very comfortably on what they have already made. But they don't.

If they were working because they enjoyed their work that would be understandable.

But how many men or women can honestly say that they thoroughly enjoy their work?

Many working men and women are pushing themselves for no reason; they are engaged in a race where the grave is the only goal and a headstone the only prize. They sacrifice their personal lives for work from which they obtain little or no satisfaction. The only goal is making money. The money is the prize, the glory, the passion and the purpose.

And the money making ritual continues because people don't ask themselves: 'Why?' and 'So what?'

Ask yourself 'Why?' you do everything you do.

Is it for applause and public approbation? Is it because you have an urgent need to say something? Is it because you want to make money for some specific purpose? Is it because you believe that you know what is right and what is wrong? Is it because you want to right a wrong? Is it because the incompetence and dishonesty of others has inspired you to action?

Not until you know *why* you do something will you be able to do it effectively. Why settle for less life and less control over your time than you could have? (And remember to ask yourself what happened to the dreams you had when you were sixteen years old.)

Remember that you are now enjoying tomorrow's good old days. You should do whatever you can to make each day the best day of your life. When you get to the end of your life will you be able to look back and say: 'I gave it my best shot!'

Make sure you are doing everything you can with your life. Ask yourself why you are doing something and you may find yourself surprised by the answer. Ask yourself 'Why?' and 'So what?' whenever you plan to do something.

The answers you get may change your life.

CHAPTER FOUR
Know What You Are Afraid Of – And Why
– And Then Banish Your Fears

'Do not fear death so much, but rather the inadequate life.'

- Bertolt Brecht

A little fear is a good thing. Fear helps us stay alive.

I remember a skiing holiday I took a few years ago. I had only been skiing once before and was with a group of beginners but within minutes of arriving on the slopes for the first time I found myself standing at the top of an extremely steep and nasty looking slope.

Everyone in my group of novice skiers expressed alarm and fear. Our very young ski instructor laughed at us and told us that he knew no fear and that we should also have no fear. I (and the other members of my group) quickly abandoned him. I have a rule never to do anything potentially hazardous in the company of someone who does not know fear.

***

But not all fear is good, useful or welcome.

Fear is one of the most potent, all-pervasive and destructive forces in our society. Fear will stop you thinking and may interfere with the way you behave. Animals, who can smell fear, know that it is a sign of weakness.

Fear, worry and anxiety lead to fatigue and exhaustion and to mental, physical and spiritual illness. (The real paradox here is that a fear of illness can create illness.)

It is because they fear what others will or might say that so many people make themselves ill with work in order to buy new and fashionable motor cars, clothes and gadgets they do not really need. Fear, together with indecision and doubt, is a major enemy of success.

150

Many people say, boldly and almost defiantly, that they fear nothing. They are either lying or deluding themselves. Everyone fears something. The variety of fears human beings have vary almost indefinitely. We fear anything which controls or handicaps us physically, spiritually or mentally.

Prison is not a happy place and yet most people shut themselves into their own personal prisons through fear, envy, self pity and an over developed sense of sin.

***

Conquering your fears is a vital step on the road to liberating your spirit and reaching personal freedom. But before you can conquer your fears you must first know exactly what those fears are. You must examine yourself and analyse your fears. Fears which are not confronted will grow and grow and eventually destroy you.

***

Animals' fears are largely pure and simple. Their needs are much simpler than ours (but don't make the mistake of assuming that they are purely physical – they aren't).

Animals need food, shelter and good health and kindness and love. They also need companionship and stability and they respond to love in a positive way.

Their fears are largely in the here and the now rather than in the future – created by the mind (as are most of ours).

We claim to be superior to the rest of the animal kingdom but we cannot find happiness quite as easily as other animals. We are much better at finding things to worry about and far, far superior at finding ways to be miserable.

***

When we think of 'fears' we tend to think of superficial fears, most widely known as 'phobias', (for example, a fear of dentists, a fear of spiders or a fear of flying or a fear of enclosed spaces).

These are very specific fears and there are fairly simple and straightforward ways in which they can be confronted and overcome. But these are not the fears which paralyse most people. And make no mistake about it: fears do paralyse. Most modern human fears are created by the culture in which we live. Naturally, we are susceptible to the basic, commonplace fears which affect other members of the animal kingdom. We fear hunger and pain, for example. But we also fear sickness, poverty, imprisonment, lack of freedom, loneliness and unemployment. We fear cancer, financial ruin, secret exposure and jealousy. We fear losing love and we fear failure.

We even fear getting old.

Many who fear old age spend much of their time and money on trying to look younger than they are. Others simply apologise for their age and use it as an excuse for everything that others criticise. Those who are most conscious of the effects of age, and most worried about ageing, are, inevitably, the ones who are most likely to suffer the adverse effects of old age. The fear of old age inevitably also includes the fears of poverty, death, ill health and pain and a loss of financial and physical freedom and independence.

And yet the fear of old age can to a large extent be eliminated by accepting it as a blessing, by realising that you have understanding and wisdom that you didn't have when you were young, and by giving thanks that at least you didn't die young.

***

We fear criticism, rejection and ridicule too. This type of fear is the basis of all kinds of modern fashions. When we buy our clothes, motor cars, jewellery and household furnishings we are conscious of the fact that if we choose the wrong items we may arouse the contempt of those around us. We are afraid that they will laugh at us if we buy the wrong things.

Millions of people have their hair cut to satisfy people they do not know and will never know.

A fear of criticism robs a man of imagination, self reliance and initiative. A fear of criticism is one of the main reasons why most people never move from their rut. Discouragement from those around ('Why should anyone care what you have to say?) is a common cause of a failure even to try.

In our modern world everyone (particularly parents and relatives) seems to have plenty of criticism to hand out – and so everyone receives plenty of it.

Most criticism (and certainly the most damaging criticism) comes from close friends, relatives and people who claim to want to help. Anyone who sticks their head up above the parapet can expect to receive a hail of criticism and so it is not surprising that most people keep their heads well below the parapet.

My office has a simple rule when dealing with my mail: letters which offer nothing but blind, crude, unhelpful criticism are thrown away, unacknowledged, before I even see them. Before I instigated this rule I once opened a newspaper cutting in which a writer began a lengthy attack on me with the words: 'I have not, of course, read any of this sorry creature's scribblings'.

Too much criticism creates resentment as well as a lack of self respect and self worth. The symptoms of a fear of criticism include nervousness, self consciousness, a weak personality, an inferiority complex, a lack of initiative and a lack of ambition ('If I try and I fail I will be criticised therefore I can avoid criticism by not trying'). Many people are so frightened of failure, of ridicule and of looking foolish that they never dare take any risks. A fear of what others will think is stifling.

***

Some people have a fear of death. They think about death so much that they become depressed. They worry that there may be no after life (or that there will be one and they will for some reason miss it).

They forget that God is merciful and that eternal pain will only afflict the evil and those who have remained silent in the face of evil.

And they forget that if there is no afterlife then death is merely sleep and, therefore, nothing to be feared.

***

One of the commonest of all fears is that of poverty.

Fear of poverty is a powerful and destructive state of mind which can destroy reason, self reliance, imagination, enthusiasm, ambition and determination.

We fear poverty because we know that few things bring as much suffering and humiliation. We fear poverty because we know that there are many cruel and rapacious individuals (and corporations) in the world who will take our money away from us without compunction − and others who will then take advantage of us and persecute us because of our poverty.

We worry about poverty because there are so many ways to become poor. You can become poor through your own fault or through no fault at all of your own. You can become poor through the dishonesty of others and through the failure of the law to provide protection.

Those for whom a fear of poverty is a significant fear tend to worry constantly about money and money related matters, are for ever expecting to be poorer than they are and frequently delay new ventures in case they fail − and lose all their money. People who are frightened of poverty are usually extremely cautious about spending money (although paradoxically some people who are poor and frightened about becoming even poorer spend their money as if they had an inexhaustible supply).

A fear of poverty often makes decision making difficult and deadens ambition; it creates pessimism and breeds doubts and excuses. Many people who worry about becoming poor spend a lot of their time planning what to do if a venture fails. They tend to procrastinate and be over cautious. And, not surprisingly, they are often also cautious about committing themselves to anything that might prove hazardous.

Our fear of poverty is enhanced by the fact that we are taught by our society that money is the key to all happiness.

(Although it is undoubtedly true that money can buy some of the freedoms which lead to happiness most people do not use money properly and certainly do not use it to buy freedom. On the contrary, most people do exactly the opposite – they give up their freedom to buy money.)

Most people do very little to confront their fear of poverty. They allow themselves to remain enslaved to an employer who, because he is the one who signs the cheques, retains control over their lives.

And even the rich – who, on the face of it, may not seem to have any need to be afraid of poverty – often fail to come to face with this very fundamental and basic fear.

The least secure individuals in our society are often those who have the biggest fiefdoms. They may have enormous amounts of money but their original and unfaced fears of poverty are enhanced because they now have the added fear of losing all that they have acquired. Those who have something to lose are far more susceptible to fear than those who have nothing to lose. The rich fear the loss of their money, the material goods and comfort it has bought, the freedom, the respect, the authority and the responsibility.

The man who already has absolutely nothing is to a very large extent unafraid of poverty. You can only be afraid of something if you think it might happen to you. And so the poor man will almost always be less afraid of poverty than the rich man. The man who has nothing has nothing to lose and so is not susceptible to fear. The man who is rich is frightened of losing his money.

This is true of all fears.

People who are comfortable are frightened of discomfort. People who are already uncomfortable have nothing to fear. People who are sick or dying do not fear sickness or death. People who are healthy are afraid of losing their health and becoming ill. The more you have, the greater your potential for fear. No human being can ever be truly secure from fear until he or she is dead. Only when you are dead are you totally secure from imprisonment, poverty, ill health or death itself.

***

When I was a medical student in Birmingham, England I ran a free discotheque in the city centre. Many of the kids who patronised the discotheque were young, homeless, jobless, penniless and without hope. They had no future. Quite often there were fights in the discotheque as other city gangs would invade the club looking for trouble – anxious to destroy as much as they could.

On the evening of the first fight I watched helpless and amazed as the teenagers around me fought with a ferocity I had never seen before. They carried knives and were not afraid to use them. Several were badly wounded. Others had to go into hiding to avoid the police.

Afterwards I asked a group of the battered survivors why they had fought so hard to protect something that did not seem to me to be worth dying for.

'We haven't got anything to lose,' said one. 'Except this.' They weren't frightened of the police because imprisonment was no great threat to them. (They were squatting in a derelict building in awful conditions.) They weren't afraid of being injured because that would just mean hospital – clean sheets and regular food. And they weren't even afraid of dying because their lives were so dull, dismal and hopeless that they did not feel that they had much to lose.

They had virtually nothing to fear because they had virtually nothing to lose. The only thing they had was the discotheque. And so they fought to protect it.

***

A fear of illness is probably as common as the fear of poverty. Those who are afraid of ill health often become obsessed with health – both their own and health in general. They constantly search for information about health care and about staying healthy. They constantly take pills which aren't needed to treat a specific illness or specific symptoms (for example, vitamin or mineral supplements) and they take greater than ordinary care to protect themselves from any possible source of illness (such as infection). They are frequently unable to work because of ill defined illnesses and they are constantly searching for symptoms and signs of illness. Those who fear illness sometimes seem to enjoy ill health. Instead of trying to forget their symptoms and doing what they can to stay healthy those who suffer most from this fear spend much of their time making themselves sicker by worrying about their symptoms.

***

Much fear is fundamentally connected to a destructive and deeply damaging lack of self worth and self respect. Most people in our society live in constant fear. Their fears are legion. And they are frightened because they have little or no self confidence.

Because we have so little confidence in our knowledge, our wisdom, our judgement and ourselves in general we constantly look to others for approval. We want – and need – others to confirm that what we are doing is good because we do not have faith in ourselves.

Why, for example, are so many people frightened of public speaking? What horrors can possibly befall the public speaker?

The simple and singular truth is that the individual who is terrified of public speaking is frightened of nothing more substantial than looking a fool. He or she is frightened not of death or pain or bankruptcy or loss of freedom but of being considered inadequate or incompetent by the audience.

Most people are so lacking in self confidence and self respect that they need others to confirm that what they are doing is acceptable. They need the approval of strangers because they do not approve of themselves. They constantly fear disapproval and rejection.

And yet public opinion is very fickle and quite meaningless. An individual who would be considered normal in one situation may be an outcast in another situation and a hero in a third situation. The object of public adoration today is quite likely to be the object of public ridicule tomorrow. The individual who, through lack of self confidence, puts himself in the hands of public opinion, is taking on a fickle mistress indeed.

(Incidentally, false modesty is an entirely fake and spurious emotion which is inspired by a constant need for support, praise or even adoration. False modesty is designed to attract praise. As in: 'I'm no good at this.' The expected response is then: 'Oh, yes, you are!'. To which the falsely modest individual will quickly reply: 'Oh, do you really think so?')

It is this deep seated lack of self confidence and desperate need for approval and support which explains why so many men are cowed by their wives (and, at the same time, why so many women stick with their husbands even when they are physically abused by them).

We are constantly frightened of being rejected, not loved or laughed at. It is these fears which stop most people daring to do anything much with their lives. It is these fears which result in our accepting mediocrity, poverty and constant, chronic and unrelieved disappointment in our lives.

The bottom line is: what does it really matter what other people think?

Everyone has the right to their own opinions and views. But you have exactly the same right. If you can persuade people to agree with you then that is fine and good. But if you fail then what have you lost? The world is much the same as it was. You have lost nothing. Is your dignity really so vulnerable that it can be damaged by the views of complete strangers?

The only person you really have to believe in, and the only person you really have to convince about your worth, is you. Have faith in yourself and many of your most fundamental and most destructive fears will melt like snow in a sudden heatwave.

***

Facing your fears is a crucial and vital part of controlling them. The best way to de-demonise a fear is to think about it a great deal. Eventually, you will take the edge off the fear by thinking about the possibilities and the ramifications. When a fear becomes boring and tedious then you have won.

This all sounds easy but I do recognise that facing and overcoming a fear can take a tremendous amount of courage. Bravery is a synonym for having absolutely no imagination, and the one quality people with fears are short of is not imagination. Physical courage is frequently regarded as the only type of courage worth praising but when physical courage is not a result of a lack of imagination it is frequently a result of stupidity. On the other hand it takes great courage to ignore public opinion, and to stand by yourself. The public does not much approve of any individual who shows indifference to its own collective opinion and conquering fear can take great tremendous courage.

***

In the end, you have to acknowledge that however much you worry there are many things in life which cannot be solved or avoided by worry or by free floating fear.

Most of the bad things that will happen to you will be unexpected. The things you worry about most will probably not happen – in part, admittedly, because your worrying and your planning will mean that you will lessen the odds against you.

If you are so frightened of the dangers of flying that you never fly then you are extremely unlikely to die in an aeroplane crash. But your chances of being killed in some other form of transport crash are inevitably and proportionately higher.

You should, of course, plan to deal with potential problems wherever and whenever you can but you should always remember that Aesculapius, the Greek god of medicine, was killed when a tortoise being carried by an eagle fell and landed on his head. What are the odds of that happening? How can you possibly plan for that sort of eventuality?

***

Most people never do anything with their lives because they spend every day worrying and thinking and scheming about what has already happened (and about which they can do nothing) and what might happen (about which they can also do nothing).

They spend days and weeks and months and years rewriting history in their minds – or (and just as futile) trying to write a script for the future or to predict what will happen to them in one, five or ten years time. Far too much energy and effort is wasted worrying about what might go wrong and what other people will think if something does go wrong, and what the authorities might or might not do.

When you are worried about something ask yourself how much it really matters.

Does it really matter very much if your car has a scratch down the side or if you are seen in clothes which are not at the height of fashion? Does it really matter very much if you have to go out with a hole in your stocking? Is the world going to stop revolving if you make a bad speech? Will your business collapse if you go away for a few days?

In order to defeat your secret inner fears you must analyse them, find out what is behind them, bring them out into the open, confront them, look at them from every possible angle, examine them in detail, make them look silly and humiliate them.

You must always look at the bottom line to find out how much harm these hidden, secret fears can really do to you. What is the worst that can happen to you if such and such a fear comes to fruition? Facing and confronting the bottom line can be a powerful way to disembowel a fear, an anxiety or a worry.

What is the worst that can happen? Would the worst really be so bad?

Finally, find yourself a passion and a purpose that transcends ordinary life and you will find it much easier to forget the day to day problems which are otherwise likely to cause you so much distress.

You will only achieve true freedom of your spirit when your life is full and you aren't frightened of anything or anyone.

CHAPTER FIVE
The Most Valuable Commodity In The World Is Not Money
(Look after the minutes and the days will look after themselves)

'In the dissipation of worldly treasure the frugality of the future may balance the extravagance of the past; but who can say: 'I will take minutes from tomorrow to compensate for those I have lost today.''

- Jackson of Exeter

'Time is the only little fragment of Eternity that belongs to man; and, like life, it can never be recalled.'

- Samuel Smiles

'Every moment lost gives an opportunity for misfortune.'

- Napoleon Bonaparte

'Lost wealth may be replaced by industry, lost knowledge by study, lost health by temperance or medicine, but lost time is gone forever.'

- Samuel Smiles

I had a telephone call from my friend G today. He is a Zulu. He was on his way to Australia and called me from Bangkok. He told me that his plane had been delayed for nine hours.

'Oh, how awful!' I said, sympathetically. I always hate delays.

'What do you mean?' asked G. He sounded puzzled.

'The delay,' I explained. 'It must be awfully frustrating for you.'

'Not particularly,' replied G, sounding as ever calm, relaxed and unflustered. 'The delay is all part of the travelling. It is part of the experience. It means I have more time at the airport. I can read and talk and ring you.'

'But it's annoying to be so late,' I said.

'A few decades ago this journey would have taken me weeks,' replied G. 'What is nine hours?'

'Aren't you worried that you will be late for your meeting?' I asked him.

'The meeting cannot take place until I get there,' said G. 'How can I be late for it?'

***

Most people abhor waste. They squeeze the last few bits of toothpaste from the toothpaste tube, they use up scraps of soap and they scribble down thoughts and notes on the backs of old envelopes.

And yet most of us regularly waste something which is much more valuable than money: time.

Einstein may have proved that time is an illusion, malleable and fragile. But on a day to day basis, time is important.

We waste it in a thousand different ways. We waste it gossiping. We waste it performing pointless and repetitive chores, many of which could be ignored completely. How many people in your life do you waste time with? How many of these relationships add value to your life? What do you offer to them that makes their lives better and what do they offer to you that makes your life better?

We waste time trying to save money.

How many people do you know who regularly spend hours (or even days) trying to save money by making a gadget for use in the house or garden – a gadget which they could easily buy for next to nothing in a local store. They use scraps of waste which they find lying around and they end up with something which doesn't work very well and looks terrible. If they had spent the time on doing something genuinely useful they could have added much more value to their lives.

***

Wandering around in Paris recently I stopped in front of a complex window display involving mannequins, streamers and a hundred or so brightly coloured balloons. I haven't the faintest idea what the shop was selling. But the window display was terribly impressive. It must have taken days to design and put together.

A smartly dressed woman in her thirties was on her knees carefully dusting the balloons; meticulously wiping each tautly stretched rubber sphere with a damp cloth. The balloons weren't overtly 'dirty'. I'd walked past the shop a day or two earlier and the display hadn't been there then. But someone in authority had obviously been alarmed by the possibility that one or two of the balloons might have been defiled by a few specks of dust.

I felt deeply sorry for that woman in the shop window. It was, I felt, one of the most futile things I had ever seen anyone doing.

I found myself imagining the conversation she might have with her husband when she got home that evening.

'What have you done today, love?' I imagined I heard her husband ask. (Although, naturally, being in France, he would have probably asked the question in French.) 'How did your day go?'

'I am exhausted,' I heard her reply wearily, in a husky, sexy, French tobacco stained voice. 'I have been dusting balloons all day.'

How terribly sad. What an entirely pointless activity.

It may sound rather comical but, the truth is that we all do some balloon dusting. We waste valuable energy, hard earned money and irreplaceable time on activities which do nothing whatsoever to improve our lives or anyone else's life.

Take a good hard look at the way you've spent your time, money and energy during the last week.

Which activities are you proud of?

And which were simply a waste of time?

How much of your life do you spend 'dusting balloons'?

***

Time is worth much more than money so don't waste it – your own or anyone else's.

For your own sake fill your life with passion and determination. – and leave the balloons undusted.

It is extraordinary to see just what you can do with those ignored and forgotten moments. (To paraphrase a well known saying I cannot resist the temptation to point out that in order to look after the hours it is only necessary to look after the minutes.)

Many men have learnt a language while travelling to work and numerous books have been written in the period while waiting for dinner to be served. One well known authoress wrote her first book while working as a governess. She wrote only in the time she spent waiting for her charge to turn up for lessons. Stephenson (of rocket fame) taught himself mathematics while working as an engineman during nightshifts. In his meal breaks he would work out sums. He used a piece of chalk for a pen and the side of a colliery wagon for a blackboard. Dr Darwin wrote down the thoughts which immortalised him while travelling from house to house in the country and Dr Mason Good translated Lucretius while riding in his carriage and visiting his patients around the streets of London.

I don't know whether it is still there but there used to be a message on the clock dial at a college in Oxford, England which read: 'The hours perish and are laid to our charge'.

Just think for a moment what you could do if you had an extra hour every day of your life.

The chances are that you could easily find another hour a day – simply by cutting out waste. Do a little time and motion study on your life and see just where the minutes and the hours get frittered away.

And, just as important, take a cool, hard look at the way you waste your time doing things that really don't matter very much at all.

The time spent (or rather wasted) on daily chores and rituals can quickly add up.

Assuming that you start at 20 and live to be 75 you will:

* Waste a total of 17 weeks if you spend 1 hour a week cleaning the car. (Why not let it stay dirty?)

* Waste a total of 40 days and nights if you spend 20 minutes a week ironing socks. (Why bother to iron socks?)

* Waste a total of well over 3 years if you spend 10 hours a week sitting in traffic jams. (Is your job really worth sacrificing so much of your life? Can't you find work nearer to home?)

* Waste a total of 836 days and nights of your life if you spend one hour a day Hoovering and dusting. (Hoover and dust for one hour a week instead of one hour a day and you will, effectively gain 716 days – that's equivalent to living an extra two years.)

* Waste a total of 3,345 days and nights of your life if you spend four hours a day watching TV. (Cut your TV watching in half and you'll have an extra 239 weeks in which to do other things. That's like living for more than another four years. Although 'self improvement' is today widely despised by the pseudointellectuals, you could learn a foreign language, write a book and become skilled at a favourite sport in that time.)

CHAPTER SIX
It Isn't *What* You Know (Or *Who* You Know) But Knowing *How* To Use What You Know (Or Who You Know)

'Every person has two educations, one which he receives from others, and one, more important, which he gives to himself.'

− Gibbon

Many graduate students mistakenly assume that just because they have completed a university or college course they are entitled to a good job, a secure position and a sound entrepreneurial or corporate future. They assume that because they have a certain amount of knowledge they are entitled to succeed.

This is not how life works.

Knowing things just isn't enough. What *is* important is knowing what to do with what you have learned. With the possible exception of 'memory men' in night clubs and circuses no one gets paid just for knowing things or for having a good memory.

CHAPTER SEVEN
Why You Should Ignore (At Least Some Of) The Rules

'Any fool can make a rule – and every fool will mind it.'
                                        - Henry David Thoreau

In any society there will always be people who like creating their own mini laws – called rules. And as our society becomes increasingly complex (in many different ways) so there are more and more excuses for rules.

Some rules are self imposed. People create their own rules out of routine and tradition. When you ask people why they are doing something a particular way, you will often hear the answers: 'That's the way I was taught' or 'Because that's the way we do it.' Those are little more than excuses for avoiding thought. Most people are shackled and constrained by many invisible, non existent, self imposed beliefs and rules which they have created for themselves, or which they have allowed others to create for them.

Most rules come from bureaucrats. Bureaucrats love rules. In particular they love rules which enable them to say 'no'. Most local and central government departments now follow the Russian way of doing things: 'If we don't say you can do it then you can't do it.'

You should not be afraid of ignoring, breaking or sidestepping the bureaucrat's rules (as long as you can do so without breaking the law, of course). If you can think of a new, different and possibly better way to do something then don't be afraid to try it. You may astound yourself and the rest of the world. Your own conscience should be the only rule maker you always obey. The only person you really have to be responsible to is yourself.

***

You might find it a revealing, enlightening and ultimately liberating exercise to make a list of all the rules which run your life. Include the rules which

164

govern your personal life as well as those which run your business life.

When you have compiled your list write the question 'Why?' by each rule. And try to decide where all those rules originated. Many of the rules which still run your personal life will have doubtless originated with your parents and schoolteachers. Some will have originated with a previous employer. Some you will have absorbed, as though by osmosis, from friends. And many you will have acquired from 'society'.

Every time you think of or come across another rule ask yourself whether the rule is essential or avoidable. Ask yourself whether the rule adds quality to your life. And ask yourself whether or not there are alternatives.

Many rules are designed to stop us doing things. Others simply convince us that we cannot do things, that we aren't good enough and that we are doomed to be poor and to fail if we do not satisfy certain preconceived conditions. What nonsense rules are.

Remember that there is no such thing as impossible. The impossible is merely the limit of your imagination. Modern scientists, invariably working for corporations and government sponsored research organisations, say that something is impossible when what they really mean is that they don't understand it and cannot explain it according to the existing rules – and that they are, therefore, more than a little frightened by it.

Don't allow yourself to be constrained by the rules – or by other peoples views of what is or is not possible. You do not have to do things the way others do them. You can play the game of life by any rules you like. If you are going to get anywhere in life then ignoring at least some of the rules is almost a prerequisite.

CHAPTER EIGHT
Put Your Heart And Soul Into Everything You Do
(But Only Do The Things Which Are Worth Doing)

'If I were confined to a corner of a garret all my days, like a spider, the world would be just as large to me while I had my thoughts about me.'
- Henry David Thoreau

'I put my sole trust in my own strength of body and soul.'
- old Norse saying

'However men choose to regard me, they cannot change my essential being, and for all their power and all their secret plots I shall continue, whatever they do, to be what I am in spite of them.'
- Jean-Jacques Rousseau

'My rule is, deliberately to consider, before I commence, whether the thing be practicable. If it be not practicable, I do not attempt it. If it be practicable, I can accomplish it if I give sufficient pains to it; and having begun, I never stop till the thing is done. To this rule I owe all my success.'
- John Hunter

People who know little about books, but who think that they might one day like to write one themselves, often ask me how long a book should be. This is an impossible question because the length of a manuscript is of absolutely no significance when trying to decide whether or not the manuscript is a book. I have seen collections of pages which were several hundred pages long but which were not books. You could pile up loose pages of neat typing until the whole mountain of paper reached a mile into the sky and still not have a book.

166

I have been a professional writer for many years and a long time ago I realised that a pile of pages (or a file in a computer memory) do not become a book simply when they reach a certain length. In order to become a book, a typescript, a manuscript or a chunk of computer memory must have a heart.

And that heart can only come from the writer.

Every book I write (whether it is fiction or non fiction) has something of myself in it. My blood is there on the pages. The pages only become a book because I put something of myself into what I am writing. Pick up a book, open the pages and start reading, and you should be able to feel a beating heart.

I believe that this is true of everything we do. A good builder, for example, will put his heart and his soul into every stone he lays.

If something is genuinely worth doing then put your heart and soul into it. Until you respect your own value and your own potential contribution to other peoples lives you will achieve nothing.

Assess yourself annually. Ask yourself if you have given the best service to those who pay your wages (either directly or indirectly). If you have failed, then ask yourself what else you could or should have done. Have you wasted energy or money? If you have how can you re-budget and change your habits. If *you* had bought *your* services would *you* be happy?

The corollary here is that if you do not think that a task merits your heart and soul then there is a very good chance that the task doesn't merit any attention at all.

When I was a child I remember school teachers always telling me to remember that: 'If a thing is worth doing it is worth doing well.'

What no one ever told me to ask myself was: 'Is it worth doing at all? Or am I frittering away my life on something that really doesn't matter a damn?'

CHAPTER NINE
Aim To Be Loved Or Hated – But Never Ignored

'One should as a rule respect public opinion in so far as is necessary to avoid starvation and to keep out of prison, but anything that goes beyond this is voluntary submission to an unnecessary tyranny, and is likely to interfere with happiness in all kinds of ways.'

- Bertrand Russell

Whatever you do you should consider it a success only if it arouses some emotion in other people.

A newspaper column is only successful if everyone who reads it feels something. It doesn't really matter whether or not all the readers agree with what they've read. (Although from the writer's point of view that may be a rather pleasing outcome, of course.) I would be happy to have "He made people think" as my epitaph.

But if a reader can put down a newspaper or magazine after reading a column and *not* feel aroused, delighted, amused, enraged or in some other way moved then in my view the column has been a failure.

What is true of a newspaper column is surely also true of everything else any of us do.

If you're making shirts, cars or apple pies you should aim to produce a reaction. The customer who buys your shirt, car or apple pie should be moved in some way. If they are moved then you will be successful because they will buy again and they will tell their friends to buy from you.

The downside to all this is, of course, that if what you do pleases some people it will annoy and upset others. You cannot possibly do anything which will please everyone. Compare a list of the ten most popular television personalities, singers, film stars, sports stars or whatever with lists of the ten most unpopular television personalities, singers, film stars, sports stars or whatever and you will see that there are many names on both lists.

Many people worry intensely if they feel that there is a chance that anything they do could arouse criticism. For example, fear of ridicule or disdain is one of the main reasons why many people are apprehensive about doing anything which could attract attention. It is a fear of criticism which stops many people attempting to explore their own artistic skills.

This is a fear which needs to be put into perspective.

Approximately half of the so called civilised world dislikes the works of Picasso and Beethoven. "One half of the world cannot understand the pleasures of the other," wrote Jane Austen.

So, why should you bother to be offended if some people don't like what you do?

CHAPTER TEN
You Have To Have A Purpose For Living

'Have we not all eternity to rest in.'

- Arnauld

'The longer I live the more I am certain that the great difference between men, between the feeble and the powerful, the great and the insignificant, is energy – invincible determination – a purpose once fixed, and then death or victory. That quality will do anything that can be done in this world; and no talents, no circumstances, no opportunities will make a two legged creature a Man without it.'

- Fowell Buxton

'Purpose is the touchstone of any accomplishment, large or small. A strong man can be defeated by a child who has a purpose.'

- Napoleon Hill

'The truest wisdom is a resolute determination.'

- Napoleon Bonaparte

'What a different story men would have to tell if only they would adopt a definite purpose, and stand by that purpose until it had time to become an all-consuming obsession.'

- Napoleon Hill

Providing your family with a constant supply of clean underwear is not a purpose for living. Making sure that your children's shirts are as white as (or whiter than) your neighbour's children's shirts is no reason for living.

The woman who dedicates her life to caring for her children may become trivialised and bitter. There is a risk that she will eventually lose their respect and their love.

Ironically, if she had retained her independence and her sense of fun she would have probably retained their respect and their love.

No one said that life was fair.

Having a lawn which is better cared for than anyone else's in your neighbourhood is not a purpose for living.

God (or evolution) did not go to all the trouble of making you simply so that you could spend your days ordering fresh supplies of paper clips, or making sure that your car is cleaner and shinier than anyone else's.

People who have no purpose quickly become bored.

The rich who choose not to work often become desperately unhappy. Some simply drink too much. Others try to convince themselves (and others) that their dilettante good and charitable works are giving their lives meaning.

Lottery winners who are unable to adjust their minds to the new possibilities their wealth offers them often end up going back to their humdrum pre-wealth jobs in order to escape the boredom they feel.

Passion and purpose are vital. Without them life is meaningless. Moderation is not a virtue. Remember that it matters not how you live and die, but *why* you live and die.

Most people go through their lives without ever finding a purpose or without ever defining a plan. They get what they settle for. They never know what they want to do − or why. Their lives are governed by a series of accidents. They choose courses at school simply because their friends are doing those courses − or because they like the teachers. They choose jobs because they are convenient. They go through their lives with no sense of direction, no realistic hopes or expectations and no sense of purpose. It is hardly surprising that they constantly feel disappointed and frustrated.

Find what you want to do − and then do it the way you want to do it. Find, know and then be constant to your purpose in life. Set your own goals and define your aims and objectives. Decide what you want out of life and then make sure that you're going in the right direction.

Look around and you will see the passionless many, chilled of hope and overflowing with responsibilities.

You can do better with your life.

*** *

You must decide what you want out of life because without purpose there can be no passion or drive. And remember that only when you have found a cause (or several causes) worth dying for will you really know the joy of living.

CHAPTER ELEVEN
Would You Like To Be Happier?

'Any pleasure that does no harm to other people is to be valued.'
- Bertrand Russell

'To be without some of the things you want is an indispensable part of happiness.'
- Bertrand Russell

'I think I could turn and live with animals, they are so placid and self contained,
I stand and look at them long and long.
They do not sweat and whine about their condition,
They do not lie awake in the dark and weep for their sins,
They do not make me sick discussing their duty to god,
Not one is dissatisfied, not one is demented with the mania of owning things,
Not one kneels to another, nor to his kind that lived thousands of years ago,
Not one is respectable or unhappy over the whole earth.'
- Walt Whitman

Few of us are blessed with Mark Tapley's attitude to life. Tapley, a character in Charles Dickens' book *Martin Chuzzlewit*, believed that it was his purpose in life to find happiness in the bleakest and most depressing circumstances. When faced with the prospect of marrying a good looking, plump widow who ran a public house and cooked sumptuous meals he ran away, claiming that there was no virtue to be found in reaching happiness under such circumstances.

In reality few of us would have the strength of mind to turn our backs on happiness if it was offered to us.

Most of us know that we have the potential for great unhappiness. Sadness besieges us daily and unhappiness, not happiness, is the natural human state for most of us.

There are two main reasons for this.

The first is that as human beings we are cursed with the ability to worry about things over which we have no power. We worry about the past (which has been and gone) and we worry about what other people may or may not do in the future (which, by and large, we cannot influence).

The second is that we do not achieve happiness by right or by luck. The abilities to achieve and enjoy happiness (not necessarily the same thing) are, like the ability to speak a foreign language, dance the Tango or play a good game of tennis, achievements; skills, which have to be fought for.

Happiness means the overcoming of endless, daily obstacles which never disappear.

The heroes of Valhalla spent every day hunting a miraculous wild boar which they killed in the evenings but which came to life again for the next day so that they had to hunt it down once more. Their daily work never ended because their work began again with each new day. (As someone who despises hunters and hunting I do not particularly like the analogy but it's an extremely apt one.)

The gardener faces the constant battle posed by weeds growing among his vegetables and flowers. The salesmen has to go out every day and find fresh orders or else the business which supports him will die. The newspaper editor has to start work every day faced with several tons of blank newsprint. No one will be interested in buying yesterday's newspapers. The chef begins each day with nothing but fresh ingredients and his recipe book. The postman starts each morning with a new sack full of mail to deliver.

Under these circumstances happiness can only truly come from within, from an attitude of mind, and, most important perhaps, from a sense of satisfaction derived from the work which is being done. The individual who enjoys his daily work, who looks forward to each day's fresh labours, will find happiness far more easily than the individual for whom daily work is a constantly repeated drudgery. The individual for whom work is the same thing as pleasure has a direct route to happiness.

Most people never achieve any sense of lasting happiness because they spend their lives doing things which they either dislike or hate doing.

Ask yourself what three things you most enjoy doing in your life. Then ask yourself whether you spend as much time as you would like doing those things. If the answer is 'No' ask yourself 'Why?'.

Make a list of the ways in which you spend an average week. Then look down the list and put a tick by each of the things you do which you enjoy. How much of your life do you spend doing dull and boring things with or for dull and boring people, and how much of your life do you spend doing things you enjoy with people whose company you enjoy?

***

People who are happy usually:

* Either enjoy good health or have come to terms with whatever illnesses they may have.

* Have a good deal of personal freedom – to think and act however they like (with the proviso, of course, that their own sense of personal freedom does not have an adverse effect on the lives or well-being of any other living creature).

* Have work which they enjoy and in which they can take pride and pleasure.

* Have a sense of belonging in some community (it does not need to be a geographically based community – it can be a community held together by a common belief or a communal cause and passion).

* Have a considerable degree of control over their own lives.

* Spend as little time as possible with over-critical, negative people who make them feel downhearted or miserable.

* Have a positive view about themselves – they have identified, faced and conquered their personal fears (or have at least begun that process) and have achieved (or are achieving) a sense of personal happiness. (In order to achieve outside yourself you must first achieve inside yourself).

* Try to maintain a sense of humour, a sense of the ridiculous and an upbeat, positive attitude about as many things as possible.

* Have the ability to walk away from, and forget, minor inconveniences and trivial worries.

* Share their lives with someone they care for and who cares for them (married people are usually happier than single, divorced or separated individuals but today 25% of Americans live alone – compared with just 8% a decade ago). In the absence of a loving, sharing partner regular contact with intimate friends with whom mental and physical problems can be shared is important.

* Have the ability to maintain a sense of balance in a cruel world.

* Have a passion or a belief for which they would give up their lives.

* Have the ability to find some good in situations which may seem exclusively bad. For example, a woman who is suddenly faced with the fact that her children are leaving home may be overcome with a sense of sadness, but she should realise that she is being given a chance to regain her life.

* Have a sense of humour and the ability to laugh. The gift of creating and enjoying laughter is under-estimated; it is one of the greatest gifts of all, for those who laugh together forge a bond. Watch people coming out of a theatre where they have laughed together. They are full of love and companionship. (As a contrast watch people coming out of a movie about violence.) It is also important to be able to laugh at yourself and not to take yourself too seriously.

* Have a tendency to smile frequently. (Remember that people can tell if you are smiling even if they can't see your face; if you smile while you are talking on the telephone your voice will sound friendlier and warmer – try it!)

* Have an understanding of what other people need and want. If you know what other people like – and you make some effort to please them – then they, in turn, will like you. If you know what your prospective customers want and need – and you make some effort to provide them with what they want and need – your business will prosper.

* Appreciate that once the basic needs of food, clothing and shelter have been met, the only difference money makes to happiness is to make it possible to buy time and freedom. An absence of wealth may make a person miserable but the presence of wealth does not guarantee happiness.

***

Remember that you are responsible for your own personal world: you chose your job, your hobbies, your friends and the way you live.

If you didn't choose these things then who did? If you didn't choose to marry the person you are living with then who did? If you didn't choose to have three children who did? If you didn't choose to work in the glue factory then who did?

You might not have had the good fortune to have been born beautiful and rich, or blessed with special physical or mental skills which enable you to earn fame and money with relative ease, but you do have the ability to take control over your life.

Most people hand over control of their lives to anyone who wants to take that control. Do not avoid your responsibilities by taking the easy way out and blaming fate or luck. You have all that is necessary for success, riches or happiness. We all have potential within us, it is merely a question of recognising and using it.

CHAPTER TWELVE
Stick Up For Yourself (And Don't Make Excuses)

'Is there one whom difficulties dishearten – who bends to the storm? He will do little. Is there one who will conquer? That kind of man never fails.'

- John Hunter

Do you often end up doing things that you don't want to do – simply because you didn't like to say 'No' when you were asked?

Have you ever agreed to give a speech, attend a dinner or luncheon, chair a meeting or act as a secretary for a volunteer group? And have you ever subsequently regretted saying 'Yes'?

Life is too short to waste time in such a way.

If you spend too much of your life doing things you don't want to do then you will be losing time and the freedom to spend your life in the way *you* want to spend it.

We all like to be liked and saying 'Yes' is much more likely to attract approval and a smile from the person doing the asking than is saying 'No'.

We say 'Yes' because we know that the other person will probably feel disappointed or let down if we say 'No'. And we say 'Yes' (when we would really much rather say 'No') when we are not clear enough about our priorities and are, consequently, prepared to let other people decide what we do with our time. It is often easy to forget that saying 'Yes' to a simple sounding request may commit you to a time and energy sapping exercise.

Saying 'No' doesn't have to mean that you annoy people or upset them. Practice saying 'No' nicely and you will find that you can avoid wasting your life doing things you really don't want to do.

Here are some practical tips:

(1) Don't be defensive. You have no reason to feel guilty for saying 'No'. Don't begin by apologising.

(2) Don't give excuses. If you give excuses you are likely to end up say-ing 'Yes' when you really mean to say 'No'. For example, if you are invited to speak at a meeting which is being held next Tuesday evening and you say you can't manage that evening because you already have another commitment there is a danger that the person inviting you will suggest another date 'which will be more convenient to you'. At this point you are backed into a corner. And it will be difficult to get out of giving the speech without being rude.

(3) Begin your reply by flattering the person who is inviting you to do something. Tell them that you are honoured and flattered by the invitation.

(4) Look the person who is inviting you straight in the eye when you reply. This will help you dominate the conversation and ensure that it goes in the way you want it to go. If you look down and avoid eye contact (a natural reac-tion when you feel guilty or embarrassed) you will be behaving in a 'passive' way. When you behave in a 'passive' way the other person will automatically become more 'aggressive' and 'dominant'.

(5) Give a solid reason for not saying 'Yes' – a reason which it will be difficult to oppose or discount. It is even better if you say something which it will be impossible for the person inviting you to try to push aside without seem-ing to be rude or thoughtless. Here are some possibilities:
* 'From experience I know that this is not something I am good at and so
    I always say 'No'. But I am flattered that you asked me.'
* 'I am so busy for the foreseeable future that I cannot accept
any more invitations. I would be spreading myself far too thinly.
If I said 'yes' I simply wouldn't be able to do the job justice.'
* 'I have to say 'No' because I have been pushing myself so hard that
    I've been endangering my health'
* 'I recently made a firm commitment to spend more time with my fam-
    ily and so I have to say 'No.'

(6) If the person inviting you presses you further you can acknowledge their difficulties and needs and try to help them solve their problem without you. For example, if you are turning down a speaking engagement you can suggest another speaker.

***

Every time you say 'Yes' it should be because you are doing something you want to do – and not because you are frightened to say 'No'.

CHAPTER THIRTEEN
How To Bamboozle Bureaucrats

'Bureaucracy is a great machine operated by pigmies.'

- Honore de Balzac

Bureaucrats are the true plague of the twentieth century. Knowing how to deal with them effectively is vital. Here are two examples of simple ways in which you can deal with bureaucrats.

1. *Use Their Own Rules Against Them*
When I was a general practitioner, a bureaucrat called to say that he would be collecting, and taking away, all the medical records in my possession. He said that he had to take them away to check for some inexplicable, incomprehensible but documented bureaucratic reason. (Bureaucrats always have inexplicable, incomprehensible but documented reasons for what they do.) I told him that he couldn't take them away. I said I needed the medical records in order to treat my patients and that even if I didn't need the medical records I regarded them as confidential. The bureaucrat said if I looked at the bottom of each medical records envelope I would see that the medical records belonged to the Minister of Health and that he, as the Minister's representative, was therefore entitled to take the records with him. With a flash of inspiration I told him that he could take the medical records – but that he would have to leave the ink behind. 'The medical records may belong to the Minister,' I explained. 'But the ink is mine.' The bureaucrat thought about this for a while, consulted some colleagues and then went away and did not come back.

2. *Remember – and use the fact that – bureaucrats are terrified of responsibility*
When patients move from one part of the country to another, and therefore from

178

one practice to another, their medical records follow them at a far more leisurely pace. It is not unknown for medical records to take several months to make a journey of just a few miles. If you allowed the medical records to make their own way they would probably get to their destination more speedily. On one occasion a new patient, a diabetic, needed treatment. I did not have her medical records.

I telephoned her previous doctor. He could not remember anything useful about the patient's condition or treatment. But, he said, all the information I needed was on her medical records which he had dispatched to his layer of bureaucrats some days earlier.

I telephoned his bureaucrats. They told me that the medical records had been sent to my local bureaucrats.

I telephoned my local bureaucrats. They confirmed that they had the medical records in question. A bureaucrat confirmed that they were, as we spoke, sitting on her desk. I pointed out, politely, that I needed them urgently. The bureaucrat said that it would be another week or so before I could have them. I explained that the situation was rather more urgent than that. I said I would drive over to the bureaucrat's office to retrieve the medical records. The bureaucrat said I could not do that. I asked if I could drive over to examine the records without taking them away. The bureaucrat said I could not do that either. I then told the bureaucrat that if the medical records were not on my desk within thirty minutes, and the patient concerned died, I would put the bureaucrat down on the death certificate as a contributory cause of death. The medical records were on my desk within thirty minutes. I had discovered the single most important truth about bureaucrats: they do not like responsibility. A vampire will recoil at the sign of the cross. A bureaucrat will recoil at the threat of responsibility.

CHAPTER FOURTEEN
Adapt And Be Ready For Change

'I don't deserve this award, but I have arthritis and I don't deserve that, either. So I'll take it.'

- Jack Benny

Many people spend much of their energy trying to be in total control of their lives; trying to clear their desks and to get everything (relationships, belongings, work) just right.

This is a recipe for constant unhappiness and frustration because every time you think you have got your world sorted out some outside influence will come bursting in to disrupt things and you will lose control again.

The only constant upon which we can all rely is that tomorrow will be different to today and when tomorrow becomes today then tomorrow will, once again, be different.

Make yourself constantly adaptable to change and you will be in a far better position to survive. The moment you think you know the future and are in control, the moment you feel secure, that is the moment when the clock starts ticking on the unseen, unidentified, unexpected time bomb that will shatter your peace of mind. The moment you start to feel content, fate will start to smile. Don't pigeon hole yourself. And don't let other people pigeon hole you either.

You will only ever be in control of your life when you accept that you cannot have control and that change is a normal and acceptable part of life.

CHAPTER FIFTEEN
Don't Let People Push You Around

'When I started writing seriously, I made the major discovery of my life – that I am right and everybody else is wrong if they disagree with me. What a great thing to learn. Don't listen to anyone else, and always go your own way.'

- Ray Bradbury

Is there someone in your life who makes you feel inadequate? Your mother? Your boss? A sarcastic or manipulative friend? Do you know someone who always puts you down and makes you feel a loser? Such people can cause immense physical and mental distress – and even create illness.

Do you get pushed around a lot? Do you spend most of your time doing things that other people want you to do?

Are you spending your life the way you want to spend it?

Are you spending your life with the people you want to be with – doing what you want to do?

To get the most out of your life you must be able to answer 'No' to the first two questions and 'Yes' to the second two questions.

Are you going in the right direction?

There are only three reasons to do anything: because it may improve the world for other people or animals; because it is fun; because it makes money.

Rate all the activities in your life for: fun, money, improving the world.

How will you spend next weekend? How much time will you spend doing things that you really want to do? And how much time will you spend doing things that you aren't looking forward to – but that other people want you to do?

Make two lists of how you're likely to spend your time.

On the first list put the things you're looking forward to – the things you'll enjoy.

On the second list put the things that you feel you ought to do, the things you think other people expect you to do and the things you're not looking forward to at all.

Put down everything: meals, TV programmes, visitors, parties, trips out, sports, chores.

Now see which list is longest.

If your second list is the longest then you need to stand up for yourself more and the chances are that you get pushed around a lot by just about everyone you know; friends, relatives and employers especially.

You probably do errands for people who could perfectly well do their own errands. You're probably the sort of person who gets lumbered with looking after the children while everyone else goes off to a party. You probably work overtime at a job you hate – without getting paid for it. You get the boring jobs when you're on a committee.

And you never dream of complaining when you get rotten service in shops and restaurants.

The chances are that you're too shy, too soft hearted and too nice to complain or say 'No'. You don't stick up for yourself. And the chances are that your health is suffering.

I'm not suggesting that you try to turn yourself into a selfish bully.

But if you continue to allow other people to push you around then the chances are that you'll not only end up physically and mentally worn out but you'll also become so frustrated and acquire so much hidden anger and resentment that you'll become physically ill.

Headaches, backache, eczema and indigestion are just four of the disorders you're most likely to suffer from.

Moreover, if you become ill then your tolerance for pain will be low and you'll take longer than you should to recover.

Learning how to assert yourself – and stick up for yourself – isn't difficult.

Here's my advice:

1. *Remember that you're an individual and you have rights*
Of course you should try to help people who are less fortunate than you are. But don't let yourself be suckered into looking after people who can look after themselves. Thousands of mums spend their days acting as slaves for teenagers who could (and should) do more for themselves. You have a right to some fun in your life.

2. *Stop apologising unnecessarily*
If you're always saying sorry and feeling guilty then people will for ever be

taking advantage of you. Only say "sorry' when you really mean it. And remember: you're not responsible for what people think or believe. Your only responsibility is to be honest and true to yourself. You can do no more than that.

3. *Build up your self confidence*
Make a list of your assets. I don't mean cash but the really important things like knowledge, accomplishments, memories and skills.

4. *Disarm your critic by agreeing with him*
When someone says: 'Your hair is a mess' just reply: 'Yes, I know.' Don't apologise. Don't try to find excuses. Just take the wind out of their sails by agreeing with them.

5. *Don't let people label you*
If someone tells you that you are always unreliable or disorganised give some examples which show that you are just the opposite. If a critic tries to stick a label on you just refuse to accept it. If you are told that: 'You're always late' point out that you are late sometimes – but who isn't – but that most or much of the time you aren't late. If someone says you're clumsy, simply deny it but refuse to get into an argument.

6. *Force your critic to expand and clarify their criticism*
Ask the critic to tell you exactly what they want you to do. People who moan and criticise are often not very good at offering practical advice. Chances are that you will put them on the defensive – you will certainly take the sting out of their attack. If someone says that you are inefficient ask them to tell you what their problem is so that you can deal with it. Invite them to give you more examples and keep inviting them to give you more examples.

7. *Stay calm*
However angry or irate your critic gets you should stay cool. Eventually, there is a good chance that your critic will lose his or her temper. You can then (if you wish) retaliate by asking him or her why he or she is so touchy.

8. *Remember that most bullies are physical cowards*
Be physically assertive. I don't mean that you should hit your critics. But stand up to them. Look them in the eye. Invade their personal space. Most bullies (and this is particularly true of emotional bullies) are cowards. Move closer to them and they'll probably feel uncomfortable, back away – and back down. Don't raise your voice but keep it firm.

9. *Walk away or put the telephone down*
Refuse to get involved in a distressing argument. You don't have to put up with abuse from anyone.

10. *Don't spend time with people who annoy you, constantly put you down or make you feel guilty*
Why waste your life on people who make your life miserable? I don't care who it is – colleague, friend or close relative – if they make you unhappy cut them out of your life.

11. *Ignore gratuitous advice*
Just because someone tells you to do this, or suggests that you do that, you don't have to react. Say 'Thank you' and then ignore them and do exactly what you want to do. If people offer minor criticisms, insults or sarcastic comments just ignore them.

* * *

Stand up for yourself – you'll be healthier. Learn how to deal with toxic people – and how to handle people who make your life miserable or who make you feel inadequate. People can only push you around if you let them.

CHAPTER SIXTEEN
Use Your Imagination And Your Subconscious Mind

'It doesn't matter where you live – where you live is really in your head.'
- Henry David Thoreau

'The subconscious mind will translate into its physical equivalent a thought impulse of a negative or destructive nature just as readily as it will act upon thought impulses of a positive or constructive nature. This accounts for the strange phenomenon which so many millions of people experience, referred to as 'misfortune' or 'bad luck'.'
- Napoleon Hill

'There is nothing either good or bad, but thinking makes it so.'
- William Shakespeare

'I believe in the power of desire backed by faith because I have seen this power lift men from lowly beginnings to places of power and wealth; I have seen it rob the grave of its victims; I have seen it serve as the medium by which men staged a comeback after having been defeated in a hundred different ways...'
- Napoleon Hill

You must develop and use your imaginative skills.

Most people are unimaginative. This is not because they do not have any imaginative skills but because they do not how to use them. Many are probably frightened of displaying any imagination. The average person's idea of variety is to own sweaters in three shades of beige; their idea of daring is to plant their runner beans a week before their neighbours.

When in prime condition you can use your imagination to rework and rearrange old ideas, to see potential where there is no apparent hope and to dis-

185

cover ways through when there seems to be an impasse. You can also use your imagination to create new ideas out of thin air. Newton, when he was asked how he had produced his great discoveries replied: 'I keep the subject continually before me and wait till the first dawnings open slowly little by little into a full and clear light.'

If you allow your imagination to develop you will soon realise that most of the things which most people regard as 'impossible' are not impossible at all. Eventually, you will come to regard the word 'impossible' as a challenge.

This will give you a tremendous advantage over all those people who think that the things you are planning to do are 'impossible'. Most people are far too aware of all the things which are impossible – and which they are convinced will not work. I suggest that you do not even allow the word 'impossible' to enter your mind. When deciding whether or not to do something ask yourself not: 'Is this impossible?' but 'Do I want to do this?' (And if you answer 'yes' to the second question use your imagination to help you decide how).

***

Your imagination has a far greater control over your life than you might realise. Put a piece of wood on the ground and try walking along it. Easy? Now, imagine that the piece of wood is suspended 1,000 feet above a swamp filled with alligators and try walking across it again. The more you can convince yourself that the piece of wood really is suspended above a swamp the more difficult you will find it to walk across.

Your imagination can work against you. But it can also work for you. You can use your imagination to help you achieve whatever you want. Create in your mind the idea of what you want. Hold the idea in your mind. Sum up what you want in a few words. Close your eyes and imagine yourself writing those words down on an imaginary blackboard.

Now think of all the facts and information you have. Hold those facts in your mind. With your eyes still closed write down the facts and information on an imaginary blackboard. Then get on with something else.

When you think about your problem next you will find that your subconscious mind will have produced several possible answers.

***

If you have difficulty in getting your imagination to work then you should buy yourself a bundle of notebooks and a pile of pens and pencils. Use the pencils and notebooks to write down everything you think of – practical plans, thoughts, fears, hopes, ideas even bits of gossip. Get into the habit of writing down everything which comes into your head. If you do this then you will free your mind to wander free and you will stimulate your imagination to work harder and more effectively.

Once you start carrying a notebook with you – and using it – you will have far more ideas than you can cope with! Your imagination is the key to success. Your imagination is your mind's workshop. And your imagination can grow and develop the more you use it.

CHAPTER SEVENTEEN
Control Your Own Health

'A great healer heals with 'only a minimum of medicines'. The superior healer knows how to heal the mind first. Even without any medicine.'

– Tao Te Jing by Lao Tsu

'Holistic' medicine (sometimes also spelt 'wholistic') has, for several decades, been growing in theoretical popularity.

Many alternative and some orthodox health care professionals describe themselves as 'holistic' practitioners.

But they aren't.

Most journalists inaccurately assume that the word is a synonym for 'alternative' or 'complementary' medicine.

But it isn't.

The word 'holistic' was first introduced in 1926 by the South African philosopher and statesman Jan Christian Smuts. He suggested that the whole human being is much more than (and quite different to) a collection of physical or emotional parts. Even in those days, it seems, there must have been doctors parading up and down hospital wards referring to the 'liver' in the end bed and the 'case of pancreatitis' in the third bed on the left.

The word and the concept lay more or less forgotten until the 1970s when the growth of high technology medicine led to a revolution among patients who felt that aggressive, interventionist medicine wasn't entirely satisfactory.

In practical terms the use of the word 'holistic' meant, in theory at least, that instead of regarding patients as sick kidneys or hearts, health care professionals would try to meet the physical, mental, emotional and spiritual needs of their patients by using natural healing methods as well as modern, pharmacological or surgical techniques.

In short, the word 'holistic' was intended to describe an attitude. An attitude which can be just as well followed by an orthodox trained doctor as by an alternative practitioner. A general practitioner in a busy city health centre can be 'holistic' in his approach just as easily as can a herbalist or acupuncturist working from a back bedroom.

There is no doubt that a 'holistic' approach to medical care is extremely good news for patients. When followed properly it means that every illness can be treated with a 'pick'n'mix' approach – choosing whichever aspects of orthodox and alternative medicine are most likely to be effective, and least likely to produce side effects, and treating and taking full notice of all aspects of the individual's being.

In many illnesses there is no point in treating what is wrong with the body unless you also treat what is wrong with the mind.

It seems to me remarkable that a modern doctor will treat the body of a patient who is suffering from high blood pressure, irritable bowel syndrome or asthma but ignore the mind, when it is now established beyond doubt that in so many illnesses the physical symptoms are produced by mental turmoil of one sort or another.

It is equally bizarre and, in truth, unscientific, for an osteopath to treat a patient's back and ignore his mind.

The advantages of a truly 'holistic' approach are colossal, not only because 'holistic' medicine offers a chance to use the best and avoid the worst but also because different types of treatment can, when used together, have a synergistic effect. A genuinely 'holistic' approach may use a modern drug, a relaxation technique and a type of massage to tackle a single collection of symptoms.

But although in theory the word 'holistic' implies an admirable change in attitude there is, sadly, little evidence that practitioners really understand what the word means or how it should be applied in practice.

It would be nice to think that everyone could find a 'holistic' practitioner to look after them. But don't hold your breath. You've about as much chance of striking oil when digging up your winter vegetables.

Today, in some so called developed parts of the Western world, more people visit alternative health care practitioners than visit orthodox medical practitioners. Judged in terms of numbers orthodox medicine is now the true alternative.

But the steady rise in popularity of alternative medicine has, regrettably, made remarkably little impact on the way that orthodox medicine is practised. There are, it is true, a few orthodox practitioners who offer alternative forms of treatment (though, sadly, many of these are best described as dabblers rather than practitioners – there are doctors around practising acupuncture, osteopathy, homoeopathy and hypnotherapy on the basis of one or two weekend courses) but the establishment view, proposed and seconded by the pharmaceutical industry and supported by a medical profession which is, as I have pointed out elsewhere, now more of a marketing arm to the drug barons than an independent profession, remains unchanged: alternative medicine is a dangerous waste of time and money which should be patronised when it cannot be ignored and suppressed whenever possible.

The myth that drug therapy offers the only true solution is now repeated unquestioningly and without hesitation or embarrassment.

The importance of drug therapy, and the reverence with which drugs are regarded by doctors and nurses, is perhaps best seen in modern health centres where doctors dispense as well as prescribe and where the dispensing counter where patients exchange their prescription slips for drugs is rather akin to a high altar. The modern consultation is, too often, a simple, uncomplicated, thoughtless three part process.

First, the patient visits the doctor and reports his or her symptoms. Second, the doctor decides which drug (or, more likely, which drugs) will be most appropriate and writes out what he considers to be an appropriate prescription. And, third, the patient takes the prescription to the high priest and has it turned into a bottle of pills, a tube of ointment, an inhaler or whichever form has been deemed appropriate. An orthodox, modern medical school training means (literally) that a doctor is trained and kept up to date by and for the pharmaceutical industry. This may sound like hyperbole. It isn't. Drug companies pay for a very large part of the education that a doctor receives.

It is not surprising, therefore, that the drug company owned and controlled medical establishment still looks with horror at alternative medicine. Attempts to organise research programmes are invariably treated with a sneer or a patronising dismissal.

It is one of the great scandals of the twentieth century that the billion dollar worldwide 'charity' cancer industry, the international drug industry and the medical 'profession' (now, more of a trade than a 'profession') would all much rather suppress an alternative cancer treatment rather than have to admit that orthodox remedies might be bettered.

The truth is that the medical establishment – and the drug industry – are terrified of alternative medicine for they regard it as a major commercial threat.

So, the bottom line is that you are unlikely to find a 'holistic' orthodox practitioner after all.

You might expect to do better among alternative practitioners.

But I fear that you would probably be disappointed.

Tragically, too many alternative care practitioners are, in their complementary way, just as arrogant and intellectually isolated as medical men and women who have been trained to hand out pills.

190

Many acupuncturists, homoeopaths, herbalists and others describe themselves as offering their patients 'holistic' medicine when in reality they offer nothing of the sort.

However well trained she may be the alternative therapist who confines herself to a single speciality is not a 'holistic' practitioner. How many acupuncturists, herbalists and naturopaths will admit that orthodox doctors and hospitals can sometimes provide the best service?

To be honest I don't think that many patients are ever going to receive truly 'holistic' treatment from their practitioners – whether they are orthodox or alternative. Most training programmes are, by their very nature, designed to produce specialists. Medical schools turn out drug dispensers and acupuncture schools turn out acupuncturists. And there aren't many health care professionals with the time or inclination to study other available specialities.

We must also recognise that there is, of course, a huge financial disincentive involved here. How many practitioners are going to suggest to a paying patient that he would obtain better treatment by visiting another professional? I know of very few truly 'holistic' centres where a patient can obtain treatment from a comprehensive variety of orthodox and alternative practitioners.

All this is sad.

But it doesn't mean that 'holistic' medicine is out of reach.

What it does mean is that if you really want 'holistic' treatment (and in my opinion you should) you're going to have to take control yourself if you or anyone in your family needs treatment.

Anyone who is ill needs attention to their mind and spirit as well as their body. Selecting a properly balanced diet may be as important as choosing the right drug. Sometimes a successful outcome to an illness may be 80% dependent on choosing the right drug. On another occasion a successful outcome may be 80% dependent on diet.

There are very few truly 'holistic' medical practitioners. But everyone can – and should – be a 'holistic' patient.

Don't trust medical advisers. Compare and contrast all the possible treatments and analyse all the available advice. Try to learn as much about health care as you can while you are still healthy. Collect books and newsletters so that you have the information you may need on hand – when you need it.

CHAPTER EIGHTEEN
Learn How To Deal With Stress

'I was rich, if not in money, in sunny hours and summer days, and spent them lavishly.'
– Henry David Thoreau

'This spending of the best part of one's life earning money in order to enjoy a questionable liberty during the least valuable part of it, reminds me of the Englishman who went to India to make a fortune first, in order that he might return to England and live the life of a poet.'
– Henry David Thoreau

Nine out of ten illnesses are caused or made worse by stress. Knowing how to deal with stress will improve the health of your body, mind and spirit. Here are some tips for dealing with stress:

(1) If you are constantly busy do a little 'time and motion' study on your life. Make sure that you don't waste valuable time. For example, is it really worthwhile spending an hour of your time to race across town in the hope of saving a few pence on soap powder? Are you making best use of your resources by using a cheap car park and having to carry your shopping a mile or two in the rain?

(2) Create 'hassle free geographical zones' in your life where you can rest and recharge your batteries without fear of being disturbed. There should be places in your world where you know that you can escape from stress. You should have a quiet room in your home where there is no telephone and where you know you can relax comfortably – certain that you are not going to be disturbed.

There should be places in your locality where you can go to 'escape' from pressure. And, ideally, there should be cities and resorts which your mind associates only with relaxation. If you visit a place often enough – and have enough good memories of that place – you will eventually feel your body and mind relaxing the minute you arrive there.

(3) Learn to turn 'dead' time into useful time. Make sure that you always have a book or some paperwork with you so that you can make the best possible use of time spent at airports or railway stations. This will help you combat boredom (a major source of stress) and will also help you make time available for 'fun' things when you get back home.

(4) If you feel under too much pressure do not be afraid to retreat to your bed and tell the world that you are 'ill'. Lots of famous people – for example, Florence Nightingale – have done this to escape from pressure and recharge their batteries.

(5) Choose the seven days of your life that are the most important and most memorable. Write down as much as you can remember about those days to create a 'magic week'. When you feel 'down' simply relive your 'magic week' to put a smile back onto your face and into your heart.

(6) Do not wait until tomorrow for the future you want. Twenty years ago a friend of mine took a job with a large company. It wasn't a job he wanted but the pay was good. He really wanted to be an artist. 'I'll do this for ten years, put aside as much money as I can and then retire,' he told me and himself. 'Then I'll be free to paint.' I think he believed himself. Today, eighteen years later, he still works for the same company. He has been promoted several times. He has a company car, a pension, sickness benefits and generous paid holidays. He is very well paid and has a beautiful house in a pleasant, well kept suburb. He will stop work when he reaches the official retirement age although he now does a job he hates and he despises himself. It is not surprising that he is constantly under a great deal of stress.

(7) Never delay action which needs to be taken. Consider the case of a friend of mine who ran a small business which had expanded too quickly and who had consequently been under a great deal of pressure at work. He also had a lot of pressures at home – he had bought a new house and he could ill afford the loan payments and as a result his marriage was under a considerable strain. As a result of the accumulated pressures produced by the problems at home and at work he had a nervous breakdown. When I talked to him he agreed that the

problems at home and work had caused his illness; and he agreed that he needed to change his life. 'I'll change my lifestyle when I'm better,' he said, announcing that he had to keep on working in order to keep earning a living. That was a bit like saying: 'I'm sitting on a hot stove and it hurts but I can't think about doing anything to deal with the problem until the pain has gone.'

(8) Make sure that you find time in your life for yourself and do not be afraid to give in to temptation occasionally.

A few weeks ago I had been working exceptionally hard and had just finished a book. It had been raining for a week or more but when I looked out of the window I saw, to my surprise, that the sun was shining, the sky was blue and the birds were singing. Temptation opened the door and poked her head into the room where I was working. 'Fancy a walk in the park?' she asked.

I sighed. 'I can't,' I answered sadly, waving a hand in the direction of the computer screen in front of me. 'I've got to write a newspaper column.'

Temptation raised an eyebrow but said nothing. I sighed, smiled and stood up.

Outside it was warm and peaceful and it was good to feel the sunshine on my back.

As Temptation and I walked through the gates I heard someone shouting. I looked around. The source of the shouting wasn't difficult to spot. He was middle aged and had staring, angry eyes, wild hair and several days worth of stubble on his chin. I couldn't tell what he was shouting about but there was spittle on his chin and he was hoarse and there was much pain in his eyes.

We walked on. Behind me, walking more slowly but still shouting, walked the man with the wild hair and the angry eyes.

We walked past the lake where young mothers and children were feeding bread to fat ducks and past military neat flower beds ablaze with red and yellow flowers. I confess with shame that I didn't know any of their man-given names but you don't have to identify beauty to appreciate it.

We walked up a long, steep path through a small, cool area of wood-land. At the top of the hill there was a clearing from which it was possible to stand and view the majesty of the surrounding countryside; in the foreground two churches, neat rows of houses and a railway station, in the middle distance small white cottages and on the horizon, the sea.

But it was not the view which captivated my soul but the deliciously haunting sound made by a man in a green corduroy suit playing a double bass.

I didn't recognise the tune but it was the melody to something the di-minutive French singer Edith Piaf had made famous. A small crowd of twenty or thirty people were standing there listening and enjoying and, for an all too brief moment, at peace for a while with themselves, one another and the world.

As the bass player finished playing the tune which had greeted my arrival he shifted his instrument an inch or two and then started to play something else.

I looked around and noticed that the man with the wild hair, angry eyes and spittle on his chin was standing beside me. He was listening to the music and the pain in his face was softened. The anger in his eyes had gone and he seemed comforted and temporarily at peace with the world.

A few moments later a thick necked, red faced policeman came along and loudly and officiously ordered the bass player to stop. For a moment nothing happened. The musician was as lost in the beauty of what he was playing as we were.

Angrily, the officious policeman leaned forward and roughly pulled at the bass player's jacket.

The musician stopped playing and the spell was broken and we were all yanked cruelly back into a mouldy, dishonest, cruel society where the Rules are all that matter and people, love, beauty and kindness are nothing.

For a moment no one moved. And no one spoke. The silence hung around us like a thick curtain. The musician stood up and started to pack his double bass back into its case. I looked around. There were tears now in the eyes of the man with the wild hair.

I felt myself propelled forwards by some unseen force. It was not of my will. I touched the fat policeman lightly on the arm.

'Please let the music continue.' The voice came from my mouth but was not of my making.

The policeman glowered at me, uncomprehendingly; a brutish weapon of a cruel state. He recited some laws which were being broken.

'The law is ours not yours,' I heard myself tell him. 'If you don't let the music continue I will arrest you for causing a breach of the peace. There is a danger that there will be a riot unless you allow this man to continue playing.'

The policeman stared at me unbelievingly.

I turned slightly. 'I need witnesses that this officer's behaviour will cause a breach of the peace.'

For a moment no one moved. Then one hand went up. And slowly a dozen more hands were raised in support.

The policeman stared around him and blinked; sweating slightly and confused. He mumbled something about riots and reinforcements and conspiracy. But he moved away from the musician.

The bass player took his instrument out of its case and started to play again.

Defeated, the policeman moved away and scurried back down the hill.

This time the music sounded even sweeter than it had before. The man with the wild hair, standing beside me, turned to me and smiled. I smiled back.

In our cruel, humourless, grey, passionless world each small victory against the harsh and senseless hand of authority is like a battle won. I was glad I'd gone for a walk in the park.

Temptation may occasionally lead you astray but she will sometimes lead you to moments of greater joy than you will ever find by steadfastly following the straight and narrow paths of righteousness.

(9) Even if you work for someone else you should be your own boss. Don't let yourself be abused or used. Remember that people who work for themselves work harder but are more likely to get business satisfaction. If you are self employed you are also far more likely to enjoy freedom in the way you live.

If you work for a company remember that the company does not love you. The company has no feelings towards you whatsoever. What is a company? It is a business owned by shareholders. Do you really think that all the shareholders love you?

Stress is created by frustration and fear and comes when there is responsibility without authority. People who are truly in charge of their own lives have to endure relatively modest amounts of all these negative forces.

You might imagine that when I talk about 'people who are truly in charge of their own lives' I am talking about 'bosses' but there are very few people who work for large companies who are genuinely in charge of their own lives. Most people who are thought of as bosses are employees who still have to report to an individual, a committee or a board.

The surprising truth is that the self employed are most likely to be in charge of their own lives. You can become the boss of your own life by differentiating between the important and the unimportant, by knowing the bottom line and making your own decisions and by taking responsibility for what you do or do not do.

(10) Pleasure is an antidote to stress – and will, therefore, protect you against the illnesses associated with stress. If you do something enjoyable every day you are less likely to fall ill.

(11) Some people can cope with a small amount of stress. Others can cope with a great deal. The trick is to reduce your exposure and increase your resistance until you feel comfortable.

(12) In order to deal effectively with stress you need to know how to use your own 'bodypower' and 'mindpower'. (These are described in detail in my books *Bodypower* and *Mindpower*.)

(13) You will be better able to withstand stress and pressure if you have a wide range of interests to keep your mind busy. If work is the only thing in your life then you will suffer more when you have problems at work.

(14) To avoid burnout and minimise your exposure to stress you should take regular breaks and holidays.

(15) When you are under stress you should ask yourself: 'Is this worth the stress it causes?'. And you should ask yourself: 'What will doing this accomplish?'

(16) Break your targets down into realistic goals. Would be slimmers are usually advised to think in terms of small losses of weight and weeks rather than large losses of weight and years. You should use the same technique when starting a huge project. If you are renovating a house, writing a book, building up an international supermarket chain from scratch or planning to cycle round the world you should plan your project in easy stages.

(17) Be yourself. Don't try to be someone you're not. Don't be frightened to appear cranky or eccentric. Don't be afraid to retain your individuality in a conformist world. Don't worry about what other people think about you. Our society criticises and disapproves far too much. Don't be afraid if people laugh at you. (Their lives are probably dull and pointless in comparison.) There is a strong correlation between the word 'brilliant' and the phrase 'a lot of trouble'. It is no coincidence that the greatest sports players, artists and others invariably get into trouble with the authorities.

(18) Protect and cherish your privacy. In an increasingly intrusive world you should make sure that you do everything you can to retain your privacy. Don't tell the authorities anything you don't have to tell them. Ignore requests for information which are not backed up by the law. Don't give information about yourself that you don't want the world to know. Remember that the paranoid may get laughed at but they tend to live longer.

(19) Go for it! If you go for it you may have regrets – but the regrets you have for things you didn't do will always hurt more than the regrets you have for the things you did (and got wrong). Straightforward regrets are far worse than disappointments. When your best isn't good enough look for a fresh angle. When things are going badly remind yourself of your goals. Regularly ask yourself if you are being taken away from your goals.

(20) Aim to achieve self reliance. Always keep the phone numbers and addresses

of people with skills you might need (with back ups). And always try to have a back up system for anything upon which you rely. If you rely on a computer for your work then you should have a back up computer – or know where you can rent, borrow or obtain one in an emergency. If your home works entirely on electricity then either have a generator which you can use in emergencies or else make sure that you keep good stocks of candles, portable stoves and so on.

(21) Know your destiny. If you died tomorrow would you look down from heaven and be proud of what you had achieved? Are you getting the best out of yourself? Will others look back at your life with respect, love and affection? Are you spending your life the way you want to spend it? Remember that money won't buy you immortality. (It isn't what you own but what you do that matters.)

(22) Don't worry about annoying the establishment. Everyone who achieves anything worthwhile annoys someone. And the people who annoy the most really important people usually achieve the most.

(23) Learn to deal with envy. If something good happens to you then try to feel happy and to enjoy what is happening without thinking that what is happening to you is not as good as something that is happening to someone else.

(24) Don't be afraid of the dull moments. The good sea captain knew that sailors were always more likely to mutiny when they were bored and underemployed.
    The Marquis de Spinola: *'What did your brother die of?'*
    Sir Horace Vere: *'He died, Sir, of having nothing to do.'*
    The Marquis de Spinola: *'Alas! That is enough to kill any of us.'*
    Today, many people are driven 'out of their minds' by the tedium of machine minding or repetitive office work. Boredom is a greatly underestimated pressure in our modern lives. And it is because the opposite of boredom is excitement that so many young people with dull, boring lives drink themselves silly and take to violence. (This isn't the only reason, of course, but it is an important factor.) Our expectations have risen and our tolerance for boredom has shrunk. In the middle ages, when people couldn't read or write (even if there had been anything for them to read or write) and when there was no television, no radio and no cinema, people used to have to sit around in the dark evenings in a smoke filled room, shivering and trying to see one another with the aid of a candle or two. Travel was more or less impossible (particularly when the weather was bad and the roads were impassable) and so visitors were rare. Most people hardly ever travelled more than a few miles away from their homes. It is hardly surprising that such a boring lifestyle led to witch-hunts and the regular use of the stocks on the village green. (It is perhaps fortunate that a high infant mortal-

ity rate kept down the population. Without contraceptives there would surely otherwise have been an incredible increase in the size of the population. After all, what else was there to do?)

Today we are better able to combat boredom but we are more afraid of it. We are always searching for something new. And we take advantage of every new piece of technology to put ourselves under constantly increasing pressure. Television and radio shows try to broadcast information in short convenient sized bites because producers and editors know that most viewers and listeners cannot cope with great chunks of information. Magazine editors know the same thing: that is why their pages are so frequently broken up a great deal. If the book is ever killed it will not be television which does the killing – but the inability of prospective readers to cope with so much text.

What we have perhaps forgotten is that some boredom is essential for a healthy, balanced lifestyle. A little boredom can add relief and even spice to a life that is full of pressure. All the best novels and films break up the action occasionally with apparently boring bits of description or shots of scenery, designed to help build up the tension and add to the timing. Jerome K Jerome's book 'Three Men in a Boat' (the funniest book ever written) shows precisely how the dull boring bits in a book can, in a strange way, be just as important to the success of the whole enterprise as the funny bits.

Learn to enjoy and take advantage of the quiet moments in your life.

CHAPTER NINETEEN
Don't Give Up!

'There is no greater calamity than to under estimate the strength of your enemy. For to under estimate the strength of your enemy is to lose the war. Therefore, when opposing troops meet in battle, victory belongs to the strategic planner.'

- Tao Te Jing by Lao Tsu

We live in a world in which resolve, diligence, perseverance and persistence are no longer respected values.

'If at first you don't succeed – give up' seems to be a watchword for modern life.

And yet patience and perseverance can overcome just about any obstacle. The individual who is determined and prepared to work hard will almost always surpass the talented individual who is not determined nor prepared to work hard. I know two tennis players. One is brilliant. But erratic. He has little drive and cannot concentrate. He plays the best tennis I've ever seen – for a few games. The other player is very good but not brilliant. He has a limited range of shots and a weak serve. But he is consistent and he knows his weaknesses. He plays steadily. When these two players meet the very good player nearly always beats the brilliant player.

What on earth do you think happens to all those 'bright' boys and girls who take all the prizes at school? Precocity is no guide to future success because there are no school rewards for endeavour or for struggle. Churchill, Newton, Sheridan, Burns, Napoleon and Wellington were all 'failures' at school. Ulysses Grant, US Commander in Chief, was called Useless Grant by his mother. Dean Swift was a failure. Robert Clive was such an embarrassment to his family that he was packed off to Madras, India so that he would be out of sight. Abraham Lincoln and Handel were both over 40 before they achieved any success at all.

The often forgotten truth is that the man or woman who fails but tries, tries, tries and tries again will have a much greater chance of succeeding in life. Repeated failure can either instil a feeling of hopelessness or else a feeling of quiet but rugged and steely determination. If you persist with your desires then you will sweep aside all the opposition and get all the opportunities you seek.

If you intend to succeed – to achieve anything at all in almost any area of life – then in addition to overcoming all the natural obstacles you will encounter, and the obstacles which your enemies will deliberately put in your way, you will probably also have to ignore and overcome endless types of discouragement and negativity from those whom you might sensibly expect to be on your side.

Friends and relatives who are close to you will think of all sorts of reasons why you should not expect to succeed and why you are wasting your time and energy in even trying.

'Don't bother, it isn't worth the effort,' a friend will say. 'You don't stand a chance, so why waste your time,' a relative will warn you smugly.

You must learn to be self reliant and you must acquire self confidence because anyone who has a purpose in life will attract jeering and sneering from those who prefer to stay in their ruts. You must be prepared for the fact that the jeering and sneering will often come loudest from close relatives or some of those whom you regard as your friends. 'You can't do that!' they will say. 'What makes you think you can do that?'

It seems that to many envy comes much easier than admiration and it is hardly surprising that however crowded about they may be with friends many people suffer agonies of loneliness throughout their lives.

If you make an effort to fulfil your ambitions, some friends will probably predict calamity and disaster and if and when things go wrong they will smugly point out that they 'told you so'.

These dismal discouragements are to a certain extent inspired by an inbuilt prejudice against success but there is, sadly, also a good deal of resentment and jealousy involved.

People who have done little or nothing with their own lives, and who have accepted their place in society with little in the way of protest, do not find it easy to watch as someone else proves that ambition, fire, determination and energy can defeat all manner of obstacles.

And when you finally succeed in your endeavour they will not cheer you or offer congratulations; rather they will stand around waiting for some new disaster to befall you so that they can cheer your downfall and remind you that they warned you that no good would come of it all.

**

Success does not often come easily. The vast majority of those who seem to have an easy talent have acquired their skill through self belief, patience, commitment, perseverance and determination and through years of practice and hard work.

The writer who produces page after page of easy to read prose has learnt his trade by writing, writing, writing and writing. And still he probably polishes and hones and worries over each new sentence. The artist, dancer, orator, singer, sculptor or sports star who attracts plaudits and praise will have learned his or her skills through repetition, constant failure, hard work, labour, sweat, tears and possibly even blood. Turner, the painter, used to get paid half a crown a night to wash in the skies on other people's drawings. He would illustrate guidebooks and do anything asked of him – not just because he needed the money but because he needed the practice. The trick that looks easy to perform is hard to learn. And luck has nothing to do with it. 'It's a funny thing,' said a great golfing star, 'but the more I practise, the luckier I get.'

***

When Mohammed the prophet had been preaching for ten years he was banished, impoverished and ridiculed. Yet before another decade was over he was dictator of all Arabia, ruler of Mecca and head of a new world religion. When the armies of Mohammed entered Jerusalem not one person was killed because of his faith (though when the crusaders entered the same city, centuries later, they did not spare a single Moslem man, woman or child).

When he was trying to produce a machine which could record and then reproduce the human voice Edison was told by those close to him that what he was trying to do was impossible. It was, they insisted, impossible because no one had ever done it before. He didn't believe them. When he was trying to create light he tried out more than 10,000 different ideas before he (literally) saw the light.

People laughed at Henry Ford's first motor car and told F.W. Woolworth that he would go broke if he tried to run a store selling items at five and ten cents. Pope Adrian IV was so poor when he was a boy that he studied by the lights of the lamps in the street and church porches.

When Benvenuto Cellini, Italian sculptor, painter, author and heaven knows what else, was told by the Grand Duke Cosmo of Florence that his model of Perseus could not possibly be cast in bronze he was determined to do the impossible.

When he had prepared the mould for the statue he purchased several loads of pine wood, filled his furnace with pieces of brass and bronze and lit his fire. The pine wood blazed so furiously that Cellini's workshop caught fire. When the roof burnt away the rain came in and started to dowse the furnace and reduce the temperature. For hour after hour Cellini threw more wood onto the fire in order to raise the temperature high enough to melt the brass and the bronze. Eventually he became so exhausted that he collapsed and had to retire to his bed, leaving his assistants to continue feeding the fire. When a workman rushed into his bedroom to tell him that the whole project was proving a disaster because the fire had gone out and the metal had gone hard Cellini obtained more wood from a neighbour and got his fire going again. Eventually the metal started to flow. But it wasn't flowing fast enough and so Cellini rushed into the kitchen and grabbed every piece of copper and pewter that he could find – around two hundred different dishes, kettles and so on – and threw them all into the furnace. Eventually the metal started to flow freely and easily and the statue of Perseus was cast.

Frenchman Bernard Pallissy spent sixteen years searching for a way to make enamel. He gave away all the furniture in his house in order to pay for his experiments and when he ran out of furniture he gave away most of his clothes to help pay his assistant's wages. His family and his neighbours constantly reproached him for his recklessness. After he had eventually mastered the art of enamel making he was arrested for being a protestant in a strongly catholic country. He was condemned to be burnt to death but his life was saved by a nobleman because he was the only craftsman able to make the enamel needed for the chateau the nobleman was having built. After many more great achievements and numerous battles Pallissy died in the Bastille at the age of 79 – a rebel, a revolutionary and a free thinker to the very end of his life.

Benjamin Disraeli's first books were laughed at. Later he became a highly successful novelist. When Disraeli made his maiden speech in the House of Commons in London he was a disaster. Other parliamentarians laughed at him. He didn't give up but worked to overcome his faults, studied the audience, practised and worked slowly and patiently for success. He became British Prime Minister.

Sir Isaac Newton had many years of elaborate calculations destroyed when his dog upset a lit candle on his desk. T.E. Lawrence (Lawrence of Arabia) lost the manuscript of *Seven Pillars of Wisdom* when his case disappeared on a railway station. Sir Thomas Carlyle had to rewrite the first volume of his book on the French Revolution after the manuscript was accidentally used by a maid to light a kitchen fire. He lent the only copy of the manuscript to a neighbour. But the man left the book lying on the parlour floor and forgot about it. When Carlyle asked for its return it turned out that the maid had been using the pile of papers to light the fires in the parlour and the kitchen. Carlyle had no draft and had to rewrite the whole massive book.

Audubon, the eminent American ornithologist, famous for his marvellous drawings of birds, put 200 original drawings in a wooden box and gave the box to a relative to look after. He then went away for several months. On his return he asked the relative for his box. The box, which had been placed in a safe place, was produced and Audubon discovered that a pair of Norwegian rats had moved in. A young family had been reared amongst and upon the gnawed pieces of paper. The drawings were destroyed. Audubon was numb for a few days but then he picked up his notebook and his pencils and went back into the woods, determined that he would make the new drawings even better than the old ones. It took him three years of work to replace the lost drawings.

Philosopher and writer Henry David Thoreau was sent to prison for fighting for what he believed in. John Bunyan wrote 'Pilgrim's Progress' after he had been sent to prison because of his views on religion.

***

It has been said that knowing how to wait is the main secret of success. (There is an Eastern proverb which says: 'Time and patience change the mulberry leaf to satin.' and an Italian proverb which goes: 'Che va piano, va longano, e va lontano', meaning: 'Who goes slowly, goes long and goes far.') And patience and persistence are frequently two of the most important factors in any success. George Stephenson worked on his famous rocket for 15 years. James Watt spent 30 years working on his condensing engine.

Success may be due to industry and application, and to achieving a mastery of a chosen subject. And men who have changed the world have often been men of mediocre talents who were blessed with passion and intensity. But rarely does success come without an untiring sense of perseverance and determination. No one can succeed without planning but persistence – which itself is usually derived from a driving sense of purpose – is a vital and frequently underestimated ingredient.

***

It is a mistake to assume that obstinacy alone denotes strength. A weak man can be stubborn. A stupid man can be stubborn. And a man who is both very weak and very stupid can be very stubborn indeed. But obstinacy – in a way just another word for gritty determination – is an essential ingredient for anyone who genuinely wishes to succeed in some aspect of life and who is prepared to overcome whatever obstacles may be placed in the way. Ludwig van Beethoven the composer was deaf. John Milton the poet was blind. Charles Dickens, the novelist, started work pasting labels on blacking pots.

Just wanting something is not enough. You must *want* it and *need* it. In order to achieve you must believe that you can reach your ambitions. Hoping and wishing isn't enough. You must believe that you can achieve.

***

At the age of ten Dr Livingstone was sent to work in a cotton factory near Glasgow. With some of his first week's wages he bought himself a Latin grammar so that he could begin to educate himself. He had to be at work at six every morning but he would sit up working until twelve or even later. Many nights he simply stayed up studying until he was sent to bed by his mother. He read everything he could. He even propped books up against the machinery on which he was working so that he could keep on reading. He put a book on a spinning jenny so that he could read a sentence at a time as he passed the book. Eventually Livingstone became a doctor and a missionary (he continued his factory work throughout his education to pay for his food and lodgings and books). His whole career is one huge story of determination and perseverance.

If you are going to persevere with your aims then you must ensure that you are 'driven'. You must give your life a purpose and specific aims. You must know what you want out of life and you must turn those wants into needs.

Your drive will give you the willpower to force yourself on but you will also need to enlist the support of those around you and you will need to accumulate the knowledge that is necessary for you to achieve your aims.

CHAPTER TWENTY
Aim To Become Financially Independent
(You Can Be As Rich As You Want To Be If You Harness Your Inner Strength)

'He who knows when he has got enough is rich.'

- Tao Te Jing by Lao Tsu

'It is necessary to plan and to organise in order to get rich. Staying poor is very easy; poverty needs no plan.'

- Napoleon Hill

'The control of the production of wealth is the control of human life itself.'
- Hilaire Belloc

'Poverty takes away so many means of doing good, and produces so much inability to resist evil, both natural and moral, that it is by all virtuous means to be avoided...Let it be your first care, then, not to be in any man's debt. Resolve not to be poor, whatever you have spend less. Poverty is a great enemy to human happiness; it certainly destroys liberty, and it makes some virtues impracticable and others extremely difficult.'

- Dr Samuel Johnson

'Not for to hide it in a hedge,
Nor for a train attendant,
But for the glorious privilege
Of being independent.'

- Robert Burns

Most poor people imagine that most – if not all – of their worries would disap-

206

pear if they could become rich. It is a simple belief which partly explains the success of gambling all over the world. Instant wealth seems to offer instant solutions to all of life's problems.

Money certainly helps: there is no doubt that having money enables you to do many things. Whoever controls the money controls almost everything else. No one (except a pathological hoarder) wants money for its own sake: people want money because of the power it offers and the choices it gives.

Of course, theoretically, you don't need money to be a great man or woman. You don't need money in order to think or create. You don't need money in order to become a great artist or a successful inventor. You don't need money to become a leader of men, a great orator or a powerful writer.

But in practise you need money in order to do all those things. Not just to buy food, clothes and the equipment you need to do your job – but also to buy the time and independence you need. Money is valueless by itself, but used properly it can buy you a lot more than mere stuff. It can buy you freedom.

The man or woman who works as a 'slave' for eight, ten or twelve hours a day, earning a living to pay the mortgage, the grocer and other tradesmen will have little time or energy left for his own work. You need money saved so that you can continue to keep a roof over your head, food in your stomach and clothes on your back even when the work doesn't come or when you are sick.

Remove the need for worry about the three basic needs (food, shelter and clothing) and you can allow your mind to roam free – and without limits. You can afford to take risks and try out new projects – which may have a lengthy gestation period with no immediate prospect of profit – without worrying about staying warm and fed. The man or woman who lives from hand to mouth will remain impotent and helpless throughout his or her life.

The big mistake most people make is not to realise that money also means self respect, freedom and independence. Savings provide protection against 'want' and against being 'used' by an unfair, unscrupulous or exploitative employer.

If you have money you can be as eccentric as you like: poor people who behave differently are described as mad and get locked away and sedated; rich people who behave differently are described as eccentric and people pander to their every whim.

We make our own independence and freedom and we make those glorious and invaluable intangibles possible through the money we make. Savings give hope, security and the ability to wait and negotiate from a position of strength. Money gives a freedom of action and can help produce a richness of the spirit.

There is a widespread feeling in some parts of society that money is in some way unclean and that the possession of money is a reason for guilt. This is no accident. The bureaucrats who run our society know that a man who remains on the edge of poverty is close to slavery. He has to take whatever work is available at whatever rate is offered. He is in no position to negotiate from strength.

With a little money in the bank you can say 'stuff you' to anyone who tries to make you do something you don't want to do.

Money can help you find happiness, long life, enjoyment, freedom and peace of mind. Anyone who tells you otherwise is either a bureaucrat (who knows that a person who has money – and is therefore independent – is a danger to the orderly world bureaucrats like to create), or rich (and protecting what they see as their own position) or poor (and looking for excuses and alibis for being poor).

**

You don't need a plan to fail or to be poor. Being poor is easy. Anyone can do it. But if you want to succeed, or you want to be rich (or both), then you need a plan.

Like a potential lover money must be wooed. You must want to be rich. And you must be prepared to be rich. Any man who wants to get rich and who is prepared to put a little effort into it can become rich by the simple expedient of spending less than he earns; putting a little money aside on a regular basis and investing wisely.

A long time ago a Parisian called Osterwald used to visit a local public house to drink one pint of beer every evening for his supper. Every time he visited the pub he collected all the corks he could find. After eight years he sold all the corks he had collected for 8 Louis d'ors – a considerable sum – which he then invested on the stock market. He became a very rich man and when he died he left a fortune worth three million francs.

The first thing to understand – and to remember – is that rich people are not normally any cleverer than other people. Rich people do not work harder than other people, they are not better educated, they don't have a better background, they do not have better chances in life, they do not have exceptional talents, they do not have better training and they don't even have more luck. (Analyse how people make money and you will see that luck plays a very small part in things.)

People who are successful and/or who make a great deal of money invariably do so because they take full advantage of the skills they have and of the opportunities which come their way.

And they have a plan. They know exactly what they want and where they want to be in five or ten years time – and how they are going to get what they want and how they are going to get where they want to be. They also ignore the rules and they take no notice of the people who say 'you can't do that' or 'it isn't done that way.'

They also know that big money isn't dug out in bits. It flows.

***

The man or woman who intends to become independently wealthy (independent in that he can choose the work he does) will be sensible with his money. He will know how to economise so that he can always save. He will save what he can not so that he can point to a growing bank balance but so that he can regain his freedom and do what he wishes with his time.

It might be expected that most people who work hard for every penny they earn, and who have great ambitions, hopes and dreams, would be sensible with their money. But they aren't. Most people waste the money they earn on alcohol, tobacco, gambling and impressing the neighbours. They try to live up to the limit of their incomes. Many men fear the appearance of poverty more even than they fear poverty. They would rather be dishonest than poor. And so they spend every penny they earn impressing strangers. The result is that they spend their lives as wage slaves – entirely dependent on others. Those who have wasted their resources will always be slaves.

***

Money needs to be told who is the boss.

Acquiring and saving money is important but you should know when to stop.

There is a tendency among many men and women who are successful to forget what their original aims were. There is a grave danger that earning and saving for a good, sound purpose – protecting oneself and one's family and acquiring a certain independence from the world – may become saving for savings sake. Too great a regard for money may lead to miserliness, greed, selfishness and a dangerous and unhealthy love of wealth for its own sake (rather than for what it can do).

Many people continue to push themselves hard long after they have achieved their original ambitions and made all the money they are likely to need. They carry on working because they never stop to ask themselves why they are working or what they are working for. There are many men and women who are driving themselves to an early grave earning money which they will never be able to spend, or striving to satisfy an employer who will never appreciate their endeavours.

There are many individuals whose sole aim seems to be to be able to leave a lot of money so that everyone will see what their score was when the game ended for them. As if anyone cares.

The trick is always to be prepared to ask yourself 'Why?' when you are earning and, when you have earned it, 'So What?'

***

You also need to know what you mean by 'rich' and, more particularly, what you consider to be 'rich enough'. My definition is that 'rich enough' means having the money to be able to afford to live the lifestyle you enjoy, to do the things you want to do, to buy the necessities you need and (perhaps most important of all) to refuse to do the things you don't want to do without worrying about the financial consequences. That is rich. Once you are rich by your own standards and definition then the accumulation of additional wealth will be of little significance. Many people who regard themselves as poor could comfortably regard themselves as rich if they would reduce wastage and unnecessary expectations.

Those who become most truly independent through the accumulation of money, and who acquire the greatest satisfaction and contentment through their money, are those who have raised their wealth above their wants. That, after all, is the only definition of 'rich' which really counts. The man who has enough or more than he needs in order to be independent is rich enough.

***

It is a mistake to think of success (and, in particular, financial success) as a satisfactory aim for life. It isn't enough. Making money by itself is not enough of a challenge and if you get there it will become boring and pointless unless you have some deeper purpose.

Remember that people who have worked hard for many years often find it difficult to know what to do with their leisure hours. A large proportion of successful men and women rarely – if ever – take proper holidays. They could afford the best holidays in the world. They could earn all the money they need by simply working for twenty or fewer hours a week. But they don't know how to enjoy themselves when they aren't working.

If money and success cost too much in terms of life itself then the money and the success are too dearly bought. Making money can, if you are not careful, eventually become the goal instead of the means to a goal. Why else would so many men and women with big salaries and comfortable bank balances fret about making even more?

***

Rich people may not have the same problems as poor people – but most of them certainly do have problems, fears and anxieties. Money can make life smoother (it means you can take a taxi instead of the bus) but it does not eradicate problems.

The commonest, biggest and most important fear rich people have is that they will one day lose all their money. Once a rich person acquires this fear it tends to increase in intensity with wealth. After all, the more money you've got the more you have got to lose.

This fear is particularly likely to strike those who have acquired their wealth through luck or good fortune rather than through skill, ambition, talent and hard work. The individual who has earned his money will know that he can probably do it all again if necessary. And, if he looks back, he will know that earning the money was probably just as much fun as having it. He will not be quite so frightened of poverty as the individual who has acquired his wealth through a legacy or a lucky gambling win.

When you acquire money you should remember that the best things money can buy you are not luxury homes, yachts, private aeroplanes or chauffeur driven limousines but security, leisure, freedom and time. And you really do not need as much money for those 'luxuries' as you do if you start acquiring millionaire toys and enjoying the sort of physical lifestyle that a millionaire should enjoy. (In the section headed 'Do You Really Need All That Stuff? I have explained how the physical trappings of wealth − i.e. the possessions with which rich people tend to surround themselves − can be a burden.)

***

You must make sure that you manage your money. Don't let it manage you.

One big mistake people often make when they acquire more money than they need to buy daily essentials is to decide to try to increase their wealth dramatically.

This can be a fatal mistake.

The businessmen who has made his money through selling a product he knows well, or the talented individual who has made a fortune through his talents, or the lucky individual who has acquired money through good fortune, may all decide that they are going to double their wealth in a matter of months through aggressive investing.

This is commonly a quick route back to poverty for being greedy will often result in disaster.

People often forget that whenever they buy something as an investment someone else must be selling. The investment that you are certain is a good buy is, to someone else, a good sell. Whenever you decide that 'now' is a good time to buy someone else must have decided that 'now' is a good time to sell.

It is wiser, by far, to find a spread of safe investments which will enable you to make a good, sound, steady return without worry. You can then get on with the work you know or, if you wish, with having a good time, free of the anxieties which will inevitably ensue if you start dabbling in a world about which you know nothing. If you can get an investment return on your money of 1% above inflation then your money is making money for you.

As far as money is concerned you must remember not to trust anyone who offers advice. Don't trust banks. Don't trust investment advisers. Don't trust stockbrokers. Don't trust insurance companies. They all want you for your money. They pretend to like you. But they want your money.

The only person in the world you can trust to look after your money properly is – *you*. Always remember that your investments do not love you and will not show you any loyalty. Just because you keep a share through good times and bad times you cannot expect the share to give you a good return.

Remember that all investment is gambling. The odds differ but whenever you invest your money you are taking a gamble.

Remember too that whatever else they may say governments and society want you to spend all your money – and to keep on spending way past your cash limits.

The more you spend the richer society will become – and the more of a slave you will become. And the individual who *owes* money is a real slave to society.

CHAPTER TWENTY ONE
Take Risks – But Calculate The Odds First

'The battle of life is, in most cases, fought up hill...if there were no difficulties there would be no success; if there were nothing to struggle for, there would be nothing to be achieved...All experience of life, indeed, serves to prove that the impediments thrown in the way of human advancement may for the most part be overcome by steady good conduct, honest zeal, activity, perseverance, and above all by a determined resolution to surmount difficulties, and stand up manfully against misfortune.'

- Samuel Smiles

The saddest words in any language are: 'If only...', 'It might have been...' and 'I wonder what would have happened if...'.

Make two lists. On the first list write down all the errors you have committed and which you now regret; the mistakes you know that you have made and which you now wish you could have avoided. On the second list write down all the errors of omission you have made; the things you haven't done but which you now wish you had done.

Whichever list is the longer will tell you a great deal about yourself – and will, perhaps, give you a hint about how you should conduct your life in the future.

If your first list is the longest then maybe you are being a little reckless – and taking too many risks. But if the second list is the longest (and many people are surprised to find that this is the case) then you should perhaps be taking more risks

***

If you are going to take risks successfully you need to be able to assess the bottom line with some degree of accuracy. Only when you know the bottom line will you be able comfortably to take chances that you might otherwise avoid.

Constantly ask yourself: 'What is the worst that can happen?' 'What will/could happen if I do/don't do this?'

Whenever you are taking a risk find out the bottom line: what is the worst that can possibly happen. You may be surprised to hear that there are not many risks which can make the sky fall in or stop the world going round.

***

Most of us regard risk taking as both hazardous and unnecessary. And many people would say that they try to avoid risks whenever they can. Some people probably seriously believe that they are wise in constantly doing all they can to eradicate risk from their lives.

But taking risks is a necessary and unavoidable part of life. Every decision worth making is potentially dangerous. There is a risk in every venture you undertake – personal, professional or commercial.

Every time you get out of bed or walk out of your home you are taking a risk. Every time you make an investment you are taking a risk. (Despite words such as 'guaranteed' there is no such thing as a safe investment. Even a government bond can be risky if the government falls.) Every time you begin a new relationship or a new business project you are taking a risk. It is impossible to live without taking risks.

But what you can do is to make an attempt to quantify the risks before beginning any new venture. Only when you have quantified the risks can you make a sound judgement about whether or not an individual risk is worth taking. You must put risks into perspective.

I know of a man who takes vitamin supplements because he believes that the vitamin will help reduce his risk of developing cancer. But he smokes heavily. If he really wants to reduce his cancer risk he would be much better advised to stop smoking.

***

One of the great tragedies of life is that we tend to take fewer risks as we get older. We become more wary of danger and more aware of the things that can go wrong. The danger is that a preoccupation with safety may reduce the possibility of success.

We should take more – not less – risks as we get older. After all, as we age we have less to lose. Regularity, habit and commonsense tend to paralyse. Not taking risks is sometimes the riskiest and most dangerous option.

The security and comfort which ordinary people enjoy has always been achieved because exceptional individuals have been prepared to take risks.

You should learn to take risks which have the highest possible upside and the lowest possible downside. In order to succeed you have to be able to assess risks accurately. You should learn from your own mistakes but (and this is just as important) you should also learn from other peoples mistakes. Knowing the bottom line leads to confidence which leads to success.

CHAPTER TWENTY TWO
You Have More Power Than You Think You Have

'Power may be defined as organised and intelligently directed knowledge.'
— Napoleon Hill

You need power to make money and to keep it. You need power to remain independent and to retain your freedom.

But where does power come from? How can ordinary people obtain power?

The answer is disarmingly simple.

If you add knowledge, ambition, faith, desire, plans and persistence together you usually end up with power.

Mahatma Gandhi obtained power by persuading over 200 million people to coordinate their minds, bodies and spirits for a single purpose.

CHAPTER TWENTY THREE
Do You Really Need All That Stuff?

*'No man ever stood the lower in my estimation for having a patch in his clothes;
yet I am sure that there is greater anxiety, commonly, to have fashionable, or
at least clean and un-patched clothes, than to have a sound conscience.'*
- Henry David Thoreau

'Happiness is found in doing, not merely in possessing.'
- Napoleon Hill

*'Fill your house with gold and jade,
And it can no longer be fully guarded.
If you set store by your riches and honour,
You will only reap a crop of calamities.'*
- Tao Te Jing by Lao Tsu

I know a handyman who earns his living painting, bricklaying and doing bits of carpentry. He's a real jack-of-all-trades and he's very good at what he does. But it's difficult to get him to come and do anything because he only works two or three days a week. The rest of the time he messes around on his boat or in his garden.

A few months ago I asked him why he didn't work harder.

He explained that he didn't see any point in earning more money than he needed to satisfy his fairly simple needs. He told me that he has paid off his mortgage, that although old and rather battered his car is his own and that he has all the furniture he wants. He has, he told me, managed to put aside a few hundred pounds in the building society for emergencies.

I asked him if his wife was happy with this philosophical approach to employment. He said that she was very happy and that they spent much of the week gardening together, walking along the cliffs or, on sunny days, bobbing around in their little boat. He also told me that he and his wife don't have holidays away from home because for them home is a pretty constant holiday but that they do spend a day every month travelling to demonstrations against hunting, vivisection and other examples of cruelty to animals.

He also told me that because his earnings are low he pays hardly any income tax.

I found his attitude enormously refreshing. This local handyman is leading the life of a true revolutionary. I suspect that Henry David Thoreau, the philosopher of Walden Pond, would have been proud of him.

Before you dismiss the handyman's lifestyle as impractical ask yourself how much of your life you spend earning money to buy things you don't really need and are only buying to impress people you don't really care about.

Here's a simple little exercise you can try.

Make a list of everything other than food that you've bought in the last six months. By the side of each item on your list make a note of the price you paid.

Then divide your after-tax annual income by the number of hours you work to find out how much you earn an hour. Don't forget to deduct any essential business expenses from your income before you do this calculation.

Now you can easily use this figure to find out how long you had to work to buy each of the items on your first list.

This can be a frightening exercise for you'll quickly realise that you've given a great deal of your life in order to buy junk that you don't really need.

Add up the cost of all the unnecessary stuff you bought last year and work out how much of your life you wasted earning money to buy stuff that hasn't improved or changed your life.

The whole point of modern advertising is to persuade people to buy things they don't need; to turn shallow wants into desperate 'must haves'.

It is skilful advertising which encourages otherwise sane people to spend a fortune on double glazing which will never pay for itself and to spend thousands of pounds ripping out a perfectly serviceable kitchen and replacing it with another, slightly different kitchen.

And, of course, the more money you have to earn to buy all this stuff that you don't really need the more income tax you will have had to pay.

If you are happy with the things the government buys with your money then you won't mind giving them great chunks of it. But are you really happy with what they do with it?

I'm not suggesting that the handyman's life style is right for everyone.

But you might like to think about all this a little for the next day or two.

***

We live in a society which encourages the accumulation of goods: a smart, shiny motor car; a beautiful home; a wardrobe full of expensive, beautiful designed clothes – these are what we are encouraged to work towards.

If you are not careful the stuff you think you own could end up owning you. Our world has been taken over by a lot of materialistic, acquisitive nonsense. We buy telephones shaped like the sports cars we cannot afford, garden gnomes, coffee table books that no one ever reads, fancy toilet roll holders, lotions to make fat thighs thin, special pens to help us pick our lottery numbers (described as 'great conversation pieces' though it is surely a sorry sort of conversation which needs that sort of boost), creams to make small breasts melon sized and to make melon sized breasts positively breathtaking and all sorts of other nonsenses. We buy things for the sake of buying. We buy presents that are neither beautiful nor useful.

Some years ago I bought myself a Rolls Royce.

I tell you this not out of pride or vanity but because I learned valuable lessons through this, and the subsequent, experiences. And maybe you can learn something too from my mistakes.

A socialist in Britain once suggested that there should be an extra tax on large and extremely expensive cars. He was wrong. Large and extremely expensive cars should not be taxed at all: they are a curse on those who own them.

My Rolls Royce wasn't a new one but a gracious, elderly classic, roughly the size of Belgium. It was so large that I needed planning permission to park it and so thirsty that I could leave the fuel pump pouring gas into the tank while I went and had my lunch.

For the first day or two owning the car was fun. But it quickly became something of a nightmare. Every time there were problems with the car – or it needed a service – I had to send it on a several hundred mile journey back to the garage from which I had bought it. Because the car was valuable it usually made the journey on a low loader. At the time I was living in a house in the country and the low loader used to have great difficulty making it through the lanes.

Eventually, there were serious problems with the paintwork on the car and I sent the car back.

But I hadn't got the idea of owning a large, luxurious motor car entirely out of my system. I had always promised myself that if I ever had enough money I would buy a Bentley. So within days of sending the Rolls Royce back I bought my first Bentley. This, like the Rolls Royce, was rather elderly, extremely large, and quite beautiful.

The snag with the car was that it was so beautiful and so well preserved that I was rather frightened of damaging it. So, believe it or not, (and I confess I now find this rather difficult to believe myself) I bought a second, more modern, Bentley for day-to-day use.

Those two Bentleys more or less ran my life for the next couple of years.

One evening I left one of the cars parked outside a Town Hall (just a few yards away from a police station) while I attended a birthday party. When I got back to the car it had been deliberately scratched. A vandal had dragged a key, a penknife or some other sharp metal object along the boot, the car doors and the bonnet.

The first respray wasn't successful because it was difficult to match the colour of the paint and in the end the car had to be completely resprayed at a cost of around £10,000. Naturally, the insurance company declined to pay the whole of this sum.

After that I didn't dare leave either of the Bentleys parked without someone to watch them and make sure that they were not damaged.

The costs of maintenance were phenomenal too (I remember paying around £1,500 for an exhaust pipe for one of the cars – and being told that I was really rather lucky to get it at such a bargain price).

Since the insurance company stipulated that both cars had to be kept in a locked garage I had to get special permission if I wanted to go away for the night and park either car at a hotel.

The final straw came when, following advice from a specialist garage, I found myself buying a high pressure hose to make sure that the cars were kept properly cleaned – there was a lot of mud in the area where I lived.

When I discovered that I had to find someone to operate the hose I suddenly realised how absurd the whole exercise had become. My two Bentleys had become a drain. I was over-Bentleyed by a factor of two.

The ownership of these vehicles, designed to give me fun, was causing me aggravation and trouble, anxiety and worry. Within a day or two of realising this, I sold both cars to a dealer for a fraction of their value. I just wanted to get rid of them.

As the cars disappeared from my driveway I felt a tinge of sadness but mostly I felt free. And I realised that I had learned a very costly but extremely valuable lesson.

Today, when I see someone driving a Rolls Royce, a Bentley or some other expensive motor car I feel nothing but pity. I had bought those motor cars to add something to my life. But although they had each given me some pleasure they had all taken far more from me than they had given back. I hadn't owned the cars – they had owned me.

***

There are several valuable and important lessons to be learned here.

First, do not allow material possessions, belongings of any kind, to take over your life. Next time you are buying something other than an everyday item ask yourself if you are making the purchase because you want it or need it or because you have been persuaded to buy it by someone else – or, worse still, by society. And then remember how many hours you have to work to earn that item.

And regularly take time to go through all your possessions and sort out those which you want to keep and those that you neither want nor need to keep. Sorting through ('spring-cleaning') your possessions has several advantages. It will enable you to see exactly what you have got (you may be surprised to discover things you had forgotten you owned) and it will also enable you to convert unwanted items into cash. You will have more space available and you will be able to find and use the belongings which are left more easily and more effectively. Clear out the stuff you own at regular intervals and throw away everything which doesn't add value to your life. If you haven't used something or worn something for six or twelve months sell it or give it to a charity shop.

And always remember William Morris's saying: 'Have nothing in your home that you do not know to be useful or believe to be beautiful.'

CHAPTER TWENTY FOUR
Use Technology – Don't Let It Use You
(You Don't Have To Use It Just Because It's Been Invented)

'Year by year we are becoming better equipped to accomplish the things we are striving for. But what are we striving for?'

- Dr Lawrence Peter

Writing in his HSL newsletter not long ago my dear friend Chevalier Harry D. Schultz said: 'Ironically, the technology of fax and answering machines, e-mail, cellular phones, and networked computers that promised to save us time and make our lives less stressful, only increased the urgency we feel to respond and 'be switched on' at all times. One would think with all these high tech 'conveniences' we would be putting in shorter work days and enjoying more leisure time. Sadly, just the opposite is true. With the pace of society spiralling frenetically, joy will become increasingly elusive unless you seek it out by taking conscious control of your life, your time, and your priorities.'

Harry Schultz is absolutely right. Instead of giving us more freedom and greater opportunities new equipment often provides more stress and greater pressure.

For example, the fax machine has made it possible for us to communicate with one another far more speedily. Before the introduction of the fax machine it would take several days to move a letter or a document from one desk to another. Today the same letter or document can be moved from one desk to another within seconds.

The result is that the recipient is under great pressure to respond speedily.

And so, in the end, everyone communicates far more frequently than they did before.

But the increase in the amount of communicating does not automatically result in an increase in the amount of profitable (in all senses of the word) endeavour.

Technology doesn't make life easier, it just makes life faster. Technology enables us to do more things and it enables us to do them more speedily but it is doesn't enable us to do them better, easier or with more style.

Think about it and I suspect you'll agree with me that Harry Schultz is absolutely right.

Most of us are surrounded by labour saving gadgets which add to our daily stress rather than reducing it. Worse still, we often allow those gadgets to dominate our lives and our thinking. Telephones, fax machines and computers bring messages to us so quickly that we feel we must attend to them immediately.

But why should you always rush to answer the telephone or fax when it is inconvenient to do so, or when you really want to rest and relax?

How many times in your life is it truly essential to produce an immediate response?

Many gadgets are expensive, complicated and unreliable. We fall for them because we believe they will make our lives easier. But often they do just the opposite.

Take a close look at every facet of your life. Throw out the gadgets which are more trouble than they are worth. Try not to bring equipment from work into your home area. And don't allow any sort of equipment (particularly communications equipment) to rule your life.

Don't be afraid to turn off telephones, television sets and computers. Make a real effort to use gadgets to *improve* your life – and reduce your workload.

And when you can feel yourself being pressurised into dealing with numerous apparently urgent and vital problems stop and ask yourself just how significant those problems will be in six months or six years time. That should help put the apparent urgency of those problems into perspective.

Just because the technology is available it doesn't necessarily follow that it is essential to use it – or, indeed, that it is or would be wise to use it.

Sometimes the simpler technologies are much better.

As I was writing this chapter I telephoned a friend who works in a very large organisation. She was out. The colleague who answered the telephone told me that he would leave a message on her computer. My heart sank. I realised that if he put a message into her e-mail it would probably lie there unnoticed for days.

'Exactly what do you mean by 'put a message on her computer'?' I asked him.

'I'll scribble a note on a yellow sticky pad and put the note on her computer screen,' said the wise man.

CHAPTER TWENTY FIVE
Never Do Another Day's Work In Your Life
(And Still Get Rich)

'Work is my chief pleasure.'

- Mozart

Work takes up a large part of most peoples' lives. And it is work which usually defines you and your life.

One of the first questions strangers invariably ask is: 'What do you do for a living?'

When describing someone to a third person their occupation is usually something we include within the first few sentences. ('He's a teacher. Tall, middle aged, slightly scruffy but has a great sense of humour.' 'She's in her mid twenties, blonde, bubbly and very bright. She works as a hairdresser at a salon in town.')

And yet, tragically, work is, to most people, a tiresome and largely unpleasant experience. If they get pleasure out of their work it is often despite the work they do – rather than because of it. Their enjoyment may, for example, come from the relationships they have with the people with whom they work. In many cases the only pleasure comes from the weekly or monthly pay check.

What a tragedy this all is. How much better it is to find work that you enjoy and look forward to. If you enjoy and look forward to your work then you will do it far better, far more effectively, far more productively, and consequently far more profitably, than if it is something which you suffer purely for the financial reward.

You should not regard work as a burden. If you do then you are doing the wrong job. You should rethink your attitude to work completely.

Almost without exception the people who make a real success of their lives – and who make a great deal of money – are the people who enjoy what they do for a living. They look forward to work because it provides many satisfactions in addition to the financial one.

As far as work is concerned the most fortunate people in the world are those who say: 'I love my job. Don't tell anyone but I'd do it even if they didn't pay me to do it.' These are people who get rich without ever doing a day's real 'work'.

Work is anything you don't want to do. If you make sure that your work is its own reward then the chances are that you will do well at it. The more you don't want to do it the more it becomes work.

CHAPTER TWENTY SIX
Don't Be Afraid To Be A Rebel

'The barriers are not erected which can say to aspiring talents and industry:
'Thus far and no farther'.'

- Ludwig van Beethoven

We should all be disrespectful to our leaders. Their duty is to lead. Our duty is to remind them that we put them there. Without criticism leaders become dictators.

What is authority there for but to be rebelled against? Unless people rebelled there would be no need for authority.

It is not unreasonable to argue that rebellion is essential for the survival of authority. Anyone who rebels could reasonably argue that he was helping to sustain authority. The sole real function of grey, politically correct authority is to provide a sounding board for the rebels whose ancestors created our present society and whose descendants will create tomorrow's society. Authoritarians should be deeply grateful to rebels and anarchists for without rebellions and threats of anarchy they would not know they had authority and would never know the joy they doubtless obtain from abusing it and finding new ways to circumvent justice.

You should not be afraid to be unconventional. The boys and girls who seemed to be the high 'achievers' at school often turn out to be life's drones. Those who are popular with their teachers and who do particularly well at school usually end up doing something dreary like managing the local sewage works.

But you must use humour in order to take the sting out of the hatred and the fury of the conventional. If you attack a conventional man for being ordinary he will hate you because, in his heart, he knows that you are right. But if you laughingly apologise for your eccentricity then he will accept you.

Throughout my career I have frequently been warned that the things I have done will ruin my career, will prevent me earning a living and will stop people publishing my work or buying my books.

I confess that I now feel uncomfortable if something I plan to do is praised or supported by those whom I regard as conventional.

Chapter Twenty Seven
Be Positive!

'Impossible is a word only to be found in the dictionary of fools.'

- Napoleon Bonaparte

Decide today that you will have no more destructive, negative or unproductive thoughts. Banish fear, jealousy, hatred, revenge, resentment, greed, superstition and anger. Fill your mind, instead, with love, faith, desire, enthusiasm and hope.

Every time you find yourself face to face with a problem try to see how you can deal with it, how you can get round it, what you can learn from it and how the experience can strengthen you. Try to discover what good you can derive from something that seems wholly bad.

If you ask yourself 'Why do I feel so bad?' or 'Why is life treating me so unfairly?' then the only answers you can possibly receive will substantiate and strengthen your feelings of failure.

You must start asking yourself questions which will lead to an improvement in your life. Try asking yourself things like: 'How can I improve my life?', 'How can I find myself a better job?', 'How can I make this job more enjoyable?'

If you constantly think in a negative way (for example: 'I feel frustrated', 'Nothing is going my way') then you will simply create further discontent and unhappiness.

On the other hand, if you say to yourself: 'What can I learn from this?', 'What can I do about that?' 'How can I change this to my advantage?' then you will move forwards, rather than backwards.

Ask yourself questions which take you further on in your life. Wallowing in the past is easy. It takes courage to move forward and to face each problem with determination.

By taking a positive attitude you will enrich and strengthen your mind.

(And remember that your mind is your spiritual estate and your body is its home. You should look after your mind and your body better than you look after all your physical possessions. Your mind and your body are the only two possessions which cannot be replaced.)

**

You should take care not to spend too much time with people who depress you with their negative attitudes. Those who are filled with negativity often spend their time mentally besieged by their own negative aura; spreading gloom, doom and a sense of failure to all those around them.

If other people tell you often enough that you are no good at something you will eventually come to believe them. And then, in due course, your belief will become reality.

The truth is that you can do anything you want to do if only you believe you can. Don't worry about aiming to win; just aim to do your best.

And learn to differentiate between positive, constructive criticism (which can be useful) and negative, carping criticism which is unlikely to add any value to your life.

A few years ago I used to worry enormously about what critics had to say. When they wrote things which were blatantly unfair or simply untrue I felt a burning need to respond. I have learnt to ignore much (if not all) inaccurately based criticism.

Most negative criticism which is published is written by individuals who have achieved nothing of value in their own lives or who are biased or prejudiced because their views have been 'bought' with a small cheque.

You should even learn to take a positive attitude towards your mistakes. Be careful not to let your mistakes depress you too much. Instead of allowing your mistakes to knock you backwards make sure that you gain something from them.

Everyone makes mistakes. If you spend your time merely regretting then you will gain nothing from your errors. But if you make sure that you learn from your errors then you will eventually realise that mistakes are an essential, vital part of progress.

Ask yourself these two simple questions. First, if you had a chance to relive your life up until today would you avoid the mistakes you made before? Second, and more importantly, would you see the warning signs – the small signs that signal the start of major problems ahead?

Remember that you do not have to explain, excuse or justify the things you do. And nor should you change what you do every time a stranger criticises you or offers some negative comment. You can be anything you want to be and whoever you want to be. All you have to do is go out and do it.

Fill your mind with positive emotions and there will be no room for the negative ones. Concentrate on looking for solutions and answers rather than worrying about questions and problems. Learn from your mistakes – and don't be afraid to keep on making them!

CHAPTER TWENTY EIGHT
Learn The Secrets Of Negotiation − And Remember That Everything Is Negotiable

---

'The family of emotions 'gratitude, friendship, respect etc' on which a stable society is based lose their meaning when it comes to the nomads, whose social conditions have created a different spirit. It is absurd to expect gratitude from the Moors, as it would be absurd to condemn them for being ungrateful. The sentiment of gratitude in its European sense follows from a set of social conditions in which contacts and needs are permanent; a given nomadic tribe will have a very different need tomorrow from the one it has today.'

- Antoine de Saint-Exupery

Everyone negotiates. The local car dealer and the real estate agent expect you to negotiate when they give you a price. Whether you are buying a product or a service you have to be capable of negotiating.

There are several simple guidelines to follow when negotiating.

First, you must know what your opponent needs and what his deadline is.

Second, don't bluff unless you are extremely adept at it.

Third, don't be afraid to change your mind. Indeed, if you acquire a reputation for changing your mind a great deal it can make it tricky for other people to negotiate with you for they will find it difficult to predict exactly what you are going to do or how you are going to react to given circumstances.

Fourth, you must be prepared to walk away from the deal. You must be always be prepared for the deal to break down. If you are negotiating for a higher salary you must always be prepared to resign. You must do everything you can to ensure that you are always in a position where you can resign. And you must be sure that the person with whom you are negotiating knows that you can and will (if necessary) resign.

CHAPTER TWENTY NINE
Beware Of Compromise

'I am the master of my fate, I am the captain of my soul.'

- William Henley

Most people accept compromises in their lives. Every day they make another small compromise. Each compromise may be very small and may seem unimportant in itself. But although each compromise may appear to be no more than an unavoidable, incidental and momentary concession to the requirements of the real world, each compromise takes them further and further from the path which will lead them to their destination in life.

You owe it to yourself to get the most out of your life and your talents – and everything you do.

***

Jack wanted to be an artist but he had difficulty selling his work when he left college. And he desperately wanted to be able to buy a car. So he got a temporary job designing chocolate box covers for a local company. And while he was working there, earning enough money to buy his car, someone offered him a job on the company magazine. The money seemed attractive and the job didn't sound too bad. And it was nice to be able to afford decent clothes and records and books and pay for a meal in a restaurant once in a while. And then he met a girl and they decided to set up home together so they found a slightly larger flat with a bigger monthly rental. And then he had commitments. And then the girl got pregnant and a full time job came up and it was important that he took the job.

And suddenly, before he knew what had happened, it was ten years later. And he was too tired to do any of the work he dreamt of doing.

One day he met a former classmate who had carved out a career as an artist, painting exactly what he wanted to paint in exactly the way he wanted to paint, who was having his first gallery showing. And Jack thought to himself what a lucky fellow the chap was.

But the fellow wasn't just lucky.

He had spent ten years in penury, with no car and no flat. He wasn't lucky. He was just determined. He knew what he wanted out of life and he went for it.

Life is all about choices.

No one does what he doesn't want to do.

Jack made his choice and he built his life on compromise.

But it is still not too late for him to change.

If he has the courage.

CHAPTER THIRTY
If Your Ship Doesn't Come In, Swim Out To Meet It

'Half the failures in life arise from pulling in one's horse while he is leaping.'
- Samuel Smiles

'Either I will find a way or make one.'
- Family crest with a pick-axe on it

Imaginative, thoughtful and creative individuals have always had a hard time.

Look back in history and you will find countless examples of citizens who were harassed or persecuted simply because they dared to think for themselves – and tried to share their thoughts with others. The history books are crammed with examples of men who fought for years against ill fortune, poverty, jealous enemies, vested interests and a thousand other hazards.

Our world has never welcomed the original, the challenging, the inspirational or the passionate and has always preferred the characterless to the thought provoking.

Today, more than ever, the individual who dares to speak out against the establishment will face ridicule and contempt. Even success itself is often derided by those who themselves have no talent and no determination. The 'posh' newspapers are full of patronising articles by self appointed icons of the world of culture who are quite free of talent or skills.

Those who dare to speak out against the establishment have always been regarded as dangerous heretics. The iconoclast has never been a welcome figure in any age.

* Confucius, the Chinese philosopher, was dismissed by his political masters and his books were burned. Those who didn't burn his books within 30 days were branded and condemned to forced labour. Two and a half thousand

years later Confucius's influence was still considered so dangerous that Chairman Mao banned his works.

* Described by the Delphic Oracle as the wisest man in the world, Greek teacher Socrates was accused of corrupting the youth of Athens, arrested for being an evildoer and 'a person showing curiosity, searching into things under the earth and above the heaven and teaching all this to others'. Socrates was condemned to death.

* Dante, the Italian poet, was banished from Florence and condemned to be burnt at the stake if ever captured.

* After they had failed to silence him with threats and bribes the Jewish authorities excommunicated Spinoza in Amsterdam because he refused to toe the party line, refused to think what other people told him he must think and insisted on maintaining his intellectual independence. He and his work were denounced as 'forged in Hell by a renegade Jew and the devil'.

* Galileo, the seventeenth century Italian mathematician, astrologer and scientist got into terrible trouble with the all powerful Church for daring to support Copernicus, who had had the temerity to claim that the planets revolved around the sun but who did not dare to publish his discoveries. Galileo lived in exile, wandering from city to city. He ended up in prison.

* Jesus Christ was crucified by an establishment which regarded him as a danger.

* Henry David Thoreau, surely the kindest, wisest philosopher who has ever lived, was imprisoned for sticking to his ideals.

I could go on with this list but I suspect that you've begun to get the idea. Original thinkers do not go down well.

But although all these individuals were persecuted for their beliefs – and many of them died for their ideals – they did at least have a chance to develop, to learn, to speak out, to teach, to write, to publish and to attempt to change things.

Today, things are worse than they have ever been for the iconoclast.

Incompetence and mediocrity thrive and are now subsidised, supported and encouraged by our increasingly bureaucratic and intrusive society. Schoolteachers and social workers encourage mediocrity because they themselves are mediocre. Talent frightens them witless.

Among bureaucrats and administrators incompetence and mediocrity are esteemed virtues; the besuited morons revere the banal and worship the bland. They support the establishment in all that it does and everything it stands for and they sneer at and scorn the unusual or the eccentric.

Politicians are frightened of anything new or challenging. They reject the innovative, the creative and the imaginative in favour of the accustomed, the comfortable and the ordinary.

It will not, I fear, be long before mediocrity and incompetence are regarded as essential virtues; the necessary building blocks for personal and professional success. In schools mediocrity will be taught as a social necessity; compulsory for commercial or personal success. Creativity will be regarded as politically incorrect and therefore unacceptable. Originality will be suffocated.

The danger now is that the great thinkers of tomorrow will never even develop — let alone survive or thrive to find themselves struggling against the eternally powerful barriers erected by the establishment of the day.

This is a tragedy of monumental proportions for the lone eccentric voice, speaking out against perceived wisdom, is often right and the experts and the officials are often wrong.

If the politically correct have their way and the social workers and bureaucrats take over the world there will be no place in the 21st century for great thinkers and leaders like Christ, Paracelsus, Galileo, Confucius or Socrates.

***

Men do not achieve distinction through luck or by accident but through industry and hard work. As Samuel Smiles once put it: 'Nothing creditable can be accomplished without application and diligence.' Perseverance often leads to success but the road to success is not always a smooth one and many of those who have made the greatest contributions to our knowledge have had to fight hard against ridicule.

Andreas Vesalius, born in 1514, achieved eternal fame but contemporary notoriety as the author of the first textbook of human anatomy: 'De Humanis Corporis Fabrica'. Vesalius rejected many of the traditional (and grossly erroneous) beliefs about anatomy but this earned him official disapproval since the medical establishment firmly believed that the traditional texts could not possibly be wrong.

Poor Vesalius was unable to cope with the outcry his anatomical researches produced. He burnt his remaining manuscripts, abandoned any further study of anatomy and lived as a vagabond. He was accused of heresy, body snatching and was nearly executed. Eventually, forced to make a pilgrimage to the Holy Land, he died in a shipwreck.

When Ambrose Pare, the great French surgeon, first started work as an army surgeon it was accepted practice to stop a haemorrhage by sealing a wound with a red hot iron. Amputations were performed with a red hot knife and the wounds which were left were sealed with boiling oil. One day Pare ran out of boiling oil and used a mild emollient to dress the wounds of the men he was treating. It wasn't an experiment. He simply had no alternative.

Pare worried a great deal about what he had done but the next day he found that his patients were not only healthy but that they were also in less pain than the men whose wounds had been sealed with boiling oil. Pare was a wise enough and observant enough man to learn from this. And from that day onwards he started dressing wounds with an emollient rather than boiling oil. He also introduced ligatures, artificial limbs and surgical instruments such as artery forceps.

Inevitably, Pare met the usual fate of innovators and reformers. He was denounced by other surgeons as dangerous and unprofessional. Older surgeons banded together to oppose him and in their attempts to discredit him they attacked him for all sorts of other things – for example, his ignorance of Latin and Greek.

Pare succeeded, however, because all the soldiers asked for him by name. They wanted to be treated by him because they knew that they would suffer less pain. They weren't interested in whether or not he could speak Greek or Latin.

British doctor William Harvey spent eight years in the 17th century researching the circulation of the blood before he published his findings. His patience was rewarded with ridicule. He won over no converts from among other doctors but he received a great deal of abuse. He lost many friends and his practice shrank in size.

The American anatomist, lecturer, poet and novelist Oliver Wendell Holmes was similarly unsuccessful when, in 1843, he read to the Boston Society for Medical Improvement a paper 'On the Contagiousness of Puerperal Fever' in which he explained his theory that the disease could be carried from patient to patient by doctors themselves. Holmes recommended that pregnant women in labour should not be attended by doctors who had been in contact with possible sources of infection. He also suggested that surgeons should consider changing their clothes and washing their hands in calcium chloride after leaving a patient with puerperal fever. His controversial recommendations annoyed a large part of the medical establishment and his advice was ignored completely.

An even worse fate befell Ignaz Philipp Semmelweiss who, three years later in 1846, at the age of 28, became an assistant in one of the obstetric wards at the Allgemeines Krankenhaus in Vienna, Austria. Semmelweiss noticed that the number of women dying in his ward was considerably higher than that in another obstetric ward at the hospital. The difference was so noticeable that women frequently begged, in tears, not to be taken to Semmelweiss's ward.

Deciding that the difference in the number of deaths had to be due to something other than the quality (or lack of quality) of his own clinical skills Semmelweiss looked for an explanation. He found one in the fact that the ward with the better survival rate was looked after by the hospital's midwives, while in his own ward medical students assisted the obstetricians with the deliveries. Semmelweiss discovered that students came into the ward straight from the dissecting room and often performed intimate examinations with hands which only minutes before had been delving into corpses. The midwives, on the other hands, never went near to the dissecting room and, on the contrary, had been taught that cleanliness was an essential part of obstetric care.

Semmelweiss's theory that the women were contracting puerperal fever from the students was strengthened when he attended the post mortem on another doctor in the hospital. This unfortunate man, a Dr Kolletschka, had died from a wound he had received in the dissecting room, and when his body was opened, Semmelweiss noticed that the internal pathological signs were similar to those seen in women with puerperal fever.

Convinced that his theory about the spread of infection was correct, Semmelweiss insisted that students and doctors coming from the dissecting room should wash their hands in a solution of calcium chloride before examining female patients. The precautions he introduced produced a dramatic drop in the number of deaths on his ward – from one in ten to approximately one in a hundred within two years.

Like Oliver Wendell Holmes, Semmelweiss came under a tremendous amount of pressure from those colleagues at the hospital and many eminent obstetricians elsewhere who disagreed with his theory, despite the evidence. Unable to cope with the opposition Semmelweiss left Vienna for Budapest, where he eventually became Professor of Obstetrics. Unfortunately, however, the pressure brought about by the controversy proved too much for this mild and thoughtful man and he died in a mental hospital a few years later. Semmelweiss had been ostracised and punished by the medical profession for daring to criticise practical procedures and for having the temerity to put patients before the establishment.

The history of medicine is full of men whose original work has been ignored or condemned by the establishment of the day. But no martyr in medicine suffered more or contributed more than Ignaz Semmelweiss, whose courage and persistence led directly to changes in medical practice which resulted in massive improvements in the quality of obstetric care throughout the world.

One of the most controversial characters in medical history, who may well have contributed as much as any other individual in the history of medical science, was Aureolus Philippus Theophrastus Bombastus von Hohenheim (known to his chums and his enemies as Paracelsus). Paracelsus made himself enemies all over Europe because he tried to revolutionise medicine and medical thinking in the sixteenth century. Paracelsus was the greatest influence on medical thinking since Hippocrates but the establishment regarded him as a troublemaker.

Paracelsus was born in 1493 in Switzerland. He died just 48 years later but in that relatively short space of time he tore into the precepts and paradigms of established medical thinking with all the zeal of an inspired missionary. Genius has been defined as common sense intensified and Paracelsus confirms that definition. He was a genius who was blessed with the two essentials: ideas and determination.

Paracelsus believed that it was possible to learn only by experience and personal study and he travelled widely in his search for useful information. He visited Spain, Portugal, France, Italy, Germany, Scandinavia, Egypt, Arabia, Palestine, Russia, Poland, Turkey, Holland and England. He wrote books, lectured, practised medicine and argued in Montpelier, Padua, Bologna, Basle, Vienna, Leipzig, Heidelberg, Cologne and just about all the major medical centres of Europe. He studied alchemy, astrology and herbal medicine and spoke to witches and midwives in his search for information.

It was Paracelsus's revolutionary belief that a doctor's job was to understand the causes and symptoms of different diseases and to prescribe specific solutions where appropriate. He also believed in the importance of preventing disease and was one of the first members of the medical profession to recognise that there is often an association between a man's employment and his physical condition. He was the first man to associate mining with certain chest diseases, to link cretinism and goitres with certain alpine areas, to use mercury in the treatment of syphilis, to advocate allowing wounds to drain instead of smothering them with layers of dried dung, and to argue that some foods contained poisons which had a bad effect on the human body. Paracelsus was the first peoples' doctor and he proudly claimed that he pleased only the sick and not the profession. He bombarded medical students and doctors with a seemingly endless collection of writings and lectures which were designed to encourage them to think for themselves and to reject the previously unquestioned preachings of the established medical authorities.

And yet this extraordinary man, who was the father of modern medicine, was persecuted and disowned by his own profession. His travels throughout Europe were not simply done in search of information; he was also constantly on the run from his formidable and vengeful opponents.

***

It is almost impossible to find anyone who has ever had a creative and worthwhile idea who has not been marginalised, ridiculed and persecuted by the relevant establishments. Individuals today have a harder job than ever to put forward new ideas – especially if those new ideas oppose the established view or conflict with the attitudes of powerful, rich vested interests. Industry, money, power and corruption are almost synonyms today.

The lesson here is clear: ignore attacks and ridicule from the establishment if you think you are right. Indeed, if you are an original thinker you should be alarmed rather than flattered if any member of the establishment, or any orthodox publication, supports what you are doing. (I decided many years ago that as long as the medical establishment continues to attack me I will be content. I would be extremely alarmed if any orthodox medical journal gave a favourable review – or even gave any review at all – to one of my books.)

CHAPTER THIRTY ONE
Remember That Your Friends Need Friends Too

'Have few friends but those thou hast, grapple them to thy heart with hoops of steel.'

- William Shakespeare

For several years I have been writing a weekly 'agony' column. Every week I receive many calls and letters from readers of the column who want my advice.

There are several topics which crop up quite regularly but one of the questions which I get asked most commonly is: 'How can I make friends?'

Sometimes the writer just wants to meet friends. Frequently, he or she wants to meet a partner with a view to developing a stable and committed relationship.

From their letters it seems to me that most of the lonely people who write to me, and who are desperate to make new friends, make two fundamental mistakes. First, they are far too serious. They approach the search for a new friend or companion with all the earnestness they might be expected to show if searching for a new species of fern. And, second, they mistakenly assume that in order to initiate a new friendship they have to show how terribly interesting *they* are when what they should be doing is expressing an interest in every new person they meet.

To captivate people you don't need to be interest*ing* You only need to be interest*ed.*

Most of the lonely people who write to me believe that their loneliness is the result of some personal fault. 'People aren't interested in me because I'm too poor/because I've got a big nose/because I don't have an exciting job/because I don't have a job at all/because of my accent/because my hair doesn't look right/because I always say the wrong thing.'

All this is nonsense, of course.

Romances and friendships are not usually built upon such things. Most people are captivated not by wealth, perfect good looks or beautiful hair but by vulnerability, honesty, passion and a sense of humour and – most important of all – by someone who is interested in them. Most people aren't as interested in other people as they are interested in themselves. And so, if you are vulnerable, self effacing, honest and interested you can get away with just about anything else.

Most of the strangers you meet don't care a stuff about your needs. But if you understand *their* needs (what they want and need out of life) they will respect you and like you.

Everyone – without exception – considers themselves to be special and different. Treat the people you meet as special and different and they will respond to you in a positive way. Remember that we all want other people to love us and trust us. In order to make new friends (and to influence people) ask not what they can do for you but what you can do for them. Try to satisfy their needs and solve their problems and in the end you will benefit too.

And try to smile. Try to look cheerful. Next time you are on a train or walking around the shops look around you. Look at peoples' mouths. So many of the people you see will have mouths which turn down at the ends in a permanent grimace of disapproval and distaste. Such people look as though they are about to say 'No' before they even speak. A grimace makes everyone feel miserable. A smile, in contrast, is warming and attractive. (Smiling can produce a change in your voice and your attitude to others. Try smiling whenever you make telephone calls – and you'll notice the difference immediately.)

***

When you are trying to build up one or more new relationships you are selling a product – yourself. Your customers are the people with whom you want to build up relationships. A man who wants a girl to like him will stand a far greater chance of succeeding if he takes the girl flowers or chocolates when he meets her for their first date than if he turns up on her doorstep clutching a bag full of his dirty laundry.

Relationships are like business – they involve selling yourself to other people. Some people are good at beginning, developing and maintaining relationships because they understand what their 'customers' want and need. In order to make new friends you have to provide a better service at a lower cost (in terms of effort as well as money).

If you meet someone who needs to be entertained and amused then you will win their friendship by making them laugh. If you meet someone who needs to talk about themselves then you will win their friendship simply by listening.

***

'I've had 120 Christmas cards this year! she said, proudly. 'Isn't it wonderful to have so many friends?'

I looked around. The bookcase, the top of the TV set, the sideboard and the windowsills were packed with colourful greetings cards.

It was an impressive sight.

But what she said made me think about the way we devalue one of the most important assets in our lives: friendship.

She didn't have 120 friends. Most of those cards were from casual acquaintances. And I wondered if she had ever really thought about the true nature – and importance – of friendship.

***

Remember there is a world of difference between friends and acquaintances. The former you can ring at 3 am in the morning for advice and help and support. The latter will simply add to your annual Christmas card collection.

Remember too that to win a new friend you must first *be* a friend. And you must work at that friendship. You must invest time and energy and caring. And if, in the end, you finish up with half a dozen true friends then you will be truly blessed. True friendship is an asset which will never tarnish and never devalue. And no one will ever be able to take it away from you.

CHAPTER THIRTY TWO
Watch And Learn!

'A non observant man goes through the forest and sees no firewood.'
- Russian proverb

Most of the world's scientists are, these days, funded either by governments, large international companies or massive multi million dollar a year charities. Their work is planned and structured by committees and so it is, perhaps, hardly surprising that they produce so little of value or note.

The ironical, paradoxical and embarrassing truth is that the vast majority of the world's most useful discoveries were made more by chance than by design; often by scientists who were doing work for which they had no formal training and frequently by scientists who had little money for equipment or laboratories.

Benjamin Franklin first captured lightning with the aid of a kite made with two sticks and a silk handkerchief. James Watt made his first model of a condensing steam engine with a discarded anatomist's syringe. Denis Burkitt, who made one of the most important cancer breakthroughs of the twentieth century by linking a cancer to a virus, did so with the aid of two grants; the first for £15 and the second for £150 with which he purchased a second hand Land Rover.

Serendipity has played a major part in a vast number of scientific breakthroughs. But serendipity only produces results when someone is prepared to look in what might, to other onlookers, appear to be the wrong direction.

Here are a few examples of how chance observation has led to major discoveries:

* Dr Priestley, to many the father of modern science and the discoverer of many gases, was first drawn to chemistry because he lived near to a brewery.

He was forty years of age and knew nothing of chemistry at the time but be became curious after noticing the peculiar properties of gas floating over the fermented liquor at the brewery.

* The Marquis of Worcester had the idea of steam power after watching the cover of a vessel containing hot water blow off. At the time he was a prisoner in the Tower of London. The Marquis later wrote a book describing his idea and Thomas Newcomen, who read the book, turned the observation into an application. James Watt, credited with the invention of the steam engine, turned the Marquis's observation and Newcomen's application into practice.

* Marc Isambard Brunel got the idea for building his tunnel under the River Thames from watching a shipworm. He watched how the worm used its well armed head to drill into wood first in one direction and then in another direction and to then strengthen the tunnel it had made by daubing a kind of varnish over the roof and the sides. Brunel simply copied this technique on a rather larger scale.

* Sir Samuel Brown got the idea of the suspension bridge when, while thinking about a proposed bridge design, he walked in his garden and saw a spider's web suspended across his path. Brown used this observation to build a suspension bridge across the River Tweed.

* Professor Wilhelm Konrad von Rontgen was an experimental physicist. In 1895 he was investigating the effects of cathode rays. He noticed that although the cathode ray tube on which he was working was covered with black cardboard a greenish glow seemed to come from a piece of paper coated with a substance called barium platinocyanide which happened to be lying on a nearby bench. A lesser scientist would have simply moved the paper and thought no more about it. But Rontgen realised that the paper must have been made luminous by some unknown rays – something other than the cathode rays he had intended to investigate. Fortunately for untold millions of patients throughout the world Rontgen decided to investigate further. He put his own hand between the cathode ray tube and the piece of paper and discovered X rays.

* Alexander Fleming was working in his laboratory at St Mary's Hospital in London on a study of the staphylococcus bacteria when he noticed that a culture dish containing the bacteria appeared to have been contaminated. The contaminant had in some way stopped the growth of the bacteria. In retrospect it seems likely that spores of a common fungus had blown in through an open laboratory window. Contamination is a fairly common problem in laboratories and normally such cultures are simply thrown away. However, Fleming was too good a scientist just to toss away the contents of the dish, regard the incident as nothing more than a spoilt experiment and forget about it. He made careful notes on the culture and the following year published a paper in which he described the way in which the growing spores (which he had identified as being those of

penicillium notarum) had contaminated the culture dish and prevented the growth of the bacteria. Fleming realised that one day the penicillin would prove useful as a drug. It wasn't until a decade later that Fleming's observation was turned into a practical reality but it was Fleming's vital observation which gave mankind one of the most important therapeutic breakthroughs of the twentieth century.

***

It is not, of course, only scientists who need to be observant – and need to be able to seize the moment.

If he was away from home without a sketch pad and he saw something he wanted to draw later the artist William Hogarth would make a sketch (literally) upon his thumb nail. (Hence the phrase 'a thumb nail sketch'.)

It is surprising how many people go through life apparently quite blind to what is going on around them. Numerous opportunities are missed simply because people do not really 'see' the things around them – and do not apply what they have seen to their own lives.

Make sure that you remain alert and observant and you will benefit greatly in many different ways.

Everyone you meet can teach you something. They may be able to teach you something big and important. Or they may be able to teach you something small and apparently unimportant. But if you remain observant, keep watching and keep listening and keep learning then in the end you will benefit enormously. You may forget much of what you have learned. New information may not seem important at the time. But there is a good chance that at some time in the future it will be important and useful.

You can learn something from everyone you meet and every situation in which you find yourself.

One of the main secrets of success is the ability to seize opportunities and to turn accidents to good purpose. Observation is, perhaps, the most important secret for gaining knowledge and success.

CHAPTER THIRTY THREE
Protest To Survive (But First Learn When To Complain And When Not To)

'The world is disgracefully managed, one hardly knows to whom to complain.'
– Ronald Firbank

'The lady doth protest too much, methinks.'
- William Shakespeare

I watched a documentary film about Anne Frank not long ago and I cried as I watched how the Germans treated their concentration camp victims during the Second World War. I cried not just because of the way the Jews were treated by the vile barbarians of Nazi Germany but because the pain, the sorrow, the indignity and the cruelty suffered by Anne Frank and millions of others has changed nothing.

The real tragedy is that there are now just as many – if not more – people in the world who would happily operate concentration camps and gas chambers if their governments told them to. We live in a world where cruelty is honoured, where dishonesty is rewarded and where power is taken by the vicious and the brutal and the uncaring. We live in a world where integrity is sneered at, where honesty is described as controversy, where passion is regarded as an embarrassment and where the truth is a dangerous commodity. We are ruled by pompous authoritarians who cloak their petty ambitions and personal greed in stolen power and glory but accept no responsibility for justice.

Morals and ethics have become abstract subjects for university debate, rather than guidelines for our behaviour. No one cares any more about what is right.

The politicians and their servants the bureaucrats have dirtied our land and polluted our air and our water. As a result we live in a filth that gets worse each day and which contaminates our very lives.

We are encouraged to applaud and reward the fat businessmen who cheat the world's poor. We are taught to kneel before the representatives of evil and daily pledge our allegiance to witless, passionless mediocrity.

We live in a world where the truth is a victim and propaganda rules. We live in a world where politicians and international businessmen rule our lives.

And yet we claim to be innocents in all this corruption of the spirit. We blame an unseen 'them' for the horrors of our world. We blame 'them' for the cruelty, the viciousness and the misery. We live in comfort and contentment; slumped in front of the TV screen; deaf to the injustices which mark our world.

But we have built this society. It is our responsibility. We cannot escape from blame by keeping silent. The evil that is done is done on our account and if we stay silent then the evil is done with our blessing. It is up to us to shout 'stop' when we have had enough of the wickedness around us.

***

It sometimes seems to me that one of the single biggest differences which separates people on this planet is that while some people are aggressive and constantly ready to argue, defending their 'corner' whenever they feel threatened and standing up for themselves and their rights, (sometimes making themselves ill through their complaining since because there are so many things in life to complain about they wear themselves out and make themselves miserable), others never do battle but simply 'roll over' and allow themselves to be walked on, never complaining but simply accepting everything nasty that life throws at them and turning themselves into human doormats. There are those who do and those who are done unto.

There are, of course, many times when it is necessary to protest and complain and stand up for yourself. It has been shown that in hospitals it is the patients who want to know what is going on, what is happening to them and what treatment they are being given who are most likely to survive. The patients who are, to put it bluntly, bloody minded may not win any popularity prizes with the staff but they will probably stand the greatest chance of surviving.

You should protest about things which are important to you. But – and it is a big 'but' – you should pick the battles you fight and you should make sure they are worth fighting.

There are many times when battling and fighting simply uses up valuable energy. The woman who feels that she has been charged twice in a shop for a small can of beans and who then spends several hours complaining about the overcharge has lost far more than she has gained.

A few years ago a friend and I both decided that for six months we were going to fight every single injustice to which we felt we had been exposed. Every time we felt that we had been cheated in a shop, or sold a faulty item by a manufacturer, we complained. If a restaurant or a hotel gave bad service we complained. If an airline or a railway didn't provide the promised quality of service we complained. If a government department failed to do what we felt it should have done we protested through the official channels. It was an exhausting and debilitating six months. We were both totally worn out by the experience. We had had little time for work and no time for fun. Our lives had been taken over by the constant need to stick up for what we believed to be right.

And, in the end, we were the losers.

You must choose your battles. You should avoid the petty squabbles. If you are careful not to waste your energy on disputes which don't really matter you will have the energy you need when you come to fight a battle which really does matter. If you complain about every trivial injustice you will go mad and waste your life on meaningless trivia.

You should give in to petty annoyances not out of a sense of despair but out of a knowledge that these incidents are trivial and beneath you, and out of a knowledge that you have more important things to do with your life.

If you let minor injustices and bureaucratic trifles upset you it will not take long for your spirit to be drained. Your body and your mind will be exhausted.

Deal with the small problems in your life without emotion and remember that it is far too easy to waste your life fretting over petty nonsenses.

Escape from the sea of trivia which washes over us all – and which causes so much frustration, stress and depression, by concentrating on your hopes, ambitions and dreams. Keep your mind and heart on the big issues.

***

You should know how to complain so that you waste the least amount of energy. If a complaint is worth making it is worth making properly – go straight to the top. If you have a complaint about a product or an organisation complain to the Chairman or the Managing Director. There is little point in complaining to a special consumer department. Complain to the top and the worst that can happen will be that your complaint will filter downwards.

Do not be apologetic (it isn't your fault). Do not say: 'Would it be possible...' but ask for what you want. Always remember that there is no point in saying 'Don't you know who I am?' (The chances are that they don't and if they did they wouldn't care.) You should try to stay cool and be firm. If you are in the right then they will probably know this and give in. If they stand firm then you have to decide whether the battle is worth fighting. If it is – then fight on. If it isn't – walk away and don't give that person or business your custom again. Don't worry about 'losing face'. You should always be prepared to walk away from unnecessary conflict. Why should you care what they think about you? They may think that you have been defeated. But you know better. Let the inconsequential bureaucrat who wins a small victory over you crow and beat his chest; at the end of the day – and at the end of his life – he will still be an inconsequential bureaucrat.

When trying to decide which battles to fight it sometimes helps (when the battle involves money) if you know what your time is worth. Work out how much you can earn in an hour. And then, if you feel that you have been cheated out of a sum of money, try to decide in advance how much time you are prepared to allocate towards recovering that money. You may, for example, decide that you will write one letter or make one telephone call but that you will then abandon the complaint.

**

If someone complains to you about something you have done wrong try to defuse the situation by asking these two simple questions: 'What did I do wrong?' and 'What can I do to make things better?'

Remember, too, that saying 'sorry' doesn't hurt and doesn't cost anything but will often save you a great deal of time, energy, money and heartache. What's wrong with saying 'sorry'? It's only a word. Most people need to be quicker to apologise – but to apologise less. The word 'sorry' is one of the most misused in any language. We say it easily and without thought when it isn't necessary. But for some strange reason we hate saying it when it is appropriate. You should stop apologising unless you genuinely feel that you should – in which case you should apologise quickly and with genuine contriteness.

When you have done, said or written something which was wrong you do not need to explain or justify. Simply say: 'I'm sorry. I was wrong. What can I do to put things right? What would you like me to do?'

Is that really all that hard to say?

CHAPTER THIRTY FOUR
You Can Be A Leader (If You Want To Be)

'The ruler must not display his weapons if he is to survive long.'
- Tao Te Jing by Lao Tsu

People can be divided into two groups: followers and leaders. Most people want someone to follow and there are never enough leaders around.

It is often assumed that all leaders are born. This is not true. Some individuals are born with leadership skills. But most people who are leaders *acquire* the skills they need.

If you don't already have leadership skills then you can learn to become a leader. Here is how:

1. You must understand yourself, your own needs and your own priorities. You must also understand your strengths and your weaknesses. Knowing your weaknesses is just as important as knowing your strengths.

2. You must know what you want. You must have short, medium and long term plans. How can you possibly get what you want unless you know what you want? And how can you lead others towards a goal unless you have a goal?

3. You must have plans. Just knowing what you want is not enough. You must know how you intend to get there.

4. You must develop a keen imagination.

5. You must understand how other people think. You must know the strengths and weaknesses of (some, at least, of) the people you intend to lead.

6. You must plan ahead.

7. You must be able to anticipate problems. Your plans will be of little use if they depend upon outside factors over which you have little control – and if the actions of someone else can disrupt your schedule. You must have alternative plans ready – so that if things go wrong with Plan A you can substitute Plan B.

8. You must master details. Both the Duke of Wellington and Napoleon Bonaparte (two of the greatest leaders of men ever known) paid enormous attention to small details. Both spent a good deal of their valuable time making sure that their soldiers had plenty of food and ammunition, suitable clothing and comfortable boots.

One of the Duke of Wellington's great skills was his ability to concentrate his mind on whatever he was dealing with – whatever other pressing matters may be waiting for his attention. He could not be intimidated or embarrassed into forgetting the issue at hand. In Spain, when he found that he could not bring food for his troops over from England he set himself up in business as a corn merchant so that he could feed his men. He brought grain over from South America and from Mediterranean ports. He then sold the surplus to the Portugese.

Napoleon was a similar master of detail. He too left nothing to chance. He constantly paid attention to such details as ensuring that his men would have level roads upon which to march, and that canals were open so that stores could be brought to where his troops were camped. He took great pains to ensure that even when he was in hostile country he had a well established line of communication with Paris and with his other generals. There are records which show that even when he was busy fighting battles Napoleon took charge of things which some generals might have regarded as 'beneath them'.

During one long but major battle he personally directed where horses were to be obtained, made arrangements for the purchase of all the saddles his men would need, ordered shoes for his soldiers, bought bugles for all his men so that they could make a great deal of noise and frighten the enemy soldiers and made sure that sufficient rations of bread, biscuit and spirits were bought and stored. At the same time he was constantly sending dispatches to Paris giving instructions on public education, dealing with administrative matters and revising budget details.

He took time out in one campaign to give instructions to architects regarding the alterations he wanted making both to the Église de la Madeleine and the Jardins des Tuileries, intervened in a squabble at the Grand Opera, wrote articles for the newspapers and carried on correspondences with the Shah of Persia and the Sultan of Turkey. His letters show that he gave instructions about where helmets were to be made and where shirts, corn, shoes, guns and great coats were to be purchased. While he was doing this he never forgot to review his troops regularly – even though this meant riding huge distances. And, of course, he attended receptions with local dignitaries and planned his battles.

Both Napoleon and Richelieu wanted the word 'impossible' completely banished from the dictionary. They also wanted the phrase 'I can't' banned.

9. You must be willing to take on responsibility.

10. You must be unselfish. When things go well and according to plan, you should be happy to give praise to those working with you. When things go wrong you should take endeavour to learn from the errors – making sure that the same things do not go wrong again – but you must take the responsibility for the errors yourself.

11. You must be able to cooperate with others. Every leader needs advice, support and information from others. A loner does not make a good leader.

12. You must have real courage. Any unimaginative fool can show a sort of courage. A fool who does not understand the consequences of his actions may appear to be a brave man. But because you will have developed your imagination, and will therefore be able to envisage the consequences of errors and mishaps, and the potential pain of disaster, you will need to show real courage in order to be brave. Muley Moluc, the Moorish leader, lay dying, worn out by incurable disease, while his troops were fighting the Portugese. He got up from his sick bed in the middle of the battle and rallied his army. He led them to victory and then sank back exhausted and died.

13. You must have a keen sense of justice. You should not administer justice according to the rule book but according to a sense of natural, honest justice.

14. You must be able to show real determination. You must be able to stick to your plans even though others may begin to show a lack of confidence. The corollary to this is that you must be prepared to change your plans if you believe that the circumstances have changed.

15. You must work harder than everyone else. A real leader always does more than he is paid to do or expected to do. During a cholera epidemic in Vienna, Emperor Francis of Austria was walking with an aide de camp in the streets. As he walked a corpse was dragged past on a litter. There were no mourners. The Emperor found out that the man had died of cholera and that his relatives would not accompany his body to the grave. The Emperor did not hesitate. 'Then,' he said, 'we will supply their place, for none of my poor people should go to the

grave without that last mark of respect.' And he did just that, and stood bare-headed throughout the burial ceremony to make sure that all the proper rites were respectfully performed. That is leadership.

16. You must understand and sympathise with the needs, wants and anxieties of those whom you are leading. The good leader will lead through encouragement rather than through punishment. The carrot is a better and more powerful aid than the stick.

17. You must be able – and willing – to do everything you expect others to do, however simple or basic that task may be.

18. You must not fear competition from those around you. The leader who is always looking over his shoulder, waiting for a challenge to his leadership, will be a weak leader. The true leader makes it constantly clear that there is no possible alternative.

19. You should lead because those who follow believe that you are worthy of the role of leader – rather than because you are officially the 'leader'. The leader who relies solely upon his rank or title will be a weak leader. The real leader doesn't get puffed up by success or unduly depressed by failure. He speaks his mind freely when the time is right but he doesn't push his views onto others. When bestowing a favour he does so with a quiet dignity rather than with a great deal of noise.

20. You are entitled to expect those who follow you to be loyal. But they, in turn, are entitled to loyalty from you.

CHAPTER THIRTY FIVE
Why Building Cathedrals Is Good For Your Soul

'Patience is the finest and worthiest part of fortitude, and the rarest too...Patience lies at the root of all pleasures, as well as of all power. Hope herself ceases to be happiness when Impatience companions her.'

- John Ruskin.

Our views of life are very short term. Television has taught us to have shorter and shorter attention spans – during the last decade or so the length of the average political sound bite on television has shrunk from a minute or two to around seven seconds.

We used to think of the short term as meaning less than a year, the medium term as meaning between one and five years and of the long term as referring to anything more than five years into the future.

Today, most people think of the short term as being within the next five or ten minutes, the medium term as being within the next week or so and the long term as being, at most, within the next six months.

Everything is done in a hurry. People want instant results. We want to see the results of our labours immediately so that we can get on to the next project.

I think that all this is a terrible mistake. It means that our views of life are gravely limited.

Back in the Middle Ages, when some of the world's most beautiful cathedrals were being built, people genuinely thought of the long term as referring to a span of several generations.

Work started on Notre Dame cathedral in Paris, France, in 1163 and didn't finish until around 1340 – over 175 years later. In Italy, St Peter's in Rome was begun in 1506 and not completed until 1615. In Exeter in England the Cathedral Church of St Peter was begun in 1275 and not completed until nearly a century later. Those are by no means exceptional examples.

In those days a craftsman would happily work on a cathedral (or some other grand building) knowing that he would not live to see the building finished. But he would know that his son would carry on his work. And when the son, in turn, grew into his own prime, he knew that *his* son would continue working on the cathedral.

Three or more generations would contentedly work on a single project. There would be a sense of continuity, of permanence, of being part of something bigger and more important than oneself, and of belonging to something meaningful. That feeling of belonging passed on from father to son and from father to son as the years and decades and centuries went by. A man's life did not end with his death because he lived on as part of something that he had begun to help create.

This feeling of oneness with future generations was not confined to builders and craftsmen working on large, public buildings.

A century or so ago men routinely planted trees for other men to sit under. Estate owners and gardeners would plant seeds knowing that future generations would enjoy the results. A rich man might arrange for an avenue of trees to be planted alongside the driveway to his newly built house (a house that might have already been two or more generations in the making) in the knowledge that the trees would not reach maturity until long after his own death.

Similarly, a farmer or small landowner might plant trees on his land so that his heirs would have wood to cut.

Today most of us tend to think far too short term. We need to change that. We need to be less preoccupied with ourselves and more concerned with the world in which we and our descendants will live.

***

Give yourself an aim, a target or a purpose that makes you part of a cause and you will be able to remain happy whatever happens to you. Even death will be just a comma in the sentence of the cause for which you are fighting.

Only when you have a cause for which you are prepared to die will you really know what living is all about. If your personal aims are tied up with a great cause in which you believe then you truly cannot lose the war. You may lose a battle or two. You may feel exhausted. You may go bankrupt. You may die. But the war in which you are engaged will go on and in so far as you are still part of that war you will not be defeated.

The best way to conquer a fear of death and dying is to achieve a feeling of oneness with those who will come after you. Your cathedral does not have to be made of stone. Make sure now that what you are doing with your life will live on after you.

CHAPTER THIRTY SIX
Focus And Take Aim

'Nothing in the world is softer and weaker than water.
But, for attacking the hard and strong, there is nothing like water.'
- Tao Te Jing by Lao Tsu

'There are no limitations to the mind except those we acknowledge.'
- Napoleon Hill

Focusing your strength can make a big difference to your ability to do things. For example, if you ever have difficulty in opening a new jar of jam or sauce simply try imagining that all your body's strength is pouring into your hands. Concentrate all your physical power on that one task. This zen technique will work for you if you believe in it.

Similarly, you can benefit enormously if you learn to focus or concentrate your mental strength on some particular task. Focusing gives you better definition and enables you to see much more clearly.

Whatever you are doing you should decide in advance what you want out of it. (Opening the jar of jam or sauce is easy. You want the jam or sauce. But what about when you go on holiday? What do you want out of your holiday? Most people go on holiday because they expect to go on holiday. They flick through some brochures, they pack a suitcase and they're off. But why? Are they going to rest? To relax? To learn? To get some exercise and fresh air? To meet people? To find a sexual partner? To practise a skill? Only when you know why are doing something will you get what you want out of it.)

In 1996 I read an interview with the 75 year old Peter Ustinov in which the actor explained that although aware of his age he had no difficulty at all in moving about when working on the stage. After working in a theatrical production of his own play 'Beethoven's Tenth' he told the Financial Times: 'I can act for two and a half hours at a stretch. But after five minutes at a cocktail party I have to sit down. It's a question of focus.' To succeed you must focus on the real problems you face.

And while you are learning to focus on the things that matter to you it is also important to learn to remove from your mind those people, things and events which are of no significance to you. Just remove them completely from your life and thoughts. Focusing accurately will enable you to do things which you previously only dreamt of doing.

CHAPTER THIRTY SEVEN
Be Loyal To Those Whom You Expect To Be Loyal To You

'If you want a friend, you must also be willing to wage war for him: and to wage war, you must be capable of being an enemy.'

- Frederick Nietzsche

'Do not forget those who fought the battles for you and bought your freedom with their blood.'

- Emile Zola

You should be loyal to your family, your friends, the people you work with and your customers. If you work for an individual and you believe that he is loyal to you then you should be loyal to him.

But you should never expect an organisation to be loyal to you – whether you are an employee, a supplier or a customer.

Organisations regard your loyalty as something to be bought with coupons, bonuses or a cheap mortgage rate. But they don't feel any loyalty towards you. An organisation isn't a live, sentient being (unless it is a very small company which is run by one or two people in which case you can, for all practical purposes, forget that it is an organisation).

Organisations have no soul. They are run by bureaucrats, administrators, accountants and lawyers.

CHAPTER THIRTY EIGHT
Are You Making Too Many Excuses?

'A difficulty is a thing to be overcome.'

- Lord Lyndhurst

'Misfortune is next door to stupidity.'

- Russian proverb

Most of us make excuses when things go wrong, when our hopes remain unfulfilled or when we do not realise our achievements. We think up all sorts of extremely convincing alibis to explain why we have failed – and to ensure that someone else takes the blame. Occasionally the excuses are designed to satisfy others. More often the excuses are intended to appease our own consciences. Ironically, the creation of excuses often requires a great deal of mental thought – sometimes more than would have been needed to achieve success in the first place.

I have compiled below a list of just a few of the commonest excuses for failure. Look through this list and see how many you can find which you have used to explain away a failure. As you look through the list remember that none of these 'excuses' are a genuine explanation for failure.

Elsewhere in this book you will find all the evidence and explanations you need to show that these problems can all be overcome.

I failed because...

* ...I don't have the necessary education.
* ...I come from the wrong social background.
* ...No one understands me.
* ...I didn't get enough support from the people around me.

* ...I didn't have enough time.
* ...I've not been well.
* ...I have too many other responsibilities.
* ...I've been unlucky.
* ...I haven't had any breaks.
* ...My family is holding me back.
* ...I made one mistake and that was that.
* ...Someone else stole my idea.
* ...I just don't know the right people.
* ...I don't have enough savings.
* ...There's a recession.
* ...I'm too old.
* ...I'm too young.
* ...I'm the wrong sex.
* ...I'm not good looking enough.
* ...I don't have enough influence.
* ...People have it in for me.
* ...They won't give me a break.
* ...My background is holding me back.
* ...I have too many other worries.
* ...I have to worry about paying the bills and daren't take any chances.
* ...No one will listen to me.
* ...I wasn't allowed to do what I wanted to do.
* ...Times are hard.
* ...There's too much bureaucracy.
* ...I don't get any support.
* ...People hold my past against me.

You can learn a great deal about yourself from the type of excuses you use.

The truth is that (at the beginning, at least) the world isn't out to get you – even if it seems like that. When you have already achieved a measure of success then you may well find that you will be opposed by people who have a personal or commercial interest in putting a halt to your successes – but at the beginning 'they' are unlikely to pay much attention to you.

In order to succeed you should find the real reason for your failure and then deal with that. Analyse your real weaknesses and find out exactly where things have gone wrong – instead of creating excuses which blame others – and you will benefit enormously.

CHAPTER THIRTY NINE
What Have You Been Doing Wrong?

'I am still waiting for something really wonderful to happen.'
- woman celebrating her 100th birthday

If you think you have been working hard all your life but you still haven't fulfilled any of your ambitions then there is a good chance that you have been doing something wrong.

Your life does not have to be dull, mundane, frustrating, boring, tiring, exhausting or unfulfilling. You *are* your reality. You can choose your own life if you want to do so. You, not the government, can rule your life. You can be immune to the vagaries of the economy. You do not need to be dependent upon the extent of your education or bank balance. You do not have to be restricted by a lack of good looks or contacts. Decide what you want and go for it. Remember that the only important battle is the last one.

1. Do you know what you want?
You must have a specific purpose. It is no good simply hoping to be 'successful', 'rich' or 'famous'. Those ambitions are far too vague. A vague desire for success alone is not enough. You need a plan and you need a purpose. Hopes and wants are not enough. Only needs succeed. Only when you have found something or someone worth dying for will your life be really worth living.

2. Do you work well with other people?
You must work with people who have the same hopes and aspirations as you do. It is impossible to do anything entirely by yourself. Whatever it is you want to do with your life you are going to have to do it with the help of other people. Acquire and show an interest in people. Learn to understand how other people think and work. Take an interest in people – talk to them and learn from them.

My book *People Watching* is packed with practical tips and hints on how to 'read' people simply by watching them. Be curious and interested in other people and you will benefit twice. First, you will learn a great deal which will be of use to you in your life and work. Second, the people in whom you show a genuine interest will like you because you have shown an interest in them. If you have a conversation which seems to be flagging simply keep on asking questions: delve deeper and deeper and people will eventually talk to you and tell you more and more about themselves. Ask yourself how other people do things – what are their strategies and tactics for life and for work.

3. *Do you have all the information you need?*
If you try to build up your life or your business with the aid of guesses and hunches then you will doing very little to influence fate to be kind to you. You need information. But do not allow yourself to be overloaded with information. We live in an age where information is readily and freely available in huge quantities. There is, indeed, so much information around that it is often possible to forget what the information is for. You must learn to know when you have acquired enough information to make a decision.

4. *Do you really want to succeed?*
In order to succeed you must be driven by a desire to do something positive with your life. You must be determined and enthusiastic. Desire and willpower will help to produce success. You must have a passion as well as a purpose. A passion, a purpose and a plan will produce action – and action will produce results. Remember: hard work alone is not enough. Never forget: if hard work alone produced wealth and success then factory workers and farm workers would all be taken home in chauffeur driven Rolls Royce motor cars.

5. *Are you good at judging risks?*
If you try to take too many short cuts – and achieve your aims overnight through gambling – the chances are that you will fail. You must learn when – and when not – to take risks. You must be aware of the hazard of procrastination (if you are for ever waiting for the perfect moment then you will probably be for ever waiting) but you must also be aware of the hazard of jumping in with both feet when you can't see your hand in front of your face!

6. *Have you been spreading yourself too thin?*
Having several irons in the fire or balls in the air is a good basic principle. By the very nature of things there will be times when one project doesn't seem to be getting anywhere. Having several projects will help you through the dull – and possibly depressing – patches. But if you involve yourself in too many projects

then your energy and your resources will probably be spread too thinly and your chances of success will diminish.

7. *Are you too undisciplined?*

In order to succeed you must be disciplined. Disciplined diligence can make up for an absence of great intellect or wealth. You must (at least, to begin with) be prepared to put in long hours (though if you enjoy what you do this will not seem like too much of a hardship). And you also need to be disciplined about money. If you are setting up a new business and you spend too much money on things which aren't strictly necessary then you will be short of capital to help you deal with the inevitable mistakes and problems. Not long ago I spoke to someone who had recently obtained a bank loan to set up a new business. He had spent more than half the money he had borrowed on vast quantities of expensive stationery and an impressive looking chair and desk for his office. Since his business was designed to be built around visiting clients in *their* offices this initial expenditure was clearly pointlessly extravagant.

8. *Do you need to be more persistent?*

Do you give up or feel disheartened every time you come across an obstacle? If so then you need to be more persistent. You don't need any great talents to become successful if you are persistent and determined. Any top sportsman or woman will confirm that hard work often beats talent. The steady sports professional who works hard and practises consistently will, over a period of time, usually beat the enormously talented professional who does not practice. 'It has ... often happened that genius has planted the tree, of which patient dullness has gathered the fruit,' wrote Samuel Smiles. Remember that one energetic attempt is worth a great deal more than all the hopes, dreams and aspirations in the world. Hopes, dreams and aspirations are an essential fundamental part of success; but alone they are not enough. Persistence (for which the basic quality is willpower) is an essential quality for success. Those who do not have your determination may describe you as cold blooded or ruthless. Remember that the four key principles for success are: desire, faith, planning and persistence.

9. *Are you going in the wrong direction?*

If you are going to do well at what you do then you must enjoy it. The people who do best in life are those who never do a day's work. They enjoy what they do so much that they don't think of it as work. Such individuals often end up winning twice: they have fun and (because they apply themselves to what they do with great dedication) they also make a great deal of money.

10. Is your private life unsatisfactory?
If you are unhappy because of problems in your private life then your chances of getting where you want to be will be dramatically reduced. You must deal with your personal problems clearly and quickly and decisively.

11. Do you have fears which you have not recognised or dealt with satisfactorily?
If you are frightened of failure, or the consequences of failure, then you will be constantly handicapped in your search for success. If you worry about what other people might think then your chances of getting where you want to be will be low. If you allow your subconscious mind to be flooded with negative thoughts then you will fail. Instead of allowing your subconscious to damage your life learn to use it in a positive way. Give your subconscious mind a difficult topic to think about – and then go back to it after a while. You will probably find that much of the hard thinking work has been done for you (while you were busy doing something else).

12. Do you lack confidence?
If you think that you will fail then you will probably fail. If you think you will win then you will probably win. If you have faith then you can rise to almost limitless heights. You must have a vision of where you want to be in one year, two years, five years time. When visualising where you want to be you must also visualise yourself working towards that end. Repeat your dreams to yourself until you come to believe them. Remember that perception can become reality if you believe in it enough. Bad thoughts can have a negative effect upon you. And good thoughts can have a positive effect upon you. Belief in a cause can be a cause of great happiness. And when you go for it – go for it in a big way. Try to change your focus from the small and the immediate to the large and the long term. Do not hold yourself back by worrying too much about failure. You must do what you can to minimise the risk of failure. But do not allow yourself to be so obsessed by failure that you spend too much time preparing for it. The more time you spend on a backup plan the more you are accepting the possibility of defeat. Remember that success often comes just one step after defeat has stared you in the face. You can get whatever you want if you are prepared to make the necessary demands upon yourself – and never to give up hope. When you believe in yourself others will believe in you too. Self confidence is contagious: those around you will also have confidence in you. Do not be afraid to burn your bridges behind you.

13. Do you use all your skills?
You must take full advantage of all your senses – including your sixth sense. When inspiration flashes into your mind, welcome it, treat it with great respect

and act upon it. Inspiration is never to be ignored. If you ignore inspiration too often it will not call again. If you want to succeed you must be prepared – and able – to light your own fire. If you want to change things then you will need every skill you can find. Changing things is much harder than maintaining or working for the status quo. Change means action and taking chances. It also often means enduring pain.

14. *Are you in a rut?*
Do not accept fate simply because everyone else does. Do not allow yourself to fall into a habit of daily routine from which escape seems impossible. Escape is possible but most people – even when they have been told the secrets of success – simply carry on as before. The man who is ruled by his own lack of determination and energy is just as much a slave as the man who is 'owned' by another or who is ruled by a wicked dictator.

15. *Are you being adversely affected by negative emotions?*
Positive emotions will take you to success but negative emotions will, just as surely, take you to failure. Hatred does far more harm to the person doing the hating than the person who is hated. Envy, jealousy and selfishness are all entirely useless and destructive emotions.

16. *Are you capable of making decisions quickly?*
You have to be able to make decisions quickly and you have to be firm – even if you may be wrong. Making mistakes is an integral part of succeeding. If you are afraid of making mistakes then you will never make any decisions and you will never achieve anything. But you must be prepared and able to learn from your mistakes. Not making decisions (through fear), or changing your mind frequently (again through fear of having made a mistake) are common causes of failure (though changing your mind because circumstances have changed is a sign of strength not weakness). Surgeon John Hunter used to say that the art of surgery would never advance until doctors and surgeons had the courage to publish details of their failures as well as of their successes. It is, of course, particularly important to be able to make quick decisions and act decisively in an emergency. To help yourself make quick decisions you can do two things: first, you should sharpen your intuitive skills so that you are better able to make a fast, but well based, intuitive decision; second, you should train yourself to assess risks quickly and effectively, weighing up the pros and cons before making a decision.

17. *Do you deal with problems decisively – or do you panic?*
There is no point in panicking when you are suddenly faced with a problem. There is rarely little point in begging, pleading, cajoling or threatening when things

go wrong. Try not to allow yourself to be bogged down in detail when you come face to face with those whose main purpose in life seems to be to stop you doing things that you believe you should be allowed to do. Our society is full of them. These are the men and women who hide behind their uniforms. Remember that winning is not a question of being the better side, or even being right. Winning is about winning. It is the problems in our lives which give us wisdom and happiness for it is through solving the problems we have to face we discover knowledge, contentment and joy.

18. *Are you spending too much time with people who depress you and hold you back?*
One famous artist always refuses to look at bad pictures. He believes that if he does this his pencil may become tainted. It has always struck me as absurd that depressed patients are placed in a ward full of depressed patients and expected to get better. You should avoid people who make you feel downhearted, depressed and dispirited. Do not allow your mind to be contaminated by the minds of those who have entirely negative thoughts.

19. *Are you spending too much time on trivia?*
Bickering over trivialities is destructive. Concentrate on the big picture. Far too many people are obsessed and overwhelmed by trivia. Pointless trivia is the bondage of the soul. Gulliver in the land of the little people was tied down by trivia. Most of us are, at one time or another, tied down by the bureaucrats and by trivial responsibilities. (But trivia need not always be pointless. While Michaelangelo was working on a statue a visitor asked him what he had done since his last visit. Michaelangelo explained that he had softened this feature and that and given more expression to the statue's lips. 'But these are trifles!' protested the visitor. 'It may be so,' said Michaelangelo. 'But recollect that trifles make perfection, and perfection is no trifle.')

20. *Don't have regrets and do not try to justify what you do.*
The more successful you become the more you will realise that there are many people around who will want to question what you do and what you have done with your life. They will demand that you justify every move you have made. You will find that some of the severest criticism you will face will come from those whom you might have imagined would have been on your side. (They may, indeed, actually describe themselves as being on your side.) Ignore them. Constantly defending yourself and having regrets will turn you into a loser.

21. *Have you been distracted from your aims?*
I know a woman who always knew exactly what she wanted to be: a nurse. She

spent her teenage years training to be a nurse. In her twenties she worked hard at her job. She was good at it. She enjoyed what she did. The patients liked her. The other nurses liked working with her. The administrators were so impressed that they promoted her to an administrative post. Too flattered to say: 'No, this isn't what I want to do' she accepted the administrative post. She then spent the next fifteen years of her life doing a job which she hated. Instead of spending her days with patients she spent her days with files and piles of paperwork. Eventually, she had the good sense and mental strength to insist that she was downgraded and put back onto the wards. She had to take a massive pay cut. But now she enjoys her work and her life again. Do not allow yourself to be distracted from your real goals and purposes − whatever they may be.

22. *Do you talk too much?*
Do not talk too much about yourself or your plans. If you tell others what you intend to do there is a risk that you will attract envy and therefore danger. And there is also a risk that others may steal your ideas and use your plans to satisfy their own ambitions.

23. *Are you capable of dealing with disappointment?*
If you want to succeed then you must be prepared for disappointments and disillusionment. You must also be prepared for dishonesty from on high.

24. *Decide who your heroes are.*
When you are in difficulty ask yourself: 'What would *they* have done in these circumstances?' Most great men and women exhibit many of the qualities on this list: an ability to inspire; courage; an ability to think clearly and make decisions quickly; a lack of unreasonable prejudice; an ability to organise; persistence; determination; charisma and poise; self confidence; faith in themselves and in what they do; an understanding of nature and people and patience. How many of those virtues do you have? How many of those virtues can you create within and for yourself?

25. *Do you make enough notes?*
You should practise writing down all your thoughts and hopes. Write down everything you have to do. Make lists. Writing things down helps to clear your head − and helps to keep the ideas flowing. The practise of writing everything down is commonplace among great men and women.

26. *Do you deal well with adversity?*
When things go wrong you should escape − in your mind. Write about your adversities, use them as experiences. Use anything and everything that happens

to you. Any adventure can be – and should be – a valuable learning experience.

27. *Do you have a sense of humour?*
When Henry David Thoreau was dying a friend asked him if he had made his peace with God. 'I didn't know we'd fallen out,' was Thoreau's splendidly laconic reply. A sense of humour can help you make friends and deal with problems.

28. *Do you have enough interests?*
You should let your interests range as widely as possible. The more potential sources of pleasure you have the more likely you are to be able to survive a crisis in some important part of your life. If you keep your life too narrow you will be prone to disappointment. Alexander the Great is said to have wept when he realised he had no more worlds to conquer. He should have thought of space travel.

29. *Are you too hostile?*
Keep your hostility for when you need it. Try to approach every stranger as a potential friend and most of the time you will not be disappointed. If you approach every stranger as a potential enemy then you will soon acquire a great many enemies.

30. *Do you overestimate your powers?*
If you *slightly* overestimate your powers you will be constantly surprised by failure and disappointment. And your life will be miserable and unhappy. If you *slightly* underestimate your powers you will be constantly surprised by success. And your life will be happy.

31. *Do you think big enough?*
Remember that large bounds are often easier than little steps. If you take large bounds you only have to move two or three times to get somewhere. If you take little, tiny steps you may have to move a dozen times to travel the same distance. And don't be afraid to miss out steps that other people may think are essential – if you can see a profitable, safe and effective short cut. Most people live in an entirely linear way. They deal with problem A, then with problem B and then with problem C. But you may discover that if you deal with problem C you automatically get rid of problems A and B.

32. *Do you know how to turn obstacles into opportunities?*
Problems are opportunities. Grasp them. If someone has a problem and you can find the solution for them then you will gain their everlasting gratitude. But if you find a solution to a problem someone doesn't know he has make sure that

you tell him about the problem before you tell him about the solution. If there is a barrier between you and potential customers use your mind to find ways to avoid or work your way through the barrier – and ways to increase your customer's perception of the benefit you are offering them. If you run a mail order business and your business is threatened by a postal strike do not regard the proposed threat as an obstacle so much as an opportunity.

33. *Are you aiming high enough?*
You should aim to get the greatest possible result from every effort you make.

34. *Are you over-complicating your life?*
Do you remember the story I told you about my two Bentley motor cars? They were beautiful vehicles. One was old. One was relatively new. But they required a good deal of care and attention. Every few months I had to take them both to a specialist garage where the cars could be serviced. An ordinary service for one of these cars cost about the same as a small car would cost to buy. On one occasion, when I was collecting one of the cars, one of the specialist mechanics told me that in order to preserve the vehicles and protect them from the elements I should buy a high pressure hose and clean them down after taking them around the muddy lanes near where I lived. I dutifully went out and bought a high pressure hose. And then I realised how absurd my life had become. I was being ruled by two motor cars. I sold both cars immediately and bought a sturdy, four wheeled drive vehicle which I have owned for three years without ever washing.

35. *Are you sure you know exactly what you want?*
Unless you know what you really want there is very little chance that you will ever get it.

36. *What do you think is stopping you getting what you want?*
Could it be, do you think, that getting where you want to be is going to be painful, difficult, inconvenient or just plain hard work? Is there going to be more pain in getting where you want to be than there is in staying where you are now? Even if you have a job – and do not ever intend to work for yourself – you should nevertheless think of yourself as self employed. Being self employed used to be regarded as a precarious way to earn a living. In fact, it is just the opposite. But being self employed doesn't just mean earning a living without having a 9 to 5 job to go to. Being self employed requires an attitude of mind as much as anything else. Many people who lose their jobs and who decide to earn a living for themselves describe themselves as 'freelance' or 'self employed' but in their hearts they are still operating like small cogs helping a large wheel to go round. The self employed work for many people but are beholden to none – as

anyone who has ever employed a self employed plumber or builder will confirm. If you have a job you should think of yourself as operating as a self employed individual within that organisation. Constantly be on the look out to try and find ways in which you can help your boss or company be more successful. Be creative. Look for ways to save money or make money or to introduce new products. And when you have proved that you can contribute wealth to the company you can be creative on your account – and ask for a percentage of the profits.

37. Do you know how to motivate yourself?
There is no point at all in waiting for others to motivate you. If you want to succeed then you must motivate yourself. You must make *not* achieving more painful than achieving. Commit yourself to your plan. Open your eyes to the world and do not be afraid to travel outside your normal boundaries – be those boundaries national, mental or spiritual. Learn from others who have been in similar situations to you.

38. Are you honest?
You must be honest in everything you do with those who work for you, your customers and those with whom you do business. Integrity in adversity is vitally important. Nothing is easier to acquire than a bad reputation. Nothing is harder to get than a good reputation. Nothing is easier to lose than a good reputation. Nothing is harder to lose than a bad reputation. But most of all you must be honest with yourself. To know when and what you do not know is vitally important. It is always dangerous to pretend to know something you do not know.

39. Are you driven by vanity?
You must not be inspired or driven exclusively by vanity – a dangerous and destructive force. A little vanity is fine. But too much can be deadly.

40. Are you constantly improving what you have to offer?
However successful you become you must always try to improve the quality of the products or the service you sell. (You are 'selling' something whatever you do for a living. A heart surgeon is selling his knowledge, skill and time. A lawyer is selling his knowledge, skill and time. A freelance gardener is selling his knowledge, skill and time.)

41. Do you find it difficult to concentrate?
You can't succeed at anything without concentrating on what you are doing. In order to concentrate you may need to cut yourself off from outside stimuli. If you are working on something which requires a great deal of continued thought

then you may need to close the door and turn off the telephone. You may find that playing music will help by cutting out any small, extraneous noises which might distract you. (Once you are concentrating hard you will probably be quite unaware that the music is playing. A few moments ago I stopped work for a second and decided to put on some music. I then realised that a tape was already playing. I had been concentrating so hard on what I was doing that I was completely unaware of the music.)

42. *Do you blame other people for everything that goes wrong?*
Some people spend their entire lives utterly convinced that they are the victims of ingratitude and treachery and that they are persecuted by named and known or unnamed and unknown enemies. Every time they fail at something they find someone else to blame. Taken individually all their complaints and protests may sound plausible but such individuals eventually fail to rise above their constant moaning.

43. *Do you get depressed by other people's failures to do what they promise to do?*
You and I would like to live on a planet inhabited by wise, compassionate, sensitive, intelligent beings. But, sadly, space travel is not yet available and so we are stuck with a planet which is dominated by the cruel, the rude, the selfish, the greedy, the unthinking and the prejudiced. You must not allow yourself to be too frustrated by people who do not do what they say they will do. Such frustration turns to stress which will make you ill. Be true and noble to yourself and to those who are true and noble to you; there is nothing else to be done.

44. *Do you worry about not being up to date with technology?*
We live in a world of constant change. On any given day anyone older than about twelve years of age will be living in a world where the technology is developing faster than they can keep up. But don't worry. It doesn't matter. You can always hire someone to handle the technology. And if the technology isn't accessible enough for you to use without understanding it then it hasn't developed properly. How many people who use a motor car, a television set or a camera understand how these pieces of technology work? Why should you feel guilty because you don't know how a computer works? The computer manufacturers will be doing their jobs properly when they sell products which anyone can understand. I believe that Marshall McLuhan was wrong. It is the message not the medium which is important. The medium is merely the route you use to spread the message. If, as I hope, this books adds in some way to the quality of your life it will be because of the ideas it contains and not because of the paper and ink with which it has been manufactured.

For a full catalogue of Vernon Coleman's books please write to:

Publishing House
Trinity Place
Barnstaple
Devon
EX32 9HJ
England